MY LIFE WITHOUT GOD

For Rev. Ken Harrell

With my regards
and prayers

Bill Murray

LK 3:16

MY LIFE

WITHOUT GOD

William J. Murray

93

THOMAS
NELSON
PUBLISHERS
Nashville • Camden • New York

Seventh printing

Published in Nashville, Tennessee, by Thomas Nelson, Inc. and distributed in Canada by Lawson Falle, Ltd., Cambridge, Ontario.

Printed in the United States of America.

Library of Congress Cataloging in Publication Data

Murray, William J. (William Joseph), 1946-
  My life without God.

  1. Murray, William J. (William Joseph), 1946-
2. Converts—United States—Biography.   3. O'Hair,
Madalyn Murray.   I. Title.
BV4935.M87A35   1982   248.2'46'0924 [B]   82-14269
ISBN 0-8407-5256-3

So my children might know the Truth.
With special love to Jade Amber Murray.

The battle in the kitchen was heating up, hotter already than the July dusk in Baltimore, Maryland. Supper was finished, and my mother and grandfather were slinging barbed insults at each other across the littered table. Having heard the same arguments hundreds of times in my eight years, I had left the room quietly, while my grandmother and Uncle Irv remained uneasily at the battle's edge.

I walked into the living room and settled into my favorite chair. The black and white television set, which we had acquired only a year before, blasted me with sound. As usual there was a shoot-'em-up western playing, and the gunshots and other noise helped block out the noise of the growing commotion in the kitchen.

Mine was not the typical American family, where a dad and a mom and the kids cuddled up on the couch with hot chocolate and popcorn to watch *Father Knows Best*. At my house we argued about the value of the American way, whether or not the workers should revolt, and why the Pope, Christians, Jews—anybody who believed in God— were morons. We rarely did anything together as a family. The hatred between my grandfather and mother barred such wholesome scenes. And instead of talking and playing games, we cursed each other and screamed.

The roar of oaths and machine gun-like retorts in the kitchen rose, and I twisted the TV's volume higher.

"I'll kill you, you old, stupid S.O.B.!" my mother screamed.

My stomach tightened. I felt the violence in her words. I ran to the kitchen door, and as I looked through the opening, a dish flew past my grandfather's head and smashed against the wall. It fell, in pieces, on the linoleum floor. Mother reached for another plate, her short, solid body flushed and rigid with rage. Grandfather, left speechless by the intensity of his daughter's outburst, cowered uncertainly as she shredded him with her tongue.

The second dish firmly grasped, Mother aimed and flung it sidearm. The white plate flew through the air, this time obviously on a straighter course. An instant before impact, Uncle Irv blocked the dish in midair with his hand. The plate shattered, slicing his wrist. Blood began to spurt from the cut with each heartbeat.

"You ignorant jerk," Mother yelled at Irv, narrowing her eyes to reddened slits. Abruptly, she whirled around and opened a drawer behind her. Grabbing a ten-inch butcher knife, she turned, then stepped slowly toward the men. Grandmother shrieked, and my heart pounded. Grandfather and Uncle Irv jumped to their feet, rushed my mother, and wrestled the knife from her hand. She cursed angrily, the sweat shining on her forehead. Now both Irv and Grandfather had deep cuts, and blood spots dotted the wall and table. Disarmed and beaten, Mother ran from the room, shouting at Grandfather as she fled, "I'll see you dead. I'll get you yet. I'll walk on your grave!"

It was 1954, just another day in my life without God.

I wasn't sure why Madalyn hated her father so much. That night, Grandfather's comments about the unborn child Mother was carrying had caused the outburst. It had been over eight years since she had borne her first bastard—me— but Grandfather's disgust for his daughter's loose morality had not changed. Not that Grandfather was a moralist, but he wanted his daughter to be pure even if he wasn't. This night he had been unable to resist a comment on her blossoming illegitimate motherhood.

Maybe if I knew more about Mother's childhood and early years I could better understand why she treated her father with such contempt. But when I was growing up, she seldom interrupted her tirades on politics and atheism to reminisce.

I do know she was born on Palm Sunday, April 13, 1919, an ironic twist of providence, I suppose. Her parents, John and Lena Mays, named her Madalyn Elizabeth. She was their second child. Uncle John, Jr., always called Irv, had been born two-and-a-half years earlier. At this time the Mays lived in Beechview, Pennsylvania, which is now a part of Pittsburgh.

It seems likely the Mayses were not well prepared to be effective parents. Each had come from families of more than a dozen children. Because of the poor circumstances at home, John had run away permanently at age twelve, wearing all of the clothing he owned—five sets. Lena was forced to leave her home as a teen-ager because there simply was not enough room. John and Lena met one night in 1912 and were married the following day.

Their lack of enthusiasm for children is shown by an incident that occurred in 1918 when Grandmother was several months pregnant with Madalyn. Hoping to abort the fetus, Grandmother jumped from a second floor window of the family home in Pittsburgh. The hard landing must have not damaged either the baby or the mother, because Grandmother carried Madalyn full term. The fact that Grandmother later related this incident to her daughter reveals the calloused insensitivity so rampant in the family. Mother certainly must have been hurt by this and other instances of early rejection by her parents.

Even Madalyn's birth had a bizarre element. Grandmother swore years later that Mother had been born with an unusual, dark membrane covering her whole body. It resembled a black shroud, and Grandmother claimed that the doctor at hand had said it was very unusual, though he offered no explanation. He gave a portion of the membrane to her, and Grandmother kept this odd keepsake for many years.

The Mayses never were enthusiastic churchgoers. However, they did arrange in 1923 the joint baptism of their son and daughter at a Presbyterian church near their home in Pittsburgh. And sometime not long after Madalyn began to speak, Grandmother taught her a good night prayer in German, which Mother faithfully repeated night after night:

> *Ich bin klein,*
> *Mein Herz ist rein;*
> *Soll Niemand drin wohnen*
> *Als Jesus allein*

This means roughly, "I am little, my heart is pure. No one can live there, but Jesus alone."

Grandmother had her children pray at bedtime, not out of any significant devotion to Christianity but because of her deep interest in spiritual matters of any kind. She also claimed to possess psychic powers. For example, when the First World War was ending and a neighbor was distressed by the lack of news from her son, an infantryman serving in France, Grandmother told the lady that her tarot cards showed the young man to be dead. Several months later, official word of the soldier's death reached the mother. This boosted Grandmother's confidence in her psychic powers, and while I was growing up, she often tried to predict the future using cards.

During my mother's early childhood, Grandfather operated a small but reasonably successful construction firm. Unfortunately the company went bankrupt in the late 1920s. Never again was he to be involved in any endeavor nearly so prosperous. Unable to find work in Pittsburgh, Grandfather moved the family from place to place and eventually opened a roadhouse. During Prohibition, roadhouses were clandestine taverns located along highways in rural areas to take advantage of laxer law enforcement. Grandfather's roadhouse, I'm told, was also a bit of a brothel.

In addition to operating the roadhouse, he did a bit of rum-running. Beneath the seat of the family's Rickenbaker, he had installed a custom-made tank to transport bootleg liquor from a West Virginia still into Pennsylvania. Because suspicious-looking cars were often searched at police road-blocks, little Madalyn would lie on the back seat—above the secret tank—where she pretended to sleep. Grandfather thought that suspicious law officers would be reluctant to disturb the child's nap. He must have been right because, to my knowledge, he was never caught.

In 1931 the family moved to Madison, Ohio, a small town in the northeast corner of the state, only five miles from Lake Erie. I'm not sure why this spot was chosen, but it's likely that Grandfather had located some employment there.

While in this locale Madalyn received a nickname that stuck. Grandfather frequently read a pulp magazine called *Spider*. The magazine featured stories of a character named Spider who used "many different faces" to see himself through various adventures. One evening after Grandfather had finished another exciting tale of the Spider, he put down the magazine and began to laugh. Grandmother walked in to find out what was so amusing. He told her that he had finally found the perfect nickname for his daughter, who he felt had many different faces. From then on in the Mays' family, Madalyn was called "the Spider."

In adolescence Madalyn became somewhat religious, perhaps in part because of some peer relationship. In her high school yearbook, she listed her goal as serving God for the betterment of man. Later she would claim to have been an atheist from about age six.

In 1941, when Madalyn was twenty-two, a young man named J. Roths became seriously interested in her. He was a local boy whom she had known since high school. As far as I know, he was an ordinary sort of guy. I have no idea what kind of romance they had, but on October 9, 1941, they ran away to Cumberland, Maryland, and were married. Two months later, after the Japanese attack on Pearl Harbor, both Mother and her groom went off to war, but not together. He joined the Marines and she the Women's Auxiliary Army Corps. After training, Mrs. Roths was shipped to Europe, while Mr. Roths went to the Pacific front.

Madalyn served in North Africa and Italy as a cryptographer and had a high security clearance. In letters home she expressed confidence in an Allied victory because "God is on our side."

Mother always relished telling one story in particular about her time in the army. Though I doubt it ever happened, it illustrates the sort of grandiose ideas about herself that her army experiences somehow fostered.

While she was in Rome, serving on General Eisenhower's staff, she and some friends went out for a night on the town. After a more or less conventional round of dining and drinking, according to Mother they arrived at the Vatican around three o'clock in the morning. Drunken and rowdy, they nevertheless gained entrance to St. Peter's Basilica by bribing a Swiss guard. Once inside, with champagne bottles in hand, they made their way to a room where the three-tiered crown used in papal coronations was on display in a glass case. Mother never said how, but she claims they managed to remove the crown from its case. Thereupon they proceeded to act out a mock coronation of my mother as the first female pope. If true, Mother's knack for attention-getting theatrics was already fully refined.

As a member of General Eisenhower's staff, Mother often found herself with officers and other dignitaries. These associations, I'm sure, made her husband, John, a mere Marine footsoldier, seem drab by comparison. Evidently she began to seek out a higher class of male companions, one of whom must have been a young Eighth Army Air Corps officer named William J. Murray, Jr. He was the son of a large and wealthy Roman Catholic family from Long Island, New York. How the two met and what was the exact nature of their relationship is unclear to me. I can guess that my father might have been the sort of man who matched my mother's dreams more closely than did Roths. They became intimate, and I was conceived in September 1945, the same month that Japan officially surrendered.

My father was already married to a New York woman, also from a large family. Even though Mother was aware of Murray's marital status, I'm sure she hoped he would honor his commitment to her and to the unborn child by obtaining a divorce. Not only did he not seek a divorce, he refused to admit he was the father of the child.

Mother later attempted to establish his paternity in court. She provoked a burst of laughter from the jury by presenting as evidence a pair of my father's pants to prove their intimacy. In the end she won the case and did receive support payments of fifteen dollars per week from my father until I was eighteen years old.

When Mother returned to Ohio after the war, she found out that her parents had moved—to a shack with a dirt floor. When Mother first saw that place, which did not have electricity, running water, or a telephone, she must have been devastated by despair. She soon learned that her father had spent on booze all the money she had sent home for savings. The whole family was destitute, she was pregnant, and her husband—not the father of her child—was expected home anytime. I believe it was during this period, as she was pacing the dirt floor of that shack and mulling over the dismal outlook for her life, that her extreme anti-God views were born. The same thing could have happened to others trapped in similar circumstances. In particular, Mother came to hate the Roman Catholic church and the Pope for preventing her marriage to a man of considerable wealth. My father had told her point blank that it was his devotion to the church that would not permit him to divorce his wife.

Using her VA loan privilege, the family purchased a farmhouse and barn near Haysville, Ohio. While Grandfather worked hard at renovation, which included cleaning the barn with lye water and buying a milk cow, Mother went out to find employment. She held several clerical jobs, none of which lasted more than a few months. I've been told there was always some fellow employee or supervisor with whom she could not get along. She has often said that the supervisors were forced to get rid of her because they were made insecure by her intimidating intelligence and wit.

When Roths returned from the Pacific, near the end of 1945, he quickly traced Mother to the farmhouse in

Haysville. I suspect that her interest in him had waned so much that she had failed to keep in touch with him or let him know of her whereabouts. He pursued her nonetheless, and when he found her and discovered that she was pregnant with another man's child, instead of being furious, he offered to remain as her husband and to be my father.

Madalyn declined his noble offer—still hoping, perhaps, to convince William Murray to be her husband—and proceeded to sue Roths for divorce.

By this time Mother's antagonism toward God had reached an advanced stage, which an incident in the family lore reveals plainly. Sometime in early 1946, while pregnant with me, she was at home with others in the family waiting out one of those violent lightning storms that raise a fear of God in most people. My mother, however, viewed the storm as an occasion to make a point. After a thunderclap sounded startlingly near the home, she announced, "I'm going out in that storm to challenge God to strike me and this child dead with one of those lightning bolts. Come and watch!"

Her mother and brother stood at the door as she strode dramatically out into the yard. When she was sure her audience was in place, she shook her hand menacingly toward the heavens and, at the top of her voice, unleashed blasphemies intended to provoke violent wrath from God. When enough time had passed to indicate that God was not going to respond, she strode triumphantly back inside, saying excitedly, "You see, you see! If God exists, he would surely have taken up my challenge. I've proved irrefutably that God does not exist!"

Her father grunted sourly and continued to read his newspaper. He, like God, paid Madalyn little attention.

Mother already had received her divorce from Roths when I was born on May 25, 1946. She named me William Joseph Murray, III, and sometime after that she began to call herself Madalyn Murray, even though my father never consented to marry her.

My earliest memories are not of happy times with family members, but rather of Laura, the milk cow Grandfather had bought for the farm in Haysville. Her former owner had sold her cheap because she was supposed to be ornery. But Laura liked Granddad, and soon her temperament sweetened and she gave plenty of rich milk. What I remember most distinctly is the birth of Laura's second calf, probably in 1949. I was fascinated with the little animal and became quite attached to it. But the calf had to be sold, to my immense grief and disappointment.

Later the same year, Mother decided she wanted to test her fortunes elsewhere. The family was struggling to make ends meet, and the mortgage payments on the property were several months late.

Some months earlier, to add a little income, Grandfather had purchased a large truck for general hauling. But he had been unable to make enough money from it to manage the payments. Meanwhile, Mother had been attending Ashland College, a Church of the Brethren private school. She also had worked a short time with the Akron Rubber Company and had been employed part time for six months by the Social Security Administration. Uncle Irv was unemployed, too. In fact, he had never been employed in his life.

It was obviously a good time to move, but where? An unusual way to decide the family's destination was chosen, according to family legend. A map of the United States was tacked to a wall, and Mother and Uncle Irv hurled darts at it simultaneously. They had agreed that when their darts hit the same state at the same time, that would be the place. Not surprisingly, considering the nature of their system, the lot fell to Texas, the largest single entity on the map.

This story is entertaining and may be true. I do know, though, that my grandfather and a cousin had already departed for Texas to work in the oilfields—an event that certainly must have influenced where the others chose to move.

In early winter we jammed our belongings in and on top of the two family cars and moved from Ohio to Houston. Mother soon found work as a probation officer for Harris County, a job she held for over two years. She also attended night classes at the South Texas College of Law. Eventually, she graduated but failed to pass the bar exam.

It seemed that the Mays-Murray clan might finally be settling down, but in early 1952 my grandfather's sister-in-law convinced him to join her family in a business venture in Maryland. Grandfather left first for Baltimore, and then Grandmother, my uncle, Mother, and I eventually followed him in November of the same year.

We moved into a small red brick row house on Winford Road across the street from Northwood Elementary School. The neighborhood at the time was white and middle-class. Row houses had been common in this area of the nation for over a hundred years. Each had a front and back yard, but the walls of the house were shared with units on either side, unless it was at the end of the row, which ours was not. The front porch was covered with a green canvas awning, which was taken down during the winter months. The property owners' association dictated the size and color of these awnings. Consequently, the houses in the row maintained a uniform appearance all year long.

Each of the row houses on our block sat on a lot twenty-two feet wide and eighty feet deep, which allowed room for twenty feet of yard in front and back.

The inside of our home was as unimaginative as the outside. The front door opened into the living room, which was dominated by an open stairway to the second floor. The upstairs had three bedrooms and a bath. On the main floor, beyond the living room were the dining room and kitchen. A stairway from the kitchen led to the basement, a large, chilly room with concrete walls.

Although I was six years old and would have liked my own room, my single bed was set up next to my grandparents' double bed in the master bedroom. Uncle Irv occupied the larger and my mother the smaller of the two other bedrooms. The house was sparsely furnished. We had abandoned most of our furniture when leaving both Ohio and Texas, and only a few family heirlooms remained, such as an antique highboy belonging to Grandmother. To have money so we could furnish the house with basic pieces, Grandmother hocked her diamond ring.

It was a noisy house, the only one on the street you could hear from half a block away. A year after moving to Baltimore, my grandfather bought a television set, which was turned on at high volume throughout the day. To carry on a normal conversation, one always needed to shout.

Voices were raised, too, during the ongoing arguments between my mother and the others. If there was a fight, you could be sure Mother was involved, swearing, pounding her fist, expressing her rabidly held opinions with enormous energy. At age thirty-three, Mother was already losing her battle with excess weight, but her stout appearance only enhanced her ability to intimidate those who shun confrontation. I often awakened in the morning to the sounds of high-volume television and loud arguments, both rising annoyingly from the rooms below.

One major and oft-repeated dispute centered on the character of my mother's male companions. By 1953 she had met a local Italian man. Grandfather so disapproved of their romance that Mother's friend almost never made an appearance at our house. But the relationship went on, and sometime in February of 1954, Mother became pregnant, the event that provoked the ugly knife incident in the kitchen.

I was now nearly eight years old and a second grader at

the elementary school across the street from our house. Each morning before instruction began, my teacher led a brief ritual that was so much a part of each day's routine that it made no strong impression on me. After we settled at our desks, the teacher swiftly read a few verses from a worn black Bible. Upon closing the book and setting it on her desk, she asked all of us to bow our heads. We did so and recited in unison the Lord's Prayer. This daily custom lasted only two or three minutes, and because it was such a normal, expected part of my day, I never mentioned it to my mother.

Actually, there was little real intimacy of any kind shared between my mother and me. She had always been remote to me, not someone I shared things with or went to when I needed or wanted something. Her image was so indistinct I didn't know clearly until I was in grade school that she really was my mother. One day we were at the supermarket together and as always when I spoke to her, I called her by her first name.

"Madalyn," I asked, "can I get some Coke?"

She turned around and stared at me oddly. "Why do you keep calling me 'Madalyn'? I'm your mother."

I didn't have the nerve to tell her that I hadn't really understood she was my mother until that moment. I had, after all, gotten most of my parenting from my grandmother. To learn Madalyn was my mother was confusing and painful, because in many ways she was a stranger to me.

Our uneasy relationship became more strained after she became pregnant, because she frequently told me, "Bill, I'm not going to marry the baby's father. He won't marry me unless I give you away, and I love you too much to do that."

This announcement always troubled me, because I never suspected she loved me very much. Later, I realized it was Madalyn's not very subtle way of blaming me for her mistakes and frustrations, a way to allow me to help bear her guilt. But at my tender age, I was too young to recognize her tactics.

In May 1954, the family gathered to celebrate my eighth birthday with a dinner party. It was a particularly special occasion because my father, whom I could not remember having met, had been invited to attend the event. He arrived, and while the adults exchanged strained and awkward greetings, I noted that my father was tall and strongly built and had chiseled features. His hair was salt-and-pepper colored, and his eyes were pale blue, unlike mine which were light green.

Although my father tried, it became obvious as the party progressed that he did not fit in with our family in the little row house. He was from a wealthy Catholic family, one of thirteen children. Before dinner, he folded his hands, bowed his head, and said a prayer—something unheard of in our home.

After we ate, I opened my presents, and my father's gift to me was a model of the B-24 bomber he had flown during the war. The party ended, and as he was about to leave, he gave me the only hint I ever received of what was in his heart toward me. We were standing somewhat alone, and he squatted down to my level. "Good-bye, son. Happy birthday . . . . You're a fine boy," he said. I thought I saw a tear in his eye, but before I could be sure, he leaned over and kissed me squarely on the mouth. With that he strode out the door, leaving me startled and confused. I have never seen or talked to him since.

My birthdays always were more troubling than fun, largely because of Mother's gifts. When I was six, she had presented me with the largest Erector set on the market. It was a huge and elaborate collection of nuts, bolts, and metal girders, and the box's label read, "For children twelve years and up." A set more suitable for children my age had been available, but Mother wanted to show that any offspring of hers had superior intelligence. The next birthday she gave me a microscope. This frustrating sort of thing happened year after year.

As Mother's pregnancy progressed, she became obsessed with an unlikely notion for an avowed atheist. She told me over and over that some Christian sects taught that an illegiti-

mate child was condemned to hell from birth without possibility of salvation. Such talk upset me, because I was
vaguely aware of the circumstances of my own birth. Some
days it seemed she could think of nothing else, and she
developed an elaborate argument to refute this supposed
teaching. But her personal turmoil on this issue may have
become unbearable, because during the final weeks of the
pregnancy, she and Grandmother asked a Methodist minister if he would baptize the baby. Less likely is the possibility
that Mother agreed to the sacrament in deference to my
grandparents' wishes about such things. When asked by *Life*
magazine ten years later why she had both Garth and me
baptized, she said: "It pleased their grandparents, and I
figured the kids would think it was like any other water
splashing on their heads. My attitude then was, 'You go your
way, I'll go mine—you think Christ was born of a virgin; I
think he's the hero of a beautiful story . . . .' "

Whatever the case, Mother promised to attend the
pastor's church for one year in return for his services in
baptizing the child.

In November 1954, my half brother was born and named
Jon Garth Murray, despite the fact his father is not Murray.
From the first we called him Garth. He was baptized a month
later, and for about seven months thereafter, our family attended church. This was to be my only contact with religion
for many years, and aside from the fact that this was an
extraordinary activity for our family, the experience for me
was unmemorable.

The bleak depravity of life in our home on Winford Road
was shown by the treatment little Garth received after he was
carried home from the hospital. He was held and touched
only when he was fed or changed. He was rarely removed
from his crib in the dining room, except when relatives came
to visit. Suffering from this cruel isolation, as he grew older
Jon Garth sought attention by banging his head against the
headboard of his crib. He climbed on all fours, put his head
down, and rocked back and forth in order to butt his head
against the wood. Somedays he would keep this up for what

seemed to be hours. I heard the thudding of his head, even above the television set. No one, however, seemed to pay much attention or to regard his behavior as alarming, least of all my mother. The days passed, and Garth continued to bang his head.

I only met Garth's father once, before Garth was born. He came to our home for a visit and managed to step on my hand while I was playing with some Lincoln Logs on the floor. He and my mother never married.

When Garth outgrew his crib, he was moved to my bed in the master bedroom. A makeshift bedroom was set up for me in one corner of the basement, a chilly, damp room where later I contracted bronchitis.

It was after the family moved to Baltimore that my mother's frustration in life began to find expression in radical political ideas. Although her education and background now provided her with higher quality employment than had her post-war jobs in Ohio, she was unable to hold any job for much more than six months or so. She worked as an accountant, probation officer, welfare clerk, draftsman, and retail store clerk, but from her perspective her superiors in these jobs were inevitably dolts who were impossible to work for. If only they would have given up and let her run the place, things would have gone so much better, or so she thought. But her supervisors invariably failed to recognize her superiority, and thus her—and their—frustration grew, and Mother would end up leaving.

While on these various jobs, she evidently came in contact with other malcontents who shared her resentment against their managers. Some of these coworkers must have expressed their discontent politically. With some legal training in her background and brimming with energy and disgust for the status quo, Mother probably found irresistible the latest causes of the oppressed.

That is conjecture. What I do remember is that she began to host Socialist Labor party study meetings in our basement, right next to my bedroom. And when I was nine, she insisted I attend these meetings to learn the "truth" about capitalism.

When mother's turn came to host a meeting, she prepared for the arrival of her guests in the most bourgeois fashion. The house had to be immaculate, the furniture and staircase freshly polished. Even the kitchen was cleansed and put in perfect order, because the guests had to walk through it to reach the basement stairs. But most important, perhaps, was the display of my mother's books which, to the extent it was possible, lined the concrete walls of the below-ground room. She and her fellow Socialists fancied themselves to be an intellectual elite, hence the books were a vital prop in the scene. The ultimate irony of these occasions, though, was the sterling silver service with which my grandmother served tea to the budding revolutionaries.

The men and women who gathered in our dark basement were just as out of sorts with the world as my mother. They shared her contempt for the established order and its managers. This discontented group of "workers," all of whom had white collar jobs—some of them with the hated government—became for me what a church group would have been for another boy.

I remember sitting at the edge of these meetings, fighting off sleep as I heard that the United States was bad because it had rich people. Rich people were bad because they did not work; instead, they exploited the labor of others. Our nation was, in fact, an enormous fascist slave labor camp. We had been tricked into believing we were free. A dramatic Socialist revolution was needed to divest the rich of their wealth. Then the workers would control the means of production under the benevolent protection of a leftist dictatorship . . . . Heated discussions of this type—always seething with righteous indignation—would continue deep into the night.

I was bewildered by this talk, but I had little experience by which to test it. Like any child I was eager to gain the approval and support of adults, so I began to work strenuously to help these closet Socialists forward their goals. I set up the tables and chairs for their meetings and stuffed envelopes with Socialist literature. I also distributed leaflets. One day I was moving through the parking lot of a neighborhood shopping center, sliding Socialist tracts under the windshield wipers of the cars. I didn't know I was being watched.

"Hey, sonny! Whatcha doin' there?"

I looked up and saw a police officer walking toward me. I froze and didn't say anything. He pulled a leaflet out from under the wiper blade.

"Hmmm. Mighty interesting," he said, looking down at me from over the sheet. "Do you know what this piece of paper you're passing out is all about, young man?"

"Well, sir, not exactly. But it's to help the poor people . . . ."

"I see," he said, frowning. "Where do you live?"

"Fifteen twenty-six Winford Road, sir."

He was jotting notes on his pad. "Okay, and what are your parents' names?"

"Mrs. Murray."

"Mrs.?"

"Yes, sir."

"What about Mr. Murray?"

"Well, he does not live with us."

"Hmmm. Okay . . . what's your name?"

"Bill."

"Okay, Bill, let me take care of your papers," he said as he took the leaflets from my hand. "You just run along home now."

When I got home my grandfather found out what had happened. He was furious. "Madalyn, what the h— were you thinking about when you sent that boy out to distribute those commie handbills?"

"Don't tell me what I can or can't make my own son do!" she yelled in reply.

"Ha, your own son! If your mother hadn't fed him and changed his diapers, he would have died for all you ever cared."

"Aw, shut up."

"Only the grave could shut me up about this. You and

your commie politics make me sick. You shouldn't make Bill part of them!"

"Look who's talking about politics, you Nazi. If you weren't blind, you'd see how the Jews in big business are running this country into the ground. The poor working man hasn't got a chance in our system."

"I'm a Nazi and you hate Jews. Madalyn, you don't make sense. You've hardly ever held a job for longer than six months at a time. How would you know how the system works? I thank God for our system. Life in this country is better for everybody than anywhere else in the world. This system paid for your education and this house. You can't own a home in Russia."

"What do you know about Russia?"

"Enough to know I wouldn't want to live there!"

"H__, you don't know anything. Russia is a strong and beautiful nation. They were our allies in the last war. They had the guts to take wealth from the rich and give it to the poor."

"Yeah, now everybody's poor. . . ."

Arguments like this one occurred often, and the longer they lasted, the more ferocious and foul they became. My mother often became violent. Grandfather, though, weakened by age no doubt, seldom pressed his ideas. He had little need to; they were, after all, the prevailing ideas of the vast majority of Americans. His ability to resist being drawn into a violent argument with my mother became his best method of getting her goat.

Mealtime often found him perfecting his technique. Mother would be unable to sit for long at the dining room table before attacking her father for his politics, religion (he believed in God but now refused to join or attend any church), his taste in cars, or whatever came in handy. His stamina for this verbal combat was not as robust as hers, so after perhaps a half hour of being subject to her harangue, he would rise to his feet and quietly announce, "I've raised a godless Communist." Having rested his case with this—his ultimate slam—he would walk into the kitchen to enjoy his cup of coffee and cigarette in solitude.

These words and his condescending manner infuriated my mother more than anything, and as he retreated gracefully from the battlefield, she would hurl accusations after him that assigned to him, among other things, personal reponsibility for the stock market crash of 1929, the depression that followed it, and both world wars to boot.

On other occasions, I would be the target of my mother's remarks. This happened most often because of my grades. I was not a spectacular student at Northwood Elementary, and my report card often upset her. I did most of my homework in front of the TV, an enjoyable place to study away from the brawls. My poor study habits didn't help, but my academic achievement was hindered most, in my opinion, by the fact that Mother made me wear short pants to school. I was probably the only kid out of 800 who wore them, and my embarrassment caused me to spend most of my class time concentrating on ways to hide my bare legs under my desk. Mother's estimate of my intelligence didn't help. One night I was "studying" while Mother reviewed one of my recently graded papers.

"Bill, how can you be so stupid?" she shouted. "Any dunce ought to be able to spell 'quite.' "

I looked at her sourly. After all, how could I learn all that stuff and pay attention to *Highway Patrol* and the family fights at the same time? I was getting sick of her thoughtless badgering.

"And look at this math problem! You're still having trouble dividing fractions. Any idiot can do that. Get out here," she said, waving me to a chair next to hers at the dining room table. "Now, watch me. This stuff is a cinch. H___, I used to do all your uncle's college papers and other work for him. He can thank me for that degree of his."

She paused, but I said nothing. I had heard it all before, and no comment was needed.

"Oh well, men are stupid. No matter what the subject,

I've always picked it up with ease. But not you, or your father, or your uncle, or your grandfather! There's not a quick-witted man in the world!"

This appraisal of men roused Grandfather, who was also trying to concentrate on the television program.

"Madalyn," he said, as he walked stiffly to where we sat, "why don't you lay off the kid? He's only ten years old. G_____ it, you're just going to discourage him with that kind of talk."

Her face reddened, and her hazel eyes bulged with fury. "Get out, get out of here, you old f_____," she screamed. "Get out of here before I kill you!"

He shrugged and walked back to his chair in the living room. The way Mother talked to Grandfather made me angry, and I wished he would shut her up. But he didn't, so I simmered in silence as she drained the rest of her anger on me.

Not long after this incident, late one evening I was lying awake in my bed in the basement. Although the room was damp and had a musty odor, at least I was by myself. I looked at my clock: 11:00 P.M. The house was unusually quiet—the television had been turned off. My mother was out at a party meeting, but I knew my grandfather was still up. He was a bit of a nightowl and treasured those few late-night moments of quiet in the home. I suddenly felt the need to be near him, so I slipped out of bed and quietly crept up the stairs. I turned the kitchen doorknob gingerly, cracked it open, and eased my head through the opening. There was Granddad, sipping his coffee at the table. He looked up at me and smiled, "C'mon in and sit down, Bill."

I smiled, too, and walked across the room and perched silently on a chair across from him. Except for an electric clock humming on the wall, there was silence. It was strange to feel such peace in the spot where so many battles had raged.

"How's the Little League baseball going?" Grandfather asked.

"Oh, fine."

"What position are you playing now?"

"First base. Sometimes they put me behind the plate."

"How's your hittin'?"

"Pretty good, Granddad. I'm at about .220."

"It makes my heart feel good to see you get involved in a man's thing like that, Bill." He paused, drawing a large mouthful of coffee from his cup. "You know, if it were up to that mother of yours, you'd be wearing dresses and playing with dolls. I watch her when you talk about baseball. She just hates it. Sometimes I think she hopes you'll get injured and have to stop playing."

My eyes widened as I listened. He might be right. I remembered one of Mother's favorite stories about when I was born. After I was delivered and the doctor told her she now had a boy, she asked if there wasn't some way he could put me back because she would rather have a girl.

"All she wants anybody involved in is those d____ commie politics of hers," Granddad went on. His face reddened, "A man'd be better off dead than living in a country run by Communists. They ruin everything. The people go hungry.

"Give me the good old U.S.A.," he continued. "I had troubles in the Depression, but that didn't stop me from feeding your mom and your uncle. You know, when my company went broke in 1927, I moved us all to Ohio, and me and this aunt of your grandma's opened a roadhouse. Do you know what a roadhouse is, boy?"

"Like a restaurant?" I asked.

"Well, yes. It was the sort of place where people could relax and have a drink during Prohibition."

"You mean you sold booze?" I asked, surprised at this revelation. I had not seen Grandfather during his drinking days.

"Yep."

"Wasn't that against the law?"

"Sure was," he laughed, "but that never stopped an enterprising American. And, let me tell you, we had the best stuff in the county. Everybody knew it, too. Why, the sheriff himself was one of our best customers. He and his lady friend came there to our roadhouse all the time—and his wife never found out about it either."

I laughed. Although I had heard Mother mention the roadhouse, Grandfather made it sound more interesting and exciting.

"You'll find out about lady friends and things like that soon enough," he chuckled. Then his smile vanished and his eyes got a faraway look. "Those were the days," he went on, his voice soft and winsome, "when we were running that roadhouse. Roosevelt ruined it, though, when he got 'em to repeal Prohibition. Then he got us into a war to boot. Mark my words, you can never trust a politician. None of 'em— Democrats or Republicans—do what they say they're gonna do. And those Communist friends of your mother's are no exception. If they ever took over, she'd be one of the first ones they'd put in jail."

I listened intently, and an hour must have passed as he told me more stories about the roadhouse. I wanted the pleasure of our companionship to stretch on, but when I began to yawn and prop my head in my hands, Grandfather sent me down to bed.

I lay awake for a while, though, still excited by Grandfather's words. He had planted some thoughts in my mind, some feelings about my country and what it meant to be a man. I loved his stories and the warmth and peace we had enjoyed while Mother was away.

aving successfully completed the field elimination tests for appointment to the position of cadet in the Inter-planetary Patrol, you are authorized to report to the commandant, Terra Base, Santa Barbara Field, Colo-rado, North American Union, Terra, on or before 1 July 2075, for further examination.

You are cautioned to remember that the majority of candidates taking these final tests usually fail, and you should provide . . .

"Bill! It's time for supper. Will you get up here!" My grandmother's voice interrupted my escape into *Space Cadet*, a science fiction book by Robert Heinlein.

"Okay, I'm coming," I yelled, putting my book aside. Like many young boys, I had begun to indulge in fantasies and daydreams about flying machines. The dream of flight, of mighty rocket engines propelling me into space to far-off worlds thrilled me. I dreamed of the day I would climb aboard one of those sleek ships and find my hands at the controls. I regularly read one or two science fiction books each week.

Although at age ten escape via fantasy was my way to cope with the chaos at home, when I was younger I had tried to anticipate my mother's fluctuating moods and find ways to win her approval.

On one occasion, for example, when I was about nine, I composed a blasphemous prayer and hurried to recite it to Mother. With a smug grin, I proudly spoke my irreverent piece, not paying much heed to Grandmother who was in the room and quickly began to frown. After finishing, I looked into my mother's face, expecting her to laugh and compliment me for my creativity. Instead, I was stunned to see her mouth twisted into an angry scowl.

"You stupid little b_____! What do you mean, doing something like that in front of your grandmother?" she yelled.

"I, uhh," I stammered, shocked by her reaction.

"Shut up and get your a__ over there and tell her you're sorry for what you did!"

My eyes clouded with tears of embarrassment and resentment as I walked to Grandmother's chair. "I'm sorry," I muttered.

"That's okay, dear," she said gently.

I turned and ran from the room. I was hardly out the door when the hot tears stopped and my heart became sullen and cold. After that, I didn't bother much to gain my mother's approval, and as best I could, I ignored her shifting moods. When life became too miserable, I could always escape by reading the latest science fiction thriller by Robert Heinlein or by turning my eyes to our ever-present and blaring television set.

At about that time I was introduced to another way of avoiding reality—one of mankind's most tried and proven methods. Each Friday my grandmother would head for the A & P and buy the family's weekly supply of groceries. Always a part of the purchases was a half gallon of wine. Every evening, after Grandmother had washed and put away the supper dishes, she would brew a pot of tea. Then she and Mother would mix the tea and wine half and half and sit at the kitchen table, chatting and sipping their warm libation. By the time I was ten, I had been invited to join them in this pastime.

The other males of the house were not included. Grandfather was too ill to drink, although I knew he had consumed more than his share as a younger man. Uncle Irv, now in his early forties, never drank. For some reason, the women wanted me to drink and talk with them, to be one of the "girls" who ran the house. If that was the price for my daily round of spiked tea, I gladly paid it. A warm high at the end of the day helped blank out the dismal reality of my young life.

In 1957, Mother grew bored with the Socialist Labor party because it didn't *do* anything. There was no action, only endless discussions about the coming revolution.

Consequently, Mother switched her allegiance to the more radical Socialist Worker's party (SWP). This was the renegade party of Leon Trotsky, the immensely powerful Bolshevik leader who had plotted the November revolution with Lenin in 1917. When Lenin had died in 1924, it seemed certain that Trotsky would succeed him, but he had been outsmarted by Joseph Stalin and eventually ended up in exile in Mexico. There he was cruelly assassinated with an ice pick by an agent of the Stalinist government on August 21, 1940.

As my mother became involved with this more vigorous and militant organization, we learned that many of its members were also government employees. Others received the government's direct benefits as welfare recipients or were students living on low-interest federal loans. Like those in the previous group, I can't recall meeting a true "worker" in their midst. None of them wore overalls or had dirt under their fingernails.

This party's members, though, did do more than talk, holding antiwar and other protest demonstrations in downtown Baltimore. Their chief endeavor, however, was to form and support the Ad-Hoc Committee against the House Unamerican Activities Committee. In this way they challenged the Congress's right to investigate dissident groups such as their own.

Mother's support of radical causes grew even more intense during the next few years. She was especially involved with the Ad-Hoc Committee and with the pro-Castro group, which formed later. But all of this activity must not have satisfied Mother's urges to separate herself from the American mainstream. She began to consider a permanent move to the Soviet Union. This idea had first been voiced about a year after Garth was born, and she had subscribed to *USSR* (now called *Soviet Life*), the official English-language propaganda publication of the Soviet government. This slick magazine was designed to resemble *Life* and *Look*, its popular American counterparts. The articles and four-color photographs extolled the virtues and superior qualities of Soviet life. Interestingly, the magazine was printed in Virginia by an American company.

Besides that, we received a monthly from the People's Republic of China and two weekly newspapers published by the Communist party of the United States—the *Weekly Worker* and the *National Guardian*. The information in the *Weekly Worker* was obviously intended for the ardent Communist.

All of this literature reinforced my mother's growing resolve to move to Russia, and sometime during 1959 she made her first application for Soviet citizenship through the Soviet Embassy in Washington.

While Mother awaited word from the Soviets, she drifted from job to job and continued to force her extreme views on the family. In addition, I was beginning to learn that the only predictable feature of her personality was her maddening unpredictability. This quality showed itself in many areas, one being her attitude toward cars. As with all things, mundane or important, any car had to be rated not simply as "good" or "bad" but as "the best" or "the worst."

Mother told me, in the most passionate way, that small cars were dangerously unsafe and that anyone who drove such a life-threatening vehicle was decidedly strange. Not old enough to be much of an authority on cars, I accepted what she had to say and shared her opinion until the day she purchased a small car. It was a small, foreign-built car, popular with intellectuals and leftists in the mid-1950s. Now I began to hear a different story: Lo and behold, large cars were "the worst," unsafe and expensive monsters, owned by strange people—a group, incidentally, that included my grandfather and uncle. And even though Mother was often unemployed, she traced our family's financial problems to the purchase of large American cars by the men in the family.

However, when the little car was traded in for a large Chevrolet two years later, large cars once again became "the best."

This flip-flopping of opinions on topics like cars, although irritating, was relatively harmless and became even humorous to me as I grew older. But more disruptive and troubling was a darker streak in Mother's unpredictable behavior—her vicious and violent temper. She erupted in many situations, but the after-dinner arguments seemed to produce the majority of her temper fits. One night her anger about some remark I had made so enraged her that she ran downstairs to my room and smashed to the floor the model airplanes I had been building and collecting for years. When I heard the sound of wood and plastic crashing and splitting I too ran to my room. Seeing the wreckage, tears welled in my eyes. Mother looked at me, cursed, and left the room.

Although incidents like this were frustrating, I probably was hurt deepest by her basic lack of interest in me. One sad memory demonstrates how this outlook wounded my childhood.

I played on a Little League baseball team that won a league championship one summer. Each member of the team received a small plastic trophy, which I carried home with great pride. This event must have made no impression on Mother, because two years later when she found the trophy in a closet, she asked me where I had bought it. When I protested that I had won the prize, she dismissed my answer as a "nice fantasy." It wasn't even clear to her that I had played baseball, so how could I have won a trophy? This incident, and others like it, dulled what little warmth I felt for her.

It seemed the only times of household peace came when Mother lapsed into periods of depression. She would withdraw into herself, and sometimes for days, the arguments and violence would cease.

One afternoon in 1959, a friendly looking Fuller Brush salesman named Bob Lee knocked on our door. Mother let him in, and after a few minutes, she discovered the man was a member of the Communist party. He had heard of her desire to go to Russia through the party grapevine. He urged her not to do it. He reasoned that there was a greater need in the United States for good agitators, those who could work here to overthrow the government.

In spite of the fact that Bob was unusually charming and friendly, Mother was unconvinced. She continued her efforts to find a way to Russia.

The decade of the sixties began, and in its early months Mother was still sending letters and documents to the Soviet Embassy in Washington. She had photographs of Garth and myself taken and sent them to the embassy. She also made the Russians aware of her vast job experience, claiming that she was, among other things, an aerospace engineer, attorney, psychiatric social worker, and a retired army field grade officer.

In April of 1960, Soviet cosmonaut Yuri Gagarin became the first man to be launched into outer space. That afternoon when I came home from classes at Woodbourne Junior High School, Mother was waiting at the door. Excitedly, she explained how "we" could use this Soviet space triumph as a way of endearing ourselves to the Russians. The plan was for me to clip every reference on Gagarin I could find in newspaper and magazine articles and glue the items into a scrapbook. When the time was right, the scrapbook would be sent to the Soviet Embassy—further evidence of our family's loyalty to Mother Russia.

Mother's idea filled me with anguish. This was not the first time she had asked me to show enthusiasm for such topics. During the school year I had surprised my teachers by submitting several pro-Soviet reports, most of them written by Mother. One had been a glowing review of a Caspian Sea resort in which I showed how the assets of this vacation spot greatly exceeded anything comparable in America. Another had touted in a subtle way the glories of the Soviet government and economic system. Papers like these did not impress my teachers, and after I submitted the report on

Russian government, a group of boys cornered me after school and roughed me up, calling me a "commie traitor" and more.

At any rate, my grumbling did not dampen Mother's zeal, and for several weeks I clipped and pasted. Not satisfied with our usual stock of periodicals, Mother gathered newspapers from New York, Chicago, and other cities.

Here was yet another project that became more important than my school work. It was a tedious job, and being only a month away from fourteen, I had other things on my mind. In particular, I wanted to pass an FCC examination for a general class amateur radio license. To do so, I would have to copy thirteen words per minute in Morse Code and successfully complete an exhaustive test on theory of radio electronics. But this would have to wait.

Eventually, Mother was satisfied. I had a scrapbook on Yuri Gagarin that must have been larger than any his own mother compiled. But about the time I was hoping to forget my Soviet space hero, Mother loaded me and the scrapbook into the car and drove toward Washington. I was dismayed. We parked at the Soviet Embassy and walked to the front door. Mother, choosing an unusually subtle approach for her, decided not to go inside herself but pushed me through the door. I sighed and walked into the lobby where I announced myself to the receptionist. After about fifteen minutes, some minor official came out and chatted politely with me. With a mumbled explanation I handed him the scrapbook.

"Yes, young man, this is very impressive," he said, with a puzzled look. "We are all very proud of Comrade Gagarin's accomplishment. Thank you very much."

I smiled and nodded half-heartedly. We said our goodbyes, and I walked back to the car.

"How did it go? Did they recognize you from our application for citizenship?" Mother asked, hopefully.

"Nope."

"Oh, well, I'll call them tomorrow," she said without noticeable disappointment. We were having as much trouble getting into Russia as some people were having getting out!

The episode, as far as I know, had no impact at all on the evaluation of Mother's application.

Mother's patience with the Russians faded as summer passed. In August she boldly announced that she, Garth, and I were going to travel to France and reapply for Russian citizenship in Paris. Mother believed this would speed up the process. The decision made, preparations proceeded with haste, including the purchase on credit of several large suitcases and assorted warm clothing to help us survive Russia's cold winters. Passage was booked on the *Queen Elizabeth*.

I prepared for our departure with mixed emotions. If the trip actually came off, it would be a great adventure, but I was wary, too, of the uncertain future. And such as it was, I would be leaving the only home I'd known.

On our departure date, August 24, 1960, we arrived early at the Cunard Line dock in New York City. The old *Queen Elizabeth* was huge, one of the most luxurious liners ever built. Only a few years later she would be taken out of service and eventually would perish in flames in Hong Kong harbor, but for now she and her sister, the *Queen Mary*, were the grand dames of the North Atlantic. Each was over a thousand feet long and had been crossing the Atlantic for Cunard since they were launched in the 1930s.

We walked to the gangplank, showed our tickets, and then boarded the ship that Mother hoped would take us away forever from the despised American shores.

arewells behind us, we quickly made our way to our quarters, a small compartment in the tourist section, deep in the interior of the ship. Our room was equipped with three single beds, a couple of dressers, and a small bathroom with a shower. There were no portholes, since our lodging was several decks below the waterline.

Now that I was fourteen and a card-carrying adolescent, the last thing I wanted to do was spend four days trapped in a small room with my mother and baby brother—under water no less. So that first day out, I gave the ship a complete search. My investigation made it plain that the quality of life improved the higher one climbed on the ship. I sneaked into areas reserved for first-class passengers and tried to act as though I belonged.

Up top, I was watching other passengers promenade by, checking to see if there were any girls on board, when a teenage boy who looked about my age approached me. He smiled and introduced himself. His name was Tom, and he quickly proved to be a friendly sort. We conversed a few minutes, and I learned that he, too, had escaped from the ship's bowels where his family was crammed in a cabin similar to ours. Tom and I agreed we should make the most of this exotic setting and remained a team for the rest of the voyage.

By stealth we entered the first-class sections and partook of the various amenities, including a large swimming pool, game room, and theater. We even sampled the first-class cuisine in the dining room. Amid these pleasures, I buried with ease any troubling thoughts of my future life in Russia. I was having the time of my life.

During several of our idle moments that first day, Tom and I slipped away from the topside luxury to visit our families below. Mother seemed unconcerned with my long absences and was busy strolling, with Garth close behind, the tourist-class corridor, telling anyone who would listen of her decision to leave decadent America for good. She tried her best to win some converts to socialism, but the passengers on the *Queen Elizabeth* were apparently too distracted to be much interested in revolution. Having heard Mother's leftist propaganda for years, I absented myself quickly and rejoined Tom and the other capitalists in first class.

Our hopes of enjoying three more days of floating paradise were interrupted by a late summer hurricane. The sea rose in fury, forcing the closing of the watertight bulkhead doors. Even the dining rooms were shut down, so Tom and I were forced to eat the first-class sandwiches and snacks. Cooped up, we passed the time playing cards and other games in the lounges. All the while the winds wailed outside, and the ship rolled and groaned.

The hurricane had passed by the end of the third night out, and the ship resumed full service. Tom and I eagerly planned our last day of self-indulgence. The weather being suitable, we had decided on a swim and were walking toward the pool when the fire alarm rang. The ship's personnel ran to their firefighting stations, and soon the voice over the loudspeaker commanded that all passengers leave their cabins. Within minutes, black smoke bellowed from the central portion of the ship, and the mammoth liner began to circle slowly at a steep angle to port. Smoke curled to the sky from the starboard portholes.

A bit frightened, Tom and I joined the other passengers in discussing the rumors racing faster than the fire through the ship. The official word came a bit later—the ship's air conditioning system had caught fire. There was no great danger, and the fire had been extinguished; but the ship would continue to circle until more of the smoke had escaped from the lower decks.

Later that evening, the *Queen Elizabeth* sailed into the choppy waves of the English channel, and shortly before dawn, we arrived at the LeHavre, France, harbor. Mother and I repacked our suitcases. I was gloomy, having already said good-bye to Tom and knowing I would have to hang around Mother and little Garth as we made our way to our new homeland.

After disembarking and clearing customs, we caught the next available train to Paris. I was only half awake as the train rocked along through Normandy. Mother studied intently a copy of *Europe on Five Dollars a Day*, then a popular travel guide. By the time we arrived in Paris, she had selected an inexpensive hotel, the name of which she gave to our cab driver who in minutes deposited us at the hotel's door. We rented a modest room and then had lunch. As we ate, Mother examined a map to pinpoint the location of the Soviet Embassy.

"Ah, here it is on Boulevard Lannes," she said. "It's probably closed today, so we'll head over there first thing tomorrow."

We passed the rest of the day seeing some of the sights near our hotel. Early Monday morning we took a cab to the embassy. Mother was nervous with anticipation.

"*Bon jour, madame*," the man at the desk near the front entrance greeted my mother.

"Uh, *bon jour* . . . do you speak English?"

He looked puzzled for a moment, "Ahh," his eyes brightened with understanding, "*Anglais? No, madame.*" He then blurted something out in Russian. But, when that was greeted by our bewilderment, he motioned us to wait while he stepped into another room.

Shortly, he returned with a young woman who was evidently a French employee of the embassy. She spoke a few words of English. After a tortured attempt at conversation, we got the idea they wanted us to come back the next morning. We showed up again the next day—to the visible disappointment of the receptionist. Once more there was a stumbling attempt to communicate, with no more success. We agreed to return—the next day. This pattern continued for several days. It was like being at the Soviet Embassy in Washington, only worse; now no one seemed to understand what we wanted.

After a week or so, Mother's persistence apparently paid off. The Soviets seemed to understand what we wanted and indicated it would be some time before a decision was made. In the meantime, the three of us set off to see the sights of Paris . . . on foot.

I rebelled: "But, Mother, why can't we just rent one of these little French cars? It wouldn't cost that much, would it?"

"Look, Bill, like I told you before," Mother answered, "my funds are limited. Coming over on the *Queen* cost a lot of money—almost half of what I had rounded up for the whole trip."

"If the Russians do let us in, will you have enough money for the fare to Moscow?"

"Oh sure, that will be cheaper than flying back to New York."

"Do you have enough to fly to New York?"

"Just barely. That's why we have to do our sightseeing on foot."

Our conversation was interrupted by a whimper from Garth. He was just five, and this vagabond existence was no fun for him.

"What's the matter now?" Mother demanded.

"Mommy, my legs hurt. I'm tired. I want to sit down."

"Aw h__! Bill! Hoist Garth on your shoulders. He'll see more from up there, and it'll give his legs a rest."

"D___, Mother," I objected. "He weighs a ton, and he's big enough to do his own walking."

"Don't give me that, you smart aleck b___! Watch your tongue. Garth would have a father if I had given you away."

I swore at her under my breath. Whenever she wanted to

make me feel guilty and bend to her wishes, she reminded me of how Garth's father would have married her if somehow she could have gotten rid of me. I thought to myself, *What a bunch of garbage;* but tired of her nagging and of Garth's whining, I loaded him on my back.

We had plenty of time for extensive sightseeing, because there was no movement on Mother's request at the Soviet Embassy. So day after day I lugged Garth around Paris, even to the top of the Eiffel Tower.

After nearly a month the Russians informed us that the Presidium of the Supreme Soviet alone could rule on our immigration request, and that would take months. My mother's disappointment would have been less had it not been for the parting words of one of the embassy's staff members.

"Mrs. Murray," he said, "I do not believe you have a true comprehension of the advances made by the Communist party and Marxist principles in our motherland. We need no welfare or food stamp programs in the Soviet Union, as everyone is employed. In fact, it is against the law to be unemployed. The punishment for not being employed is hard labor at half pay. As a result we have been able to abolish our unemployment commission."

He paused for a moment and glanced at some papers in his hand. He continued. "In looking at your work record, it would seem you would be working for the most part at half pay." He paused again and smiled. "Besides, you do not speak the mother tongue. More than likely your two fatherless boys would become wards of the state. Perhaps you and your children would be better off working for the revolution in your native land."

I do not believe his words represented an official response but were rather a personal observation. But on the other hand, in a totalitarian state many decisions and comments of this nature are determined at the highest level.

Nikita Khrushchev was in power at the time. My best memory of him was when he had pounded his shoe on a table at a General Assembly meeting of the United Nations.

Now, in my adolescent mind, I envisioned him in the Kremlin moving his shoes on his desk to find the red-jacketed dossier labeled "Murray." After reading it I could hear him say, "We can use this family. We need these people! Send them back to America where they can be of use."

I was certain that folder also contained the comments of good party members from the United States, including reports from Bob Lee and the chairman of the Maryland branch.

Mother counted her remaining francs and gave up. She went posthaste to the American Express office and purchased the least expensive tickets to New York she could find.

Ironically, the lowest airfare was available on the Israeli airline, El Al. Mother didn't care much for Israel because of that country's anti-Soviet posture and Jewish heritage. But we were nearly broke, so principles had to bow to financial realities.

After midnight on a day late in September, we boarded a Lockheed Electra at Orly airport. I remained awake during most of the flight. The moments of euphoria I had felt while cruising the Atlantic on the *Queen Elizabeth* did not return as I looked out the window at the red glow of the turbo-prop engines. I wondered what would happen when we got back to Baltimore. I had told a number of my classmates at Woodbourne Junior High School that my family and I would be leaving for Europe that summer, never to return. It had felt so good. No one had been able to top it for startling announcements.

As the engines droned on, I stared out into the blackness. I hated the thought of having to eat a considerable amount of crow. But there was another side to it—I was going home. The familiar is generally easier to contemplate than the unfamiliar, and I was glad to be returning to a place where at least the people spoke my language. Besides, the Soviet Union didn't seem to want us, while America would be willing to take us back.

The plane landed at New York's Idlewild International

Airport shortly after dawn. Mother was unusually nervous and irritable. When we entered the terminal, I saw on the front page of a newspaper the pictures of Richard Nixon and John Kennedy, candidates for president in the coming election. Their campaign was in full swing, and the big news this morning was their agreement to debate face-to-face on national television.

We hurried on to customs, and as we waited our turn in line, I realized why Mother was trembling; some months before, she had written to the U.S. State Department and formally renounced her American citizenship. I don't think she ever had received a reply, but I suppose she wondered now if she would be intercepted and refused entry.

We were waved through the public health station without comment after showing our yellow "International Immunization Cards." By now Mother was in a full sweat. When we reached the immigration officer, I honestly thought she might blurt out a full confession. She warily handed him the single passport containing our three names and pictures. He flipped through the pages looking for visa stamps and, without looking up, asked, "France on vacation?"

Mother froze and could not speak, so I answered for her. "No, sir, trying to defect," I said with a wide smile.

The agent liked my sense of humor, smiled back, and said, "Very funny, young man." He stamped the passport "Entered USA, New York, New York," and we moved along.

At the customs position an officer dug through the long underwear, sweaters, and other heavy clothing in our bags but found no contraband. We moved on to the passenger reception area. Waiting there was Grandmother and a couple who lived next to us in Baltimore. We had sent a telegram from Paris to the Mayses telling them of our arrival time.

When Mother saw our greeting party, she grunted, "Oh, it's those d___ next door neighbors, the Hydes. I suppose that lazy brother of mine wouldn't drive Mother up here! As for you smart a—," she said to me, "that comment could have gotten me nailed. I'll fix your loud mouth."

When we reached Grandmother, she gave each of us a

quick hug; but for the most part, the greeting was noticeably low-key. We walked out of the terminal and waited while Mr. Hyde brought up his car, a large American model with a trunk big enough to hold our suitcases. We climbed in, Grandmother, Garth, and I in back, and Mother in front with the Hydes.

"Well, how was Paris?" Mr. Hyde asked, making a stab at conversation.

"Yes, did you have a nice vacation?" his wife added.

Mother shot a dirty look to Grandmother, then smiled, "Beautiful, just beautiful. We couldn't have had a nicer time. And the tourist crowds weren't so bad because we went in the off season."

"That's nice," Mrs. Hyde commented. "I didn't realize the off season started so early."

"Yes. You know we went over on the *Queen Elizabeth*. Cunard puts off-season rates into effect for eastbound voyages on August twenty-third. We sailed the twenty-fourth. Saved about forty dollars right there. . . ."

It was all becoming clear to me. Grandmother, out of embarrassment no doubt, had not told the neighbors that her daughter and grandchildren had gone to Paris hoping to defect to the Soviet Union. Instead, she had said we were on a vacation. Why not? Grandmother had gambled that our chances of being ushered into Moscow on a red carpet were slim. She later attributed her accurate prediction to her tarot cards.

Back in Baltimore, we found Grandfather in the kitchen, his coffee cup and Camel cigarette in hand. He forced a weak smile when we clattered in, but his excitement at seeing us, if he had any, was skillfully hidden.

Mother looked through the stack of mail and opened the bill for our luggage. She had no money to pay it but soon found a creative solution.

"Bill, what did you do with those boxes the suitcases came in?" she asked.

"They're probably still in the basement, why?"

"You'll see." She then told me to get the pliers from

Grandfather's toolbox and to break several of the latches from the suitcases, which I did.

"That's good, Bill," she said when I had finished. "Now take these suitcases downstairs. I'll pack them up in those boxes and mail them to the manufacturer. I can say that the latches were defective and came apart during our trip."

"Do you think you can get away with it?" I asked in disbelief.

"You let me worry about that, d___ it! Now get busy!"

"Okay, okay. No need to blow a gasket," I muttered as I picked up the now-damaged luggage. It turned out that she was right—not in what she did but in her guess that the luggage manufacturer would fall for it.

That evening at supper, Mother told me I would have to enroll in school the following day. I groaned aloud, dreading the thought of having to face my classmates. Their taunts on my short "permanent" stay in Europe would turn out to be minor, though, in light of other events. My first day back at school would change my life forever.

I did not leap out of bed enthusiastically that morning during the last week of September. After Grandmother woke me with a yell from the top of the stairs, I stayed buried under the covers, listing in my mind the dreadful events I expected my first day back at school. First, there would be mounds of past assignments to complete. And the cracks and jeers of my peers already rang in my ears. I groaned and shut my eyes, hoping I could sink back into sleep and somehow the day would pass without my being a part of it. My semi-slumber was broken soon, though, by a profane threat from Mother. I crawled out of bed and tugged on my clothes. Soon we were on our way out the door.

Mother, having quit her job before our attempted defection, was again unemployed and had the time to drive me to school and explain my late enrollment. The weather was pleasant, and as we drove through the residential streets, warm air flowed in through the open windows. My spirits revived a bit—it was good to see the familiar sights of Baltimore. But my dread resurfaced when I saw the red brick walls of Woodbourne Junior High.

We arrived several minutes before eight and readily found a parking place. The first bell had rung to indicate school would begin in five minutes, so the sidewalks were clear. We walked up the steps and into one of the school's main hallways, which was deserted.

"How come it's so quiet in here?" Mother asked.

"Everybody's still in their homeroom," I answered.

We walked down the long hall in silence, following the signs pointing to the school office. The doors to the classrooms stood open. As we passed one class we saw the students standing with their hands over their hearts, reciting the pledge of allegiance to the flag. My mother's face reddened. "Do they do this every day or is this something special?" she demanded.

"Every day."

She stopped dead in front of another open classroom door. Mother's eyes widened. The students were standing beside their desks with their heads bowed, reciting the Lord's Prayer. "Why in h__ didn't you tell me about this?" she spat in a hoarse whisper.

"We were on our way to the Soviet Union to become great commissars, remember?"

"You smart-a_ b____," she hissed, raising her hand menacingly. I ducked back to avoid the expected blow, but she changed her mind and just froze, a glare in her eyes. "You should have told me about this!"

I shrugged. I knew why I hadn't told her. Every time I mentioned anything about school, she found some reason to belittle or strike me. It seemed wise not to tell her the true reason now, though, since she was steaming with anger. Instead, I just drew a deep breath and walked on toward the office. She strode along behind, her stocky body now tense and ready for battle.

In moments we found the counselor's office, and as we entered, a young, slender man looked at us expectantly. "Hello, may I help you?" he asked pleasantly.

"You sure can, but first I want to know why those kids are praying?" Mother shouted, advancing to within inches of his desk. "Why are they doing that? It's un-American and unconstitutional!"

The man swallowed. "I, uhh, well . . . Is your son a student here?" he asked.

"No," she answered. "But he will be starting today. I'm an atheist, and I don't want him taught any g_____ prayers."

"Look, Mrs.—uhh, what is your name?"

"Murray—Madalyn Murray."

"Look, Mrs. Murray, nobody's ever complained about this before that I know of." He paused, searching for more ammunition. "Besides, even those who aren't very religious still think this sort of thing helps improve the tone of the school day . . ."

"Nonsense! That's just a bunch of g___ nonsense, and you know it!"

"Hey, I don't want to fight with you about this. Nothing you or I do here this morning is going to change anything. Besides, let me tell you this. There were prayers in the schools of this city before there was a United States of America. If our forefathers had wanted us to stop the practice, they would have told us that when they formed the government. Now, shall we enroll your son?"

Mother was so furious she had nearly turned purple. The counselor filled in the late enrollment forms for her to sign. When he was finished, he drew a large "T" on the label of my file. I learned later it stood for "troublemaker."

Mother aimed one last verbal shot at him. "This won't be the last time you hear from me about your g___ prayers in this school!"

"Madam," he replied sternly, "I don't have to take this! If you don't like what we do here, put your son in a private school."

"It doesn't matter where I put him. You people have to be stopped," she replied.

"Then why don't you sue us?" he asked.

Mother stared at him, then motioned for me to leave. Unknowingly, the counselor had given Mother what would turn out to be a very devastating idea.

In any event I was enrolled in the ninth grade and scheduled to start classes the next morning. The counselor had explained that I would have to complete all the back homework I had missed. We left the building and got in the car.

During the drive home, Mother questioned me more about the prayers and Bible reading. When I told her I had been participating in these for years at school, she cursed me roundly, accusing me of being stupid and brainless like all men. We were almost back to the row house on Winford Road when an idea interrupted her criticism of me. "Hey, I know what we can do!" Mother said, her mood brightening.

"Tomorrow morning, I want you to start keeping a log of what happens during the school day. Make special notes on any activities that smack of religion in any form: prayer, Bible reading, songs. You know why, don't you?"

"No, Mom, I don't really. The guy said the majority wants . . ."

"You stupid fool!" she said, slapping me hard across the face. "Don't you understand what is going on yet?" Her face was flushed again. "Listen, kid, the United States of America is nothing more than a fascist slave labor camp run by a handful of Jew bankers in New York City. They trick you into believing you're free with those phony rigged elections. Just because we can run around the street free doesn't mean we are really free."

I sighed. *Why do I have to listen to this garbage over and over?* I thought.

"The only way true freedom can be achieved is through the new socialist man—an entire race that lives for the state. Only when all men know the truth of their animal sameness will we have true freedom. Russia is close but not close enough, or they would have let us in. The CIA probably passed bad information on us."

We halted at a red light, but Mother didn't stop talking.

"Well, if they'll keep us from going to Russia where there is some freedom, we'll just have to change America. I'll make sure you never say another prayer in that school!"

Now I was to become a spy. I had to log information on the school and my fellow students for a purpose not yet clear to me. I foresaw trouble—trouble in the form of my fellow students who had worked me over after I turned in the reports on Russia and the Black Sea resort.

The next day I began the log. A girl in my homeroom read two or three verses from the Bible. Then we all recited the Lord's Prayer. Next came the pledge of allegiance to the flag, which included the phrase "under God." These same events happened each day, but I observed little else that was particularly religious. At the end of the week there was a general assembly of the student body in the school auditorium. Here students and teachers both recited the pledge and said the Lord's Prayer with heads bowed reverently. I noted this in my notebook.

That weekend Mother read the log I had kept. She grunted, a bit disappointed I think that I had not discovered more. In the meantime she had looked through my textbooks with greater success.

"Have you read much of this world history text of yours?" she asked.

"No, not much. I've been too busy keeping prayer logs," I answered, trying out a bit of my adolescent sarcasm.

"Well, I have, you smart a__. I can't believe all the hogwash in there. It treats the parting of the Red Sea just like it really happened. It's incredible! Later on it talks about Jesus and says he was the son of God, that he performed miracles and rose from the dead. Damnedest stuff I ever read. It has no place in a public school textbook!"

I nodded in agreement, hoping the discussion would end so I could steal away to watch some TV or read some more science fiction. It did. Mother's time was already filling up with other dissident activities, even though we had only been back from the Paris escapade for a few days. Mother's ardor for things Soviet had not cooled a bit, even though she had been rebuffed by Russian bureaucrats in both Washington and Paris. She had plunged back into the causes of leftist politics with greater vigor than ever. One night she told me that the Fuller Brush Communist had been right: People like her were needed more in America than in the Soviet Union.

This political busybody stuff bored me. I had become disenchanted with communism and leftist causes after the trip to Paris. All I wanted to do was merge into the teen-age masses at school and do my share of girl watching and chasing. But hard as I tried, Mother would not let me be normal.

After two weeks of my undercover work on religion at school, Mother sat me down on Sunday evening, October 9, and told me of her plans. "First of all, I've already written a report on this situation for the Soviet Embassy in Washington. Maybe, when they understand our situation with you, they'll be more sympathetic to our request," she said.

Now I was really puzzled. But she was so intense, I decided it would be unwise to mention what she had said about needing to remain in America and work for communism within its borders. Instead, I simply asked, "Is that all you're going to do?"

"No, of course not!" she banged her fist on the table. We were seated across from each other in the dining room. "I'm going to insist that the school authorities permit you to be absent from the room during the Bible reading and prayer. And, if they don't allow this, I'm going to withdraw you from school."

"Really, do you mean it?"

"D___ right I do."

I smiled. I might avoid all that back homework after all. I could imagine those school administrators and teachers fuming and fussing. I might not have to worry anymore about getting beat up because of my mother's activities and views.

"Well?" Mother's voice broke up my thoughts.

"Well what?"

"Do you agree with my plan?"

"Well, sure. I don't want to go to that school anyway. I was so far behind in my homework that they put me in a dumbbell class. I can't stand it there."

"Good, that's what I wanted to hear. Tomorrow morning I'm going to send letters to your principal and the superintendent of schools. Then, I'm going to call and tell them the letters are coming and that I want you excused from Bible reading and prayer."

"What if they won't do it."

"I'll pull you out of school," she shot back, the fight hard as steel in her voice.

Mother mailed her letters and made the calls, and on Wednesday, October 12, Vernon S. Vavrina, assistant superintendent for secondary schools in Baltimore, told my mother that the school system would not comply with her demand. The next morning I stayed in bed and did not go to school.

For the next two weeks, the school system basically ignored my mother's harangues and my absence. It was the Russian bureaucratic treatment all over again. Dorothy Duval, the principal of Woodbourne, did send out a letter saying she might have to charge us with truancy if I didn't come back to school. But it was a routine note and did not contradict the school system's policy of trying to outwait us while maintaining a low profile and avoiding publicity.

For eight days my mother played the game according to the rules. Nothing happened; her grand, earth-shaking gesture was the city's best kept secret. Somehow the public had to be awakened to this hidden cause, so Mother wrote a letter to the editor of the Baltimore *Morning Sun*.

Mother has always had an ability to use words in such a way that people are goaded to respond—most often with bloodthirsty anger. This letter, which read more like an essay, was no exception. She argued fiercely that the rights of atheists were trampled on in the United States. In one paragraph she mentioned three issues that she has harped on ever since: prayer before public meetings, the phrase "In God we trust" on U.S. coins, and the words "under God" in the pledge of allegiance. She ended the letter by saying she had "had enough" and was now protesting this mistreatment of atheists by keeping me out of school so I would not have to pray or hear the Bible read. She claimed that the board of education had violated the First and Fourteenth Amendments of the U.S. Constitution, and she closed with this line: "And may my conscience now Rest in Peace."

The next morning, Friday, Mother drove to the nearest newsstand and picked up a copy of the morning edition of the *Sun*. Her letter had not been printed—nor was it printed on Saturday, Sunday, or Monday. She was disappointed, but her left-wing political experience had taught her that it was extremely difficult to get publicity for unusual or unpopular causes. Still, one had to keep trying.

In the meantime she had taken some measures to insure that my absence from school did not result in total leisure for me. She assigned me lessons from various books she had checked out of the public library. I should have known there would be some hitch in what had looked to be an ideal situation.

On Wednesday morning, October 26, the phone rang. My mother answered, and it was obvious from her excitement that the person on the other end was saying something that pleased her. She hung up and bounded into the dining room where I was doing my homework. "Guess what!" she exclaimed.

"They're going to print your letter?"

"Better than that! That was a reporter from the *Sun*. They won't print my letter, but instead this guy wants to come out here and interview us for a news story. He's even bringing a photographer!"

"A photographer? My picture will be in the paper?" The idea did not thrill me. I knew some boys at school who would make me pay for this latest weird escapade.

"Yeah! I can hardly believe it," Mother went on.

"When's he coming?"

"Around four this afternoon. . . . D___! I've got to do some house cleaning. Get out the vacuum cleaner . . . ."

The cleaning and polishing were done by the time the doorbell rang late that afternoon.

"There they are!" Mother almost shouted as she ran toward the door. "Somebody turn off the TV," she yelled as I trailed along behind.

"Mrs. Murray?" inquired the short, soft-spoken man at the door.

"Yes, and you must be . . . "

"Stephen Nordlinger from the *Sun*." He introduced the photographer who was with him, and they both stepped through the small hall and into the living room. We walked to the dining room and sat down at the table. Grandmother, who had been dismayed at the recent events that had kept me from school but was excited by this chance to chat with newspapermen, brought in steaming cupsful of tea. Nord-linger pulled out his note pad, and we got down to business as best we could, since the TV was still blaring. In response to Nordlinger's questions, Mother recited the facts as she saw them. "I'm determined that my son is not going to bow down to any concept of what an average American is given to be," she said. Later she stated that she was willing to go to jail and, if jailed, would start a hunger strike. I was glad she wasn't speaking for both of us.

"If you meet with an unfavorable verdict here in Bal-timore, will you appeal the decision? Is that what you mean?" Nordlinger asked.

"You bet I will, all the way to the Supreme Court."

"What about the possibility of truancy charges?"

"I know that withdrawing Bill from school violates the law, but this is the only way I can see to challenge this unconstitutional activity."

"What about putting your son in a private school?"

"That would defeat my purpose."

"I see. Ah, Bill, do you mind if I ask you a few ques-tions?" Nordlinger asked, turning to me. "What do you think about your mother taking you out of school."

"I don't mind it at all!" We all laughed. "But, more seri-ously," I went on, "I think my mother has done the right thing. As an atheist I shouldn't be subjected to prayer and Bible reading in order to get a free public education." Mother smiled. I knew I was saying the right things.

"I only entered Woodbourne last February. During the seventh grade, I was in a private school, which I had to leave because the campus was too far away. But since I entered Woodbourne I've run into some problems with both teachers and students."

"I see," Nordlinger said, scribbling furiously on his note pad. "What kind of problems?"

"I guess they started when I turned in a report about Russian government last spring. Afterwards, several guys from that class roughed me up. They accused me of being a Communist." My mother stared at me intently, now perhaps not as pleased. "Another time, one of my teachers opened a class by saying, 'We will now have a free discussion on why Russia shouldn't complain about U–2 flights.' I complained that this wasn't the proper way to phrase the question."

Nordlinger seemed intrigued by my term paper, and although Mother was obviously displeased, I went to my room and found my copy, which I gave to the reporter. He had already interviewed the school officials, and he wanted to see for himself if the paper was as inflammatory and pro-Russian as they had claimed. He scanned through the short essay and seemed disappointed. "Is this all?" he asked. I assured him it was. He asked Mother a few more questions, the photographer took some pictures, and then they both left.

When the sun rose on Thursday, October 27, Mother's daily trip to the newsstand bore fruit. There on page 1 of the *Morning Sun's* local news section was my young face. The headline above read, "Boy, 14, Balks At Bible Reading." Mother and I eagerly read the long article, which splashed across three columns. Nordlinger had done his homework. After stating the skeletal facts of the story, he noted that this was the first reported challenge to the school board rule since its adoption in 1905. The rule required that the Bible or the Lord's Prayer or both be used in the opening exercises of all schools under the board's jurisdiction. He added the background information that the board had approved the Bible for use as a reading book in all schools in 1839, ten years after the system's founding.

He then reviewed his interview with me about the paper and my trouble with teachers and classmates. After that, he reported that Dr. George B. Brain, the city's school superintendent, was consulting state educational authorities about the proper course of action in my case. Meanwhile, Brain said, since the rule made no provision for those who did not want to participate in these exercises to be excused from them, I and others like me must remain in class and be respectful.

Nordlinger also wrote that my mother had asked initially

that I be excused from the exercises. When her request was denied, she had notified Dr. Vernon S. Vavrina that she was withdrawing me from school.

He said Mother had also protested the use of the text-book, *The Story of the Nations,* in my world history class. Then he quoted me, "All of the religion in the book was given as fact." I also supposedly objected to a reproduction of the Last Supper in the book. Nevertheless, my mother was reported to have said that the textbook question was secondary and negotiable. The matter of the opening exercises was primary and nonnegotiable.

The rest of the article was devoted to the conflict over my paper about the Russian government and economy. In this section Nordlinger reported that Miss Dorothy Duval, the principal, had said that I had a great deal of ability but was arrogant and not using my ability to the best extent. He also wrote of my complaint that one was not free to express one's views at Woodbourne. Miss Duval insisted that this was not true and that the fact my paper on Russia had been admitted as legitimate class work demonstrated the school's basic fairness. The article concluded with a reprinting of my entire report on Russia.

It was still early in the morning and we had only skimmed the story when the telephone began to ring. We soon found that we had ceased to be private citizens. At last Madalyn Murray had found her cause, one that would be noticed.

The calls early that Thursday morning were from local radio and television stations, each eager to pounce on every tidbit of this unusual human interest story. Being opposed in Baltimore to anything religious was not a popular practice in the early 1960s. The city was predominantly Roman Catholic, so the Murray crusade was instant news.

Before long the local affiliates of NBC, CBS, and ABC had called to arrange filming of interviews. A reporter for a TV station in Washington, D.C., also wanted a story, as did a network news team in New York. Reporters from the news services showed up as well. Some calls came from other parts of the country, and Mother sucked up the attention like a dry sponge. No one was denied. It was a circus.

Sometime that morning one of the calls made Mother particularly happy. "That was Fred Weisgal of the ACLU," she announced. "He says they're entering the case now. The b___ wouldn't do anything for me before," she chuckled triumphantly.

"What did he say?" I asked.

"He wants you back in school right away."

"How come?"

"He said I'm muddying the legal waters by having you out of school altogether."

"What do you mean?"

"Well, it's sort of an overkill. Since the issue is the prayer and Bible reading, he says we've got to make sure the courts clearly see us protesting that and that only. Right now we could get hung for truancy. Weisgal wants us to force the school into expelling you for no reason other than your refusal to be in the room during the Bible reading and prayer."

"I knew it was too good to last. When do I have to go back?"

"First thing in the morning, after I set it up with our news media friends."

I muttered. Now that the whole world knew what we were up to, I doubted I could survive more than a few hours at school. But Mother was insistent that I return to Wood-bourne Junior High. She wasted no time and called several of the TV stations and told them I was going back to school in the morning. The reporters sensed the potential of the story and promised to be at our house early the next day.

That evening the whole family gathered in front of the television for the airing of the local news, followed by the network national news broadcasts. We were featured on both, and I must confess, it was an exhilarating thirty minutes. Trying to catch the brief news items on each of the national broadcasts was hectic. Mother kept flipping from station to station during the entire half hour to make sure we didn't miss any of the reports. The networks aired their coverage almost simultaneously, so it was impossible to get a relaxed impression of any one of them. I was distracted anyway. At Mother's direction I was attempting to photograph our faces on the TV screen with my 35mm camera.

The next morning, Friday, October 28, I woke up at 6:30. I dressed and ate hurriedly. As usual, I planned to walk to school. Mother had decided my walk to do battle with the public schools would provide compelling TV film footage. On cue, the TV film crews and reporters arrived, and I overheard Mother discussing strategy with them. It was decided that the reporters and photographers would trail along in cars a short distance behind me. That way any "Christians" along the route who wanted to throw rocks or punches at me would not be scared off by the media. One reporter actually asked her what hospital I would be taken to if I were injured.

By this time I was beginning to feel like shark bait. I looked out the living room window and saw that some of our neighbors were gawking, obviously displeased by the commotion. I felt excited and sick at the same time. Needless to say, I was not in the most optimistic frame of mind when I started out the door at a little after 7:15 A.M. to walk my two-mile expedition. After leaving the crowd near our door, the sidewalk was clear, and I strode ahead at a comfortable pace. The early autumn air was brisk, and a few cumulus clouds hung brightly in the morning sky. The trees lining the streets still sported their gold, red, and yellow leaves. The beauty of the morning calmed my fears.

I had been absent from school eleven class days since our return from France. The morning newspaper was already on the streets with a second article by Stephen Nordlinger devoted to me. Today's headline read: "Boy to Seek to Return to School Today." A subhead noted, "Brain Says He Will Be Suspended If He Avoids Exercises."

The article reviewed the previous day's story and explained Weisgal's advice. And it detailed a scenario for a dramatic showdown this morning. The plan was for me to arrive at school and report my presence to my homeroom teacher. Then I would withdraw from the room conspicuously to avoid participation in the Bible reading and prayer exercises. According to the newspaper, the school superintendent, Dr. Brain, had said I would be expelled if I did that.

The fallen leaves stirred under my feet as I sauntered down the sidewalk toward the school. Occasionally, I looked back over my shoulder to check on the newsmen. I saw their cars creeping along about a block to my rear. Two reporters strolled together on the sidewalk at about the same distance from me.

By 7:40, I was about a mile from school and began to see other students on their way to Woodbourne. I recognized one or two of them, but they seemed to pay me no notice.

Finally, about a block from the school, the expected abuse began. "Why don't you move to Russia?" a voice sounded from behind me and across the block. I wanted to answer "We tried, but they wouldn't take us!" but realized this was no time for humor. I walked straight ahead and did not look back.

Soon someone else yelled, "Commie lover!" Several other kids laughed. The closer to school I got, the more catcalls I heard. Interestingly, few if any of these remarks concerned my atheism. The possibility that I was a Communist seemed to be my most horrid fault.

I burned with embarrassment and resentment, but I suffered no physical wounds. If any missiles were hurled, I neither saw, heard, nor felt them. The newsmen, I'm sure, were disappointed.

A little before 8:00 A.M. I reached the main entrance of the school, along with hundreds of other students. Standing at the door were several teachers who had been stationed there to prevent the reporters from following me inside. I had just entered the foyer when another teacher stopped me from walking to my homeroom. "You're supposed to go to the office," the man told me.

"Why?" I countered.

"Because you're supposed to talk to Dr. Vavrina."

"Why should I want to talk to him?" I was bewildered. Vavrina was the big wheel from the downtown office.

"Look, young man, why don't you just do as you're told. Dr. Vavrina asked to see you in the office."

"No thanks. If I don't report to my homeroom, I'll be counted absent. I'll go there first. Then I'll go see Dr. Vavrina."

"Things will go a lot easier if you just cooperate."

"Things would seem a lot easier to me if you'd let me pass by and get to my homeroom. I'm going to be late!" I was getting angry. The excitement of the whole situation was fading fast with me. I just wanted to be in a normal situation and left alone.

The teacher rolled his eyes, "Have it your own way." He let me go on.

By now the hall was empty. I reached my homeroom door only to find it locked. I peered through the little window in the door and saw Miss Duval, the principal, speaking intently to the students. The room had a second door, which I tried to open, but it was locked, too. I had no choice; I walked down the corridor to the school office.

"I was told to come here and see Dr. Vavrina," I said to the lady behind the counter.

"Oh, yes, you're Bill Murray?"

"That's right."

"Please go into that room," she pointed to the principal's door.

Inside, sitting behind Duval's desk, sat Dr. Vavrina, looking as uncomfortable as I felt. A pained look molded his round face. "Hello, Bill. My name's Vernon Vavrina. I usually work downtown, but I came out here today to see if I could help things go a little more smoothly. Have a seat, will you?"

"Thanks." I sat down.

"I understand you have some objection to our opening exercises. Is that true?"

"Yes, sir."

"I see. What is it you object to?"

"To the prayer . . . and the Bible reading."

"And why is that?"

I was beginning to get frustrated. Didn't this man read the newspapers? "Well, we don't believe in God." It was harder to say than I thought it would be.

"By 'we,' whom do you mean?"

"My mother and I."

"Was there ever a time when you did believe in God?"

"Well, my grandparents. . . . I don't know! Why are you asking me all these questions? I just want to go to school!"

"Okay, okay. It's time for your first class now. But, on Monday morning, I'd like you to report here rather than to your homeroom again."

"We'll see," I said as I walked, red-faced, from the office.

Nothing was said that day about my extended absence from classes. My presence was met with an embarrassed silence. Only one teacher had prepared a list of make-up assignments for me, which she placed without comment on my desk while returning homework to the other kids. The other students, most of whom I did not know, ignored me, too, until I showed up for physical education period on the playing field.

"Hey, commie," yelled a boy who was shorter but more solidly built than I. "You think you're gonna change this place just to suit yourself?"

I was about to answer when I was shoved hard from behind and fell to the ground. The boy and two others had sneaked behind me and now had me in a spot.

"C'mon, you b____, get up and fight!"

I scrambled to my feet and began to turn when a fist caught my left cheekbone, knocking me back a foot or so. Whoever the guy was, he had a strong right arm. The three turned to walk away, laughing. I wasn't laughing. Madalyn wasn't the only one in our family with a temper. Enraged, I leaped to my feet and charged after them, jumping on the back of the one who had called me "commie," wrestling him to the ground. I had surprised him, and my hot anger overcame his slightly larger size for a moment and I landed a few good punches before the other two got to me. One of them kicked me in the stomach. I gasped and squirmed with pain on the ground. The boys left hurriedly, escaping before a crowd could gather and draw attention to their mischief.

The following Monday and Tuesday, the pattern of silence in the classroom and violence on the playground continued. In the morning I would be intercepted by one of the male teachers and escorted past my homeroom down to the principal's office. There I would sit until homeroom period and the Bible reading and prayer were over. As long as I was prevented from being present for the opening exercises, Mother and I could not complain that I was being forced to participate. The treatment I was receiving from the teachers and students was so irritating to me that I thought up a plan to sneak into the school building and avoid my escort.

On what I remember to be Wednesday morning, November 2, I entered the school through a back door I normally did not use. The teachers guarding the hallway thought I had gone to the office. I stayed in a restroom, and then just as the bell rang, I ran down to the homeroom and slid into a chair near the back. My heart was beating fast—from my run and the fear that I would be discovered and evicted before the opening exercises began.

The other students looked at me curiously. Then the teacher asked us all to stand. I stood, too, self-consciously because I was quite tall and it would be hard for me not to be noticed. The teacher saw me but decided to ignore me. She flipped through her Bible, the pages rattling noisily in the hushed room. After what seemed an age she found the page she had been looking for. She cleared her throat and began to read.

I listened for several seconds, and now, to be honest, I was filled with disgust and anger. What was taking place— the Bible reading and the prayer—had caused me so much pain at the hands of my fellow students, teachers, and others that I had come to loathe it.

"This is ridiculous," I blurted out, my face hot from emotion. I picked up my books and coat and walked from the room.

"Communist pig," someone hissed as I turned down the hall toward the office.

I had done it. I had accomplished my goal. And what I wanted to do most that moment was keep moving. I wanted to run away from that school and its prayers, from the city of Baltimore, from the state of Maryland, and—most of all— from my family and the house at 1526 Winford Road. This longing to escape had smoldered within me for years, but from that day on it became a burning, driving desire that nearly possessed me.

But taking a new identity or joining the Foreign Legion would have to wait. When I entered the school office some reporters were waiting. They were elated that I had finally officially challenged the Bible reading and prayer. Now they could write some more hot copy. The office secretary was peeved and curtly sent me to my first-period class. My dramatics did not change the way I was treated the rest of the day; as usual I was ignored.

When I saw Mother later that day and told her what had

happened, she laughed and said excitedly, "That's great, Bill. Let's see what they do about this!"

We didn't have to wait long. The board of education already had asked the attorney general of Maryland, C. Ferdinand Sybert, to rule on our complaint. In his decision, which was announced the first week of November, he said that reading the Bible in school was constitutional and that anyone who absented himself from school to avoid it could be prosecuted for truancy. Sybert also recommended that pupils who objected to the Bible reading or prayer be allowed to remain silent or be excused from the opening exercises.

In a sense this ruling was a small victory for our cause. We had won the right for me to be excused from fouling my virgin ears and mind with the "religious propaganda" passed out in opening exercises. It seemed a reasonable decision—the majority of students could do their praying if they wished, and I could read science fiction books in the hallway.

But Mother sensed she had a meaty issue in her teeth, and she hung on to it like a bulldog. The attention we were receiving proved her right. We had become celebrities—the media wanted interviews, the phone rang constantly, and the letters poured in. Even though much of the response from average citizens was vehemently negative, the whole matter was just too gratifying for Mother to give up. And about this time we received some low-budget legal help.

The ACLU apparently had been only moderately interested in the case. According to Mother, they did not want to get involved because they were already fully committed to a nearly identical case, *Abington Township vs. Schempp* in Pennsylvania, as well as another related case in Florida. The Pennsylvania case had begun in 1958 with much less fanfare than our own.

With the ACLU unwilling to assist, Mother began looking for other legal help. A local attorney named Leonard Kerpelman had called several times expressing interest in the case, but Madalyn was not impressed with his credentials. He was put on hold. Mother kept looking, and a discussion one day with Bob Lee led to an appointment with Harold Buchman, who at the time, I was told, helped represent the Communist party in Maryland on some legal matters. Mother claims to have been leary of dealing with Buchman, so she invited Kerpelman to attend this appointment with her. At this meeting, or subsequently, Buchman must have agreed to take the case because his name—along with Kerpelman's—appears on the original legal papers filed. Soon after the petition was presented to the Superior Court of Baltimore, for some reason Buchman dropped out, and by default Leonard Kerpelman became the attorney who guided the case to the U.S. Supreme Court. His services were free of charge, as Mother had agreed only to pay his expenses.

Although Madalyn and Mr. Kerpelman were definitely an odd couple (he was an Orthodox Jew), initially she adored him because he allowed her to do most of the work. She was, after all, a bit of a lawyer herself. She had obtained a law degree from South Texas College of Law but had never been able to pass the bar exams in Texas or Maryland.

Kerpelman was no stranger to unusual cases, having at one time won the right for a South American man to hold bullfights in Baltimore's Memorial Stadium.

While Madalyn and the attorneys prepared to fight in court, I was waging my own battles in the hallowed halls of Woodbourne Junior High.

Sadly, other teachers had now found time to prepare my back assignments, which at the time seemed excessive. I had only missed a total of about twenty school days since the beginning of the term, yet I received a typewritten list of make-up work that was over twenty pages long. Besides all this back work, I also had to maintain my current work. I was crushed by the load, and Mother was forced to help me finish the assignments. Of course, many of the answers she came up with made me even more unpopular with my teachers and fellow students. But who else was there to turn to? I felt isolated, and my longings for escape could not be satisfied.

Few of the other students at Woodbourne spoke to me, and some thought it great sport to try to beat me up whenever possible. I was a strong young man and could defend myself in any one-to-one situation. One afternoon, however, the small army of teen-age commie beaters I clashed with was more than I could handle. I nearly lost my life.

It was a chilly, overcast day in late fall. I had been shopping for some radio gear at a small shopping center near our home. As I left a store, a group of boys spotted me and began to taunt me.

"Hey commie! Go back to Russia!"

"Where's your mommie, commie?"

"How's Mr. Madalyn Murray today?"

My ears burned a little, but seeing how many of them there were, I decided the better part of valor would be to make a strategic retreat. In other words, I ran as fast as I could.

The bus stop was two blocks away and I made it—but no bus was in sight. I turned, gasping for air, and saw to my horror that there were now at least ten young men in the pack chasing me. I was caught with no avenue of escape. I was terrified, and I knew I would have to stand pat and fight.

"You stupid commie!" one of them yelled. "You need to be taught some lessons."

Then I heard a snapping sound and felt a sharp pain on the back of my neck. Something made of metal had struck me. I swore from the pain, and as I wheeled around, my raised arm deflected the second blow. I saw the weapon I was facing. It was a newspaper carrier's webbed belt with large metal buckles at each end. I danced and weaved, trying to avoid the belt. Others blocked any escape route I tried to take. I did my best to fend them off and managed to protect my head and face with my hands. Fortunately, I was wearing a heavy jacket which offered me some extra protection. They were taunting me viciously and were caught up in a mob fever. Then I heard the bus approaching. The thugs heard it, too.

"Hey, shove him in front of the bus!" one of them yelled and gave me a push. I fought wildly, fearing for my life. In the scramble, one of my attackers tripped and fell to the ground. I saw an opening in the circle and lunged out of it. The others were now sufficiently distracted by the arrival of the bus that I was able to leap through the vehicle's door and up the steps. I dropped my coins in the slot and slumped in a seat—sweating and badly shaken, but still in one piece.

Our home was just a few blocks away, so I was still damp with sweat when I wearily clambered up the steps, opened the door, then dropped on the couch in the living room. As usual, the place sounded like a riot. The television blared at full volume; Mother was on the phone, speaking at a near-yell to be heard above the background noise; Jon Garth was smashing some new toy with a hammer; Grandmother banged pots and dishes preparing dinner; only Grandfather, now retired and quite weak from a heart ailment, sat quietly in the kitchen, his hands cradling a fresh cup of coffee. He continued to be the only island of stability and peace in my chaotic world.

I wished deeply that the noise would stop and that I could walk the streets in peace. But knowing this was impossible, I thought again about running far away. Now that I was older, the idea of a real escape encouraged me more than the imaginary adventures I used to envision while reading science fiction.

The school prayer events for the most part had worsened relations in the family. At first the media attention had seemed glamorous, and Grandmother had appeared to enjoy the excitement. But the reports of our stand against Bible reading and prayer had enraged the entire community. Grandfather clearly sided with the community, and now his aged wife was adopting his view on the matter.

Grandmother thought herself to be an upstanding citizen and religious person—even though she had not been in church since the baptism of my brother. The whole spectacle became a terrible embarrassment to both her and Grandfather, besides being a twenty-four-hour-a-day interruption of their normal affairs.

To make things worse, the soapbox the media had built for Mother had caused her to become even more vehemently attached to her views, and she thought or spoke of little else. There were no breaks from her surging tide of ideas and hot words. All of this drew Grandfather and Mother into horrible, foul-mouthed fights. Their hatred for each other became so intense that one night she ordered Jon Garth and me never to speak to him again.

"Why?" I pled.

"Don't argue with me!" she snapped. "The old f___ doesn't deserve to have his grandchildren speak to him."

I didn't obey her, of course, but this incident only added to the strained atmosphere of our home.

Only a few nights later, another incident ripped the family further apart. We were all sitting at the dining room table having dinner. As usual the conversation centered on the prayer issue. Grandfather got fed up. "Oh, h___," he said. "This godless crusade you're on is just a way to get your name in the papers, Madalyn."

Mother's face turned red as she tried simultaneously to eat and argue. "Why, you old s___," she sputtered.

Suddenly my disgust with this endless arguing at the table could not be restrained: "Why don't you lay off him?" I shouted at Mother. "What do you care what he thinks? It won't make any difference to your case in court! Why do you have to fight like this at home?"

She turned and just glared at me for a moment. Then she grabbed a cup of fruit cocktail and hurled its contents point blank into my face. I wiped the juice from my face with my napkin and picked the larger chunks off my lap and shirt. I no longer could control my anger and hurled a piece of fruit at her. This was one of the first times I had defied her in a physical way, and my audacity inflamed her. She lunged at me, and as I reached to fend her off, she sank her teeth deeply into my arm. I cried out in pain, and as she recoiled, the blood began to ooze from several puncture wounds. Grandfather cursed her roundly and took me to the doctor for a tetanus shot.

Only a few nights later Mother and Grandfather were at it again. But he was wearing down, not fighting back as strenuously as he once had. Mother's energy, though, seemed boundless. Suddenly and unexpectedly, Grandfather just stood up from the table. His movement stopped her barrage for a moment.

"This is it," he said, his voice tinged with bitterness and resignation. "I cannot eat at my own dinner table in peace. I will not return to this table again."

He leaned over, picked up his plate, utensils, and coffee cup, and then retreated to the kitchen. True to his word, never again—not even at holidays or on his birthday—did he budge from his refuge in the kitchen to share a meal with his family.

On December 7, 1960, our attorneys filed a petition for writ of mandamus with the Superior Court of Baltimore. In effect, with this legal maneuver we were asking the court to force the board of education to stop the "illegal" Bible reading and prayer exercises. The petition stated, among other things, that my religious liberty was being threatened by placing a premium on belief as against non-belief. The petition also said that even by being permitted to leave the classroom during these "offensive" proceedings, I was losing "caste" with my fellows and was "being subjected to reproach and insult."

Mother was thrilled with the petition because the attorney had agreed to include a statement she had written about what atheists supposedly believed. The ideas expressed sounded so lofty and noble, but from personal experience, I already knew the words were nothing but deceitful propaganda. Mother's statement read:

> An atheist loves his fellowman instead of a God. An atheist believes that heaven is something for which we should work now, here, on earth, for all men together to enjoy. An atheist believes that he can get no help through prayer, but that he must find in himself the inner conviction and the strength to meet life, to grapple with it, to subdue it, and to enjoy it. An atheist believes that only in a knowledge of himself and his fellow can he find the understanding that will help him in a life of fulfillment. He seeks to know himself and his fellowman

rather than to know God. An atheist believes that a hospital should be built instead of a church. An atheist believes that a deed must be done instead of a prayer said. An atheist strives for involvement in life and not escape into death. He wants disease conquered, poverty banished, war eliminated. He wants man to understand and love man: he wants an ethical way of life. He believes that we cannot rely on God, channel action into prayer, or hope for an end of troubles in a hereafter, that we are our brother's keeper, we are the keepers of our own lives, that we are responsible persons, that the job is here and the time is now.

Christmas vacation came, and I was relieved to be away from the day-to-day torture at Woodbourne. We celebrated Christmas, or "Solstice" as Mother referred to it. Mother would begin playing Christmas carols at Thanksgiving and played them continually until after New Years. We also put up a traditional tree with all the trimmings and an angel on top.

In mid-January the school board filed a brief demurrer or objection to our petition. In summary, the school board argued that the facts as we had presented them were true but did not result in a worthy case. The demurrer meant a decision would have to be made by a judge. We had no idea when this would happen.

My life at school had not improved. I was still struggling to complete my make-up homework, and the hostility from students and teachers was intense. Sometimes the tests I wrote in school "mysteriously" disappeared and on occasion my homework papers were lost after I turned them in. I knew by now that people hated my mother and what she stood for. Since they couldn't always apply the whip to her, I was a convenient target.

Admittedly, at times I found clever ways of getting some laughs at the expense of other students. Some of the harassment I received was nothing more than typical teen-age teasing and sparring. One noon I found a small sign sitting on my lunch table, which was otherwise bare. I set my tray down and read the sign. Crudely drawn on a sheet of note-book paper was the outline of a cross. Inside the crosspiece some wiseguy had written the words "Jesus Saves." An idea floated through my adolescent mind that caused me to smirk.

I sat down, pulled out a pen, and with a flourish befitting a "godless atheist" added my own phrase to the vertical part of the cross. The message now read, "Jesus Saves Green Stamps." I boldly propped the sign back up on the table and began eating lunch. I snickered. I knew the person who had baited me with the sign was probably watching me, knowing I had outwitted him on this round.

On March 2, Judge J. Gilbert Pendergast heard our case. He took eight weeks to release his decision, in which he dismissed our petition. Some of the statements in his memo-randum outraged Mother. For example, Judge Pendergast wrote:

> It is abundantly clear that petioners' real objective is to drive every concept of religion out of the public school system. If God were removed from the classroom, there would remain only atheism. The word is derived from the Greek *atheos*, meaning "without a god." Thus the beliefs of virtually all the pupils would be subordinated to those of Madalyn Murray and her son. Any reference to the Declaration of Independence would be prohibited because it concludes with the historic words of the sign-ers, ". . .with a firm reliance on the protection of Divine Providence we mutally pledge to each other our Lives, our Fortunes and our sacred Honor." Any mention of Lincoln's Gettysburg Address would be anathema be-cause in it the Great Emancipator prayed that "this na-tion, under God, shall have a new birth of Freedom." It is even possible that United States currency would not be accepted in school cafeterias because every bill and coin contains the familiar inscription, IN GOD WE TRUST.

On April 28, the day after the Baltimore Superior Court threw our petition out, Mother and Kerpelman appealed the case to the Maryland Court of Appeals, the state's highest court. Mother was now more vehement than ever: If necessary she would press the case to the U.S. Supreme Court.

Only days after this appeal was filed, Mother entered the Veterans Administrations Hospital in Baltimore to have a cyst removed. While Mother recovered from her surgery, I kept on trying to avoid being wounded in the treacherous halls at Woodbourne. Although I had finally finished the make-up work, my grades fell almost to ruin—the pressures in school and the tensions at home being the reasons. I began to consider which of the city's high schools would offer me the best chance to live a normal life as well as match my academic interests.

In addition to more than forty neighborhood high schools in the city, there were also four specialized high schools, two for boys and two for girls. Of each pair, one was devoted to college preparation with emphasis in liberal arts, and the other stressed the sciences. One of these, Baltimore Polytechnic Institute, was the science and engineering preparatory school for boys and in the 1960s had a widespread reputation for academic excellence. I wanted to go there, but in spring 1962 I was barely passing ninth grade at Woodbourne. I applied to Polytechnic anyway and was elated when I was accepted. I was required to take some supplementary courses that summer, though.

During these long periods when the prayer case was inching along through the court system, Mother kept herself occupied with various left-wing causes and groups. Being rejected by the Soviet Union had not diminished her enthusiasm for activism. Bob Lee visited our home often, and it wasn't because we bought cartons of Fuller brushes. He and Mother discussed communism, and eventually Bob introduced Mother to the man who I was led to believe was the chairman of the Communist party in Maryland.

Sometime after our trip to France, Mother had penned a letter to Fidel Castro offering her services to his new Cuban government. Word of this offer eventually may have reached Communist party leaders in the United States, because Mother was asked to be chairman of the Maryland chapter of the Fair Play for Cuba Committee. Supposedly this committee was formed to insure that alternate viewpoints on the Cuban revolution and its leaders were presented to the American people. The committee was a front organization supported by the Communist Party of the United States of America. Mother eagerly accepted the post.

To this day I'm not sure what the Communist party thought of my mother and vice versa. Mother's flair for publicity and her aggressive personality did not ideally cast her in the role of a loyal, unquestioning, low-echelon comrade. Over the years Mother has repeatedly denied that she ever was a Communist. However, I am aware from personal experience that she had frequent contacts with the party, particularly during the early 1960s.

In 1961 Mother traveled with Garth and me to visit the Communist party headquarters in New York City. I'm not sure what I expected the headquarters to look like—perhaps a large room with no private offices and everyone dressed alike, equally sharing the burdens of office work. I was in for a surprise.

The modern, well-lit offices were equipped with the latest IBM typewriters and business machines. The carpets were thick and new. The decor and coordinated furnishings indicated that a talented interior decorator had been involved in setting the place up. And the background music system was not emitting the sounds of stirring revolutionary anthems but rather bourgeois melodies akin to Muzak.

Although Mother's fervor for leftist causes had not abated, the hubbub over school prayer had unexpectedly presented Mother with the opportunity to become the queen of thousands of America's dissidents of various stripes. Within that first year, the mail poured in. Surprisingly, there were large numbers of people who shared Mother's anti-establishment views and wanted her to know it. Every dissident in the country, it seemed, had to say something to my mother. In time the volume forced the post office to deliver our mail in big canvas bags. My mother was amazed that many of the letters contained donations of both cash and checks. The donors said they wanted to help her suit to remove prayer from the schools.

Notable, though not uncharacteristic, among the donors was Carl Brown, a wealthy Kansas farmer. He was both an atheist and a nudist. He believed man was simply an animal and should live accordingly. The first time he wrote to my mother, he sent a check for five thousand dollars. More donations followed, so that his cumulative gifts mounted into the tens of thousands of dollars. In addition, he also sent special birthday gifts to my brother and me in the form of stocks and bonds.

By the spring of 1961, the mail was so heavy that Mother could no longer write personal replies. I was sent to Sears to purchase a mimeograph machine. It was a cheap model, but with some experimenting, I was able to print readable copies with it. That was the start of Mother's monthly newsletter. In its pages Mother detailed and exaggerated the abuse I was receiving "at the hands of Christians." She was convinced that the worse the situation sounded to her readers, the more money they were likely to send. Consequently, according to her, I was beaten severely at least twice a month and suffered several nervous breakdowns. She probably was right about what motivates people to give: After mailing out the first newsletter, we received over a thousand dollars in contributions.

In the newsletters Mother frequently requested funds to help pay legal expenses. There were expenses, of course, but they were lower than Mother's supporters would have assumed, since Kerpelman was not receiving a fee. I don't wish to imply that Mother became vastly wealthy during this time, but we did live comfortably. A considerable amount of money came in, and our overhead was not excessive. The expenses of the paperwork and court fees involved in pursuing the appeal through the courts were not too high. In fact, as I recall, removing prayer from U.S. public schools cost less than $20,000.

In September 1961, I enrolled at Baltimore Polytechnic

Institute, wondering if I would receive the same petty harassment of the past school year. I learned it was a no-nonsense place, a factor that worked to my advantage. The school's strict dress code (shirt and tie) was representative of how all academic and nonacademic matters were handled.

After my chaotic ninth grade year at Woodbourne, the order and discipline at this school made it seem like paradise. I was determined that in spite of the handicaps created by my home environment, I was going to stay in school and maintain a respectable grade average. I began to set my alarm for an early hour so that I could get dressed, eat a quick breakfast, and take an early number three bus to North Avenue downtown where the school was located. I rode the city bus daily to school, arriving shortly after the school doors were unlocked for study hall at 7:00 A.M. This allowed me nearly an hour of study time before the first class period. I did my homework there or in the hallway. There was seldom enough time to finish it at home.

Before long I realized I would not suffer from violence, as I had at Woodbourne. The teachers and students evaluated me on my performance, not on whatever cause Mother had in the news at the moment. And the work load wouldn't have left much time for fights anyway.

I found a few friends and joined some clubs, such as the United Nations Club and the Amateur Radio Club. I had obtained a novice class amateur radio license when I was in junior high. Then, just after entering high school, I passed the Morse Code and technical tests for a general class amateur radio license. Being able to have some normal teen-age interests again helped free my mind from the continuing fights and tensions at home.

Mother was running full throttle—helping Kerpelman prepare to argue our case before the appeals court, picketing with pro-Cuban and antinuclear groups, and working at a new job with the Social Security Administration. At Christmastime, she paused long enough to send out a few of her traditional cards, which contained in her opinion "the true meaning of Christmas." Each card's message began with

"Greetings on the Winter Solstice Season!" It then went on to tell how Christians had taken over the ancient pagan holiday as the birthday of their "mythological Christ."

In January 1962, the case was finally heard before the court of appeals. Mother took Jon Garth and me out of school, and we went with her and Grandmother to Annapolis to listen to Kerpelman present our arguments. After it was over, Mother was furious with our attorney, believing he had blown the whole thing with a weak performance. She had been disenchanted with Kerpelman almost from the beginning, but it would have been nearly impossible for her to find another attorney who would work at cost on such an unpopular case. Mother constantly bad mouthed Kerpelman's abilities and nicknamed him "Sammie the Shyster."

Soon after our trip to the appeals court we were informed that the whole seven-judge court wanted to rehear the constitutional arguments of the case before making a decision. After this second presentation we waited and waited. It wasn't until nearly three months later, on April 6, that the court ruled 4 to 3 against us. The majority opinion stated in part that "neither the First nor the Fourteenth Amendment was intended to stifle all rapport between religion and government."

Mother had no choice now. On May 15 she and Kerpelman appealed the case to the United States Supreme Court.

The day after sending the case to the Supreme Court, Mother lost her job with the Social Security Administration. Mother has claimed that she was booted out because of her fight against prayer in the schools. In fact, when given the job earlier, it had been with the understanding that she needed to pass the Maryland Bar exam within a year of her employment. She never took the exam and thus was released. Sometime before she lost this job she told me she thought she would be terminated. She already had plans to use her being fired "for the anti-prayer cause" as a way of exciting her donors to contribute more money. And with hostility against her in Baltimore now reaching new heights, Mother knew it would be impossible to find another job anyway. Since the newsletter was producing some income, it seemed wise to expand the atheist mail order business to boost revenue even more.

In the spring of 1962 a man who had been publishing a magazine called the *Free Humanist* became too busy with other business interests and asked Mother if she would be interested in taking over the publication. He offered to turn it over to her, complete with the 600-name mailing list, for free. Mother said yes immediately. This was precisely what she needed to broadcast her views more widely and to raise greater funds at the same time. And, best of all, it was a ready-made situation. Those 600 names represented the more radical participants of the humanist movement—just the sort of folks who saw eye to eye with my mother.

Immediately, I was sent to look for a different printing press. Our mimeograph machine would be too small to handle the *Free Humanist*, and Mother did not want some capitalist enterprise making money on the printing. Mother wanted to enlarge the magazine's trim size, and I learned that the only press in our price range was an A.B. Dick 330, which cost about $3,000. I helped place the order for the press and then learned how to operate it. The press was installed in our basement near my bedroom, in the large open room where the Socialist Workers party meetings had been held.

Mother became the editor, and she helped set the type for each issue on an old VariTyper she had purchased. This copy was then handed to me, and I was expected to finish the job—platemaking, printing, folding, collating, saddle stitching, labeling, and mailing.

We published the first issue on July 1, 1962. With the larger format came a new name as well, the *American Atheist*. As the magazine's chief production employee, I received only my regular allowance—$7.50 per week. Later, though, I negotiated my salary to $50 per week. The compensation, in some measure at least, helped make up for what I was sacrificing in friends and grades.

Mother expected everyone in the house to work on her projects. Grandmother and I did, but not my uncle nor my grandfather. Grandfather steadfastly refused to work on anything he regarded as godless. My uncle just didn't want to be bothered. Mother found it easier to excuse Uncle's apathy than Grandfather's antagonism.

"Why won't he come down here and help us?" she yelled one night over the clatter of the machines in the basement. "He's just sitting up there with that d___ cup of coffee, reading the paper. I can't stand it!"

I didn't reply. Secretly, I admired how Grandfather stood up to her.

"You know, we ought to get rid of him," she went on.

"How? By killing him?" I asked in jest.

"I'll bet there's some drug—I think I read about something like it one time—some drug that, if your grandfather took it, he'd die and it'd look like he had a heart attack."

I couldn't believe it. She actually sounded serious.

"I'm sure I read about that," she continued. "Where was it? G___, I wish that old b_____ were dead and gone."

"Mom, I've got to get back to work," I said, still wondering if this was just more of her hot air. I changed the subject. "You know, this basement isn't going to hold much more equipment."

"Tell me about it."

"Don't get the wrong idea. I really don't mind sleeping on the printing press," I said, trying to lighten the mood. I didn't want her to say anything else about Grandfather.

She chuckled. "I hear you. I've been thinking about it. We can probably afford to rent an office somewhere. We need more storage for all these pamphlets and books I'm selling. It's a good thing we're hauling in some dough on this operation."

We talked a few more minutes about what sort of place the business might need. Actually, by this time Mother wasn't compelled to depend exclusively on the proceeds from her magazine and related activities. The Communist party had already come to her rescue.

Sometime early in 1962, the party had decided that Baltimore would be a good spot to open its third bookstore. Two others already were doing business in New York and Los Angeles. Apparently, enough dissidents, leftists, Socialists, and Communists resided in the Baltimore area to make the idea feasible. These bookstores were generously subsidized by the Soviet Union so that the chance of failure was remote.

In any event Madalyn became manager of the New Era Book Shop, which opened at 101 West Twenty-second Street on July 30, 1962. Madalyn's job was to sell books and help recruit new members for the party. The location was just above a small coffee shop near the downtown shopping district. Party officials later recognized that their potential clientele were more likely to be found near skid row. They followed the lead of the local Nazi party bookstore and moved New Era to a less fashionable location where they might make contact more easily with the down-and-outers of society, who supposedly would find the Communist line appealing.

The Soviet subsidies for the bookstore came in terms of radically discounted merchandise—books mostly—that the bookstore could secure very cheaply and then sell at full retail price. The pools of cash created by such profits were used to underwrite the expenses of projects like the Fair Play for Cuba Committee.

The remainder of 1962 passed, and preparatory work on the prayer and Bible-reading case continued. Our cause had received a boost in June when the U.S. Supreme Court had ruled that a general, prescribed school prayer ("Almighty God, we acknowledge our dependence upon thee, and we beg thy blessings upon us, our parents, our teachers, and our country") used in New York was unconstitutional. But the announcement of the decision had brought a thunderous negative public reaction, and officials in many states were openly not enforcing a prayer ban. With public opinion so bitterly opposed to the 1962 decision, we wondered if the high court would back off.

The new year, 1963, was not two weeks old when a personal tragedy hit our family. The morning of January 9,

Grandfather and Mother had a fierce argument before breakfast. Before she stormed from the house, she stopped at the door and screamed, "You old b_____! I hope you drop dead. I'll dump your shriveled body in the trash for the niggers to pick up!"

She slammed the door and was gone. Grandfather sat down, his hands shaking as he lifted his cup of coffee to his lips.

Later that day, he and Grandmother went to the A & P to do some shopping. He drove his huge white Oldsmobile 88. Once at the shopping center, he pulled a case of empty pop bottles out of the car's trunk and carried them into the market. After he obtained the refund for them, he walked over to his favorite cashier to say hello. As he reached out to touch her, he suddenly pulled back his hand and grasped his chest. He slumped to the floor . . . dead. He was sixty-nine years old.

Mother arrived home an hour or so later. She walked into the house and, when she didn't see Grandfather in his usual chair, she called to her mother in the kitchen, "Where is the old man?"

Grandmother walked into the front room and looked her daughter squarely in the eye. "You got your wish, Madalyn."

"What do you mean?"

"Exactly what I said. You wished your father dead this morning and dead he is. He had a heart attack at the A & P."

"Well, I'll be. Where's the stiff?"

"At the Memorial Hospital Morgue."

"Have you made any arrangements?"

"Not yet."

Mother then turned to me, "Bill, call up some undertakers and find the cheapest one. Then have them pick up the stiff from Memorial."

I dutifully called several mortuaries and explained, "My grandfather has died, but he was not very popular in our home. We need an inexpensive funeral."

"Tell 'em we want a cheap wood box," Mother droned in the background.

Finally, I found the Ruck Funeral Home. They assured me the body could be disposed of for less than $500, including the plot. They explained, though, that state law required that the body be embalmed unless it was to be buried within twenty-four hours after death.

"Mother, we have to embalm him. It's the law," I reported.

"Just a bunch of s___ to make money for the undertakers. The body is going to rot eventually anyway. Let's see if we can talk your grandmother into planting him right away. He didn't have any friends left anyway."

Yeah, no friends left, I thought, *thanks to his daughter.*

Grandmother's response to Mother's idea was predictable. "Oh, my G___, no!" she said, bursting into tears. We left for the mortuary, and by the time we arrived, sentiment had won out and Grandfather's body was embalmed. The guilt Mother was experiencing because of her outburst toward her father that morning began to surface. Soon Mr. Ruck was told that I had been in error and that because of her love for her father, she wanted the most expensive casket money could buy.

Mother kept a solitary vigil next to Grandfather's casket throughout Thursday and Friday. She had paid the mortician in full for his services, and before the casket was closed for the last time, she carefully deposited the invoice—marked "paid"—next to the body.

Mother arranged for a Presbyterian minister to conduct the service and burial, telling him that her father had been a Presbyterian and would have wanted a religious ceremony. She made it clear to the minister, though, that she was an atheist and regarded it all as nonsense.

The funeral service was set for Saturday, January 12. A small group of us huddled in the chapel, and the minister had just begun when laughter filled the air. A loudspeaker had been left on. Mortuary personnel in some other room were standing near a microphone cracking jokes.

Mother became enraged and stormed out the chapel door and into the hall. Even after the door closed, her scream was easily heard: "Shut that d____ thing off! My father's service is going on in there!"

It was a dreary, misty day. The temperature was so cold that several of the pallbearers failed to show up and I had to help carry the casket. The cemetery grounds were damp. Everything fit my mood perfectly.

After the graveside service, the small group of mourners stood together quietly. Mother broke the mood and walked toward what was now her Olds 88. She stopped and turned toward us. "I don't know what the rest of you are going to do," she called out, "but I'm hungry." Thus we all drove several blocks and consumed the mourners' meal in a restaurant.

As we ate and Mother heaped her ideas on anyone who would listen, I thought about Grandfather and the times we had talked, man to man. A brewing argument around our table in the restaurant interrupted my memories. I thought to myself, *This is one fight Grandfather is going to miss. He's found some peace at last.*

CHAPTER • 8

With Grandfather gone, I plunged more earnestly than ever into activities that would keep me away from home, where Mother now ruled uncontested.

Thankfully, my school life had become quite normal. I was very active in the United Nations Club, and in the middle of my junior year, early in 1963, I was elected president of this organization. I served also as its representative to the United Nations Association. My dabbling with Marxist causes in the past actually facilitated my election. All of the students in the U.N. Club at Polytechnic were either Marxists or very sympathetic to Marxism. This was true of U.N. Club members from other schools in Baltimore as well. I also attended meetings of Students for a Democratic Society (SDS), a Communist front group.

Oddly, my only real enemy at Polytechnic was a Polish boy. He had been born in Poland, but his family had escaped in 1948 while he was still an infant. He too had studied hard to obtain the knowledge required to become an amateur radio operator. When he went to take his test, though, he received the bad news. Only *natural* (that is, born in the United States) American citizens could obtain an amateur radio license. He was crushed. Yet I, belonging to a family dedicated to the destruction of the government, could obtain one.

On Tuesday, February 26, the debate of our case before the Supreme Court began. That morning the alarm clocks rang early, and we arose and put on our finest clothes. Even Mother dolled herself up and donned a white fur-like coat, matching hat, and leather gloves. Normally, Mother took delight in shunning the latest fashions and dressing as "she d_____ well pleased." She also often did not wear makeup, but today was an exception.

Only Uncle Irv had decided not to go along since the trip would interfere with his job at Bendix. Kerpelman and his wife joined us in the Oldsmobile for the drive to the capital city, fifty miles away. Mother jabbered excitedly at the wheel, making sure Kerpelman had his arguments in order. The principal in the case—William J. Murray III—sat in the back seat, hoping that this dreary segment of his life would soon be resolved and forgotten.

A bright sun was easing the morning chill as our group climbed the majestic steps of the nation's highest court. I noted the phrase carved in stone above the columns that ring the building—"Equal Justice Under Law." We entered through the huge brass doors and passed into the court-room. We were ushered to very good seats, right up front. It was an impressive setting. Directly in front of us was an elevated, mammoth platform—the bench—behind which sat nine, high-backed leather chairs. In front of the bench, at floor level, was the "pit," the spot where attorneys stood and presented their oral arguments. The stately room had a high ceiling and was ringed with twenty-four marble columns that appeared to be at least forty feet high. Long, dark red curtains framed the windows. In some ways the place reminded me of the cathedrals we had visited in Paris.

The gallery was full and a good number of reporters were milling about. At 9:30 A.M., the robed justices filed in. The entire audience stood up and a clerk said in a loud voce: "Oyez, Oyez. God save the United States and this Honorable Court!" The irony of this announcement was not lost on Mother; she scowled and shook her head in disgust.

After the preliminaries, Kerpelman rose and walked rather wobbly to the pit to face the judges. He cleared his throat and began his presentation, saying that prayer in the public schools had been winked at for so long that its supporters now claimed it to be traditional. He said that anything that is unconstitutional does not become constitutional through tradition. He continued on, saying that the Constitution had erected a wall of separation between church and state.

Justice Potter Stewart interrupted, asking where such wording on this separation occurs in the Constitution. Of course, it does not. The relevant portion of the First Amendment reads: "Congress shall make no law respecting an establishment of religion, or prohibiting the free exercise thereof."

Kerpelman was stumped, at least momentarily, and there was an embarrassing silence. Finally, he admitted that the amendment is not explicit but has been interpreted to mean separation of church and state.

This contention opened up a modest free-for-all with the judges asking questions of all the attorneys and each other. The "free-exercise" clause in the First Amendment was also discussed at length.

The arguments continued throughout the day, and after adjournment we returned to Baltimore. The next morning the family was up early again. The one-hundred-mile round trip journeys to Washington continued daily through Friday. Two days were devoted to debating our case and two days to the Schemp case.

My interest vanished after the first day, and I returned to school for the rest of the week. We could only guess when the decision would be announced, but our experiences with the lower courts made us believe it would not be anytime soon.

Speculation continued as to how the Supreme Court would rule. As with any controversial issue, there were strange bedfellows on both sides. In addition to the expected liberal and humanist organizations, we now had the National Council of Churches and several Jewish groups on our side.

Officially opposed to our stand were the attorneys general of eighteen states who had filed *amicus curiae* briefs in support of the defendants. (Interestingly, no Christian organization filed a brief in support of our opponents.)

In a March editorial, *Life* magazine argued that the nation's founding fathers had wanted the leaven of religion in public life and spoke against outlawing Bible reading and prayer in school. The title of this piece was "The Bible—Better in School Than in Court." Mother wrote a letter to the magazine denouncing its stand. It appeared, along with Mother's picture, in the April 12 issue. It read in part:

> . . . The atheist's position (I am that Maryland atheist you mentioned) is one arrived at after considerable study, cogitation and inner search. It is a position which is founded in science, in reason and in a love for fellow man rather than in a love for God.
>
> We find the Bible to be nauseating, historically inaccurate, replete with the ravings of madmen. We find God to be sadistic, brutal, and a representation of hatred, vengeance. We find the Lord's Prayer to be that muttered by worms groveling for meager existence in a traumatic, paranoid world.
>
> This is not appropriate untouchable dicta to be forced on adult or child. The business of the public schools, where attendance is compulsory, is to prepare children to face the problems on earth, not to prepare for heaven—which is a delusional dream of the unsophisticated minds of the ill-educated clergy. . . .

This letter revealed again Mother's talent to infuriate people with acid-coated words.

To help pay the postage costs and other expenses of the *American Atheist*, Mother had formed a nonprofit corporation in May of 1962. She had extracted the name for the organization from another one called Protestants and Other Americans United for the Separation of Church and State. This group was composed largely of liberal Protestants who opposed church involvement in government, especially if the church involved was Roman Catholic. At any rate, Mother had seized upon the expression "Other Americans" to describe her constituency. She had felt certain that she would be better able to represent these people than some group of clergymen.

By the time the prayer and Bible-reading case was well on its way, Other Americans had begun to pay sweet returns for Mother's efforts. One of her wealthy supporters helped acquire a small building for the cause on North Calvert Street. There she established the headquarters of Other Americans and housed the equipment she had accumulated.

I was still the chief production specialist and now had added aluminum plate making to my skills. This process, whereby a reverse photographic image of the type was etched onto an aluminum plate that was then affixed to the printing press, was then somewhat complicated. I became quite good at it and took pride in my work. Since I was picking up two hundred dollars each month for these tasks, which I did each afternoon after school, I was quite well bankrolled for a seventeen-year-old.

Occasionally I felt sorry for myself because doing this work removed any opportunity to join sports activities at school. It also interfered with time I might otherwise have had to raise my grades, which were still quite low.

Each month I single-handedly printed, folded, collated, stapled, trimmed, and mailed about one thousand copies of the *American Atheist*. Of those, several hundred were sent free to various holders of public office. Sometimes, I would convince one of the guys from the U.N. Club, or some other buddy, to come give me a hand—for the minimum wage my mother was willing to pay. But, most often, I did it alone. And while I did, I dreamed of doing other things—like building my amateur radio station or taking girls to parties.

On June 17, 1963, after most public schools had let students out for summer vacation, the Supreme Court announced its decision. By an overwhelming 8 to 1, the court reversed the Maryland Court of Appeals decision and ruled that the opening Bible reading and prayer exercises were unconstitutional. This ruling applied not only to Maryland but to all states. Only Justice Stewart dissented. The court's written decision was carefully worded and somewhat cautious, a result, perhaps, of the uproar caused by the 1962 decision and the high volume of mail the justices had received on the case. But still the deed was done; prayer and Bible reading were out of the schools. The majority opinion said in part:

> . . . the place of religion in our society is an exalted one achieved through a long tradition of reliance on the home, the church and the inviolable citadel of the individual heart and mind. We have come to recognize through bitter experience that it is not within the power of government to invade that citadel, whether its purpose or effect be to aid or oppose, to advance or retard. In the relationship between man and religion, the state is firmly committed to a position of neutrality. The breach of neutrality that is today a trickling stream may all too soon become a raging torrent, and in the words of Madison, "It is proper to take alarm at the first amendment on our Liberties."

Mother was elated; I was relieved. The ordeal was over, or so we thought. In some ways the announcement of the decision was just the beginning of another barrage of attention—from the media, fellow dissidents, and opponents. The story was on the front page of newspapers across the country and became a lead story on many radio and TV newscasts. The headline on page 1 of the *New York Times* read, "Supreme Court, 8 to 1, Prohibits Lord's Prayer and Bible Reading As Public School Requirements." In all, there were three stories in the *Times* that day on the case, as well as a picture of Mother, Grandmother, and Jon Garth smiling in victory on the front steps of the Supreme Court Building in Washington.

One of the stories told how mainstream Protestants and Jews favored the decision while Roman Catholics, conservative Protestants, and fundamentalists deplored it. Billy Graham was quoted as saying, "I am shocked at the . . . decision. Prayers and Bible reading have been a part of public school life since the Pilgrims landed at Plymouth Rock. Now a Supreme Court in 1963 says our fathers were wrong all those years."

Senator Strom Thurmond of South Carolina called the decision "another triumph for the forces of secularism and atheism."

Some weeks later, even ex-president Harry S Truman commented to a reporter that when he was in fifth grade the teacher had opened each day with prayer. "It never hurt anybody," said Mr. Truman. "It made good citizens out of them."

The final story in the *New York Times* on June 18 told how the decision would affect the nation's public schools. In total, an estimated forty-one percent of the nation's school districts, in thirty-seven states plus the District of Columbia, would have to change existing practices. At the time of the decision, only eleven states did not permit Bible reading. Our little altercation at Woodbourne Junior High, now nearly three years in the past, had finally borne fruit with ramifications from shore to shore.

The attorney who had represented the city of Baltimore in the case, Francis Burch, started a group called the Constitutional Prayer Foundation—its aim being to restore prayer to the schools via a constitutional amendment. Before long Burch's group had won the support of former President Dwight Eisenhower, William Randolph Hearst, Jr., Francis Cardinal Spellman, Conrad Hilton, and the governors of several states.

Congressmen were besieged with mail—most of it against the Supreme Court prayer decisions—and within a year the U.S. House Judiciary Committee would hold hearings to evaluate 147 resolutions proposing 35 different constitutional amendments relating to prayer and religion in the public schools.

Several governors and other high state officials openly said they would defy the court's rulings. Among them was Governor George Wallace of Alabama who vowed to stand in the schoolroom himself, if necessary, to read the Bible.

There were very few—but some—humorous results of the court decision. *Newsweek* magazine reported that a Chicago High School had responded to the decision by immediately removing a praying mantis from its biology collection. It seemed that not even insects could escape the runaway cause we Murrays had launched.

As is true with most teen-agers, my social life had become very important to me. The first girl I dated seriously was also the first girl with whom I did more than kiss. Jennifer's parents owned an enormous home across town where they often allowed her to host parties for her friends. Afterwards, she and I inevitably had some time to ourselves on the couch in front of the fireplace. Since Mother had imposed no curfew on me, I was able to try getting away with as much as possible. Thus, alone in that romantic setting, we kissed and petted as much as Jennifer would permit.

Despite my unusual upbringing and public notoriety, I was a normal, hot-blooded male teen-ager—my Marxist background having had no noticeable effect on my physical desires. On top of that, I had been given no moral foundation at home, so the traditional value of virginity meant nothing to me. I was, therefore, often quite frustrated after two hours of heavy breathing on Jennifer's couch. Usually, just after midnight, her father called her on the telephone from his bedroom (the house was actually that large). That was my cue to leave, a disappointing conclusion to a busy evening, especially since Jennifer was exceptionally good looking.

Ironically, it was Jennifer who introduced me to Susan, a plain-looking girl with hazel eyes and bright auburn hair. She and I, finding we had similar teen-age passions, hit it off from the start.

"You and Jennifer do a lot together, don't you?" she asked the evening we met.

"Well . . . you know. I mean, how do you know about that?" I felt myself turning red.

"Oh, just girl talk."

"Well, we've done just about everything," I bragged.

"Everything?"

The conversation didn't have to progress much further before I knew that Susan's interest was more than passing. She and I slipped away into a little anteroom for some privacy. A short while later, Jennifer stuck her head into the room.

"Excuse me!" she scolded, then slammed the door, leaving us alone again.

Susan resnapped her bra and started to button her shirt. "I think we should leave. It's her house."

"You're right," I replied. "Do you have a car here?"

"No, Jennifer picked me up." We looked at each other. "Well, she is my best friend!"

I laughed. "That makes things simpler. Come on, we'll take my car." I now had my own wheels, a 1963 Oldsmobile Cutlass.

We drove to her home in the wealthy Jewish section of the city. There, parked in front of her large house, we resumed our amorous explorations.

Jennifer had introduced us because Susan was the president of the U.N. Club at Western High School, one of the city's two girls' schools. Jennifer thought we would have some common interests. Sure enough, we did.

Besides sex, Susan and I shared some interesting similarities related to how our families had influenced feelings about ourselves. One night, as we sat in a favorite coffee house, she confided in me.

"My dad is Jewish, but my mother is Gentile. Dad had my mom 'cleansed' by the rabbi to make her officially Jewish. But the Jewish community in this town is pretty conservative—you know, worried about assimilation."

"I see," I said, trying to show interest in the topic. It seemed as though I just could not escape religious talk of one type of another.

"Anyway, that makes people like me and my brothers and sisters suspect. We go to synagogue, but I get the feeling that a lot of the old families there look at us like—well—halfbreeds." A sadness filled her voice. This I found very touching; I understood her feelings.

"So you don't feel like you belong anywhere, do you," I commented.

"No. I'm glad we met. We have a lot in common."

"Me, too," I said, smiling.

When Susan and I started going steady after school started that fall, her parents were not pleased. Her father was of some reputation and means in Baltimore. Given the shaky ground he had put himself on with the Jewish community by marrying a Gentile, it was little wonder that he greeted my arrival with nothing but grave alarm. It wasn't long before relations between him and his daughter chilled. She and I both reacted with the self-righteous indignation so characteristic of adolescents.

"I don't know where he gets off saying that kind of stuff to you," I said one Saturday night while we were having dinner at one of Baltimore's nicer restaurants. All the money I was making from helping with Mother's causes was now handy for such luxuries.

"Oh, Bill, it's just horrible. I don't know what I'm going to do." She began to sniffle.

"I don't get it," I said. "I thought he was supposed to be a big liberal—the New Frontier, elect Kennedy, all that stuff. What gives?"

"I don't know. When I remind him that he married a Gentile and that it worked out okay, he just explodes. Says it's not the same at all. Oh, Bill, I love you. I wish we could just run away together."

"Yeah, well, we'll see," I said, trying to drop the topic. I was not ready to use the word *love* no matter how great the times we enjoyed in my car.

In late November, 1963, I went one afternoon to conduct some business at the United Nations Association headquarters in downtown Baltimore. It was about two o'clock in the afternoon when I heard the news: President Kennedy had been pronounced dead at Parkland Memorial Hospital in Dallas.

My memories of the assassination include an odd event that occurred later in the evening on the day Kennedy died. I was at home with the family, watching the ongoing news coverage of the day's grim events. The phone rang.

"I'll get it," Mother snapped, rising from her chair and heading to another room to answer.

I couldn't hear her side of the conversation, because her voice was unusually subdued. She hung up shortly and came back into the room.

"Come on, Bill. I want you to drive me over to Bill Moore's place." She was impatient, her voice tinged with a note of urgency.

"Why now?" I didn't want to miss the news coverage.

"Never mind. Get the keys and let's get going!"

As we drove, Mother sat silently and peered out the window. I couldn't quite figure it out. Bill Moore was a postman who was separated from his wife and held dissident ideas similar to Mother's. She had located her personal office in his apartment and stored her most important documents there. With this arrangement, she had a standing excuse to drop by and see him. Tonight, however, I sensed that her motive for going wasn't purely romantic. I tried to pry with a few questions, but she was not talking.

"Do you want me to come back and pick you up later?" I asked, as we pulled up outside of Bill's place.

"No, that's okay. I'll get Bill to bring me home."

Mother didn't come home that night until almost 3:00 A.M. I learned later that the call early in the evening had come from Communist party headquarters in New York. Mother had been informed that the man arrested in connection with the shooting of President Kennedy was a member of the Fair Play for Cuba Committee. Even though his membership had been in the committee's New Orleans branch and Mother said that she did not know him, the caller had ordered her to go immediately to the Fair Play for Cuba office in Baltimore. There she was to search the files carefully for any reference to Lee Harvey Oswald or others in New Orleans who might be connected with him. She was to destroy whatever she found.

Subsequent media information on Oswald revealed an

embarrassing similarity to Mother's own experience. He, too, had sought to defect to the Soviet Union and had been rebuffed. Oswald had made it all the way to Russia in 1959 and had remained in an attempt to convince the Presidium of the Supreme Soviet that he was worthy of Soviet citizenship. He was turned down but did marry a Russian woman who returned with him, along with an infant daughter, to New Orleans in 1962.

I suspect that Mother was embarrassed to discover that she was an officer in an organization that had welcomed a presidential assassin into its ranks, even if it was before the fact and had happened elsewhere. I say this because from then on her love affair with the Communist party cooled rapidly. It probably helped that with the Supreme Court victory, Mother was now a celebrity and could be more selective about the causes and groups she embraced.

Mother's latest cause of the moment was a real winner. The prayer case completed, she had turned Kerpelman loose on bigger fish by suing the city of Baltimore to prevent them from exempting churches from property and other taxes. This action so troubled churchmen in Baltimore that Roman Catholic and Episcopal dioceses in the city had joined together as codefendants. Mother welcomed the controversy. Staying in the news as a foe of religion made it easier to support what, in effect, was the atheist empire she was building.

I did my best to ignore what Mother was doing, because I had my own battles to fight with Susan's dad. He still could not stand even the thought of me. I was not overly offended. He had made it quite clear that my inability to qualify as a proper suitor for his daughter had little or nothing to do with atheism, or the school prayer case, or other Murray crimes against humanity. My unforgivable quality was my family tree: I was not a Jew. As might be expected, his unrelenting opposition to the romance drove Susan and me closer together. I became her chief source of comfort and solace. And in her arms, I found what seventeen-year-old boys long for the most.

As 1964 got underway, the family pressures generated by the relationship grew more intense. Susan bore most of the strain, however. All that was required of me was to show up when she could escape from the house. Mother was quite supportive in this amorous adventure. She believed, too, that Susan's father was narrow-minded and backward.

Then, on a pleasant afternoon late in March, my little romance became untidy. I arrived home about six o'clock, feeling cocky because I had just been elected second secretary of the Radio Club. It was the first elective office I had ever held in a group that wasn't political and revolutionary. I was proud and eager to tell the others. When I saw Grandmother waiting for me on the front porch, I knew something unusual was up. Her drooping face showed she was bothered about something.

"I have some news for you, *young man,*" she said without even a "hello."

"The way you're standing here, it must be serious."

"It is—more than you think."

"Well?"

"That girlfriend of yours has moved in."

"What?"

"You heard me."

"Where is she?"

"Where do you think? Down in the basement."

I ran past Grandmother, through the kitchen, and down into the basement. Susan was standing by my bed. Two suitcases stood nearby on the floor. A third lay open on the bed before her. A determined look covered her face, and I could see she'd been crying.

"What's happened?" I ran up to her and took her hand.

"I'm sorry, Bill. I'm sorry, but I just didn't know where to go."

Then she let go and sobbed for several moments. She spoke angrily after wiping her eyes. "I guess I should have been telling you. Things have been impossible between Dad and me the past two weeks. I couldn't believe some of the things he was saying to me. Even mother told him to stop it, but he was like a man possessed." She paused and looked up at me, "Bill, I couldn't take it any longer. He was driving me crazy."

"I understand; it's okay." The words somehow slipped from my lips, but even the numbness in my head could not cover up the thought, *No, this is not okay!*

"Well, yesterday I called your mother. I told her how it had been going and asked her if I could come live with you. I figured we were practically married anyway, what with all we have done together."

"I guess my mom said yes?" A sickness was building in my stomach.

"Oh, yes. She was really nice about it and said, 'Sure, come on ahead.' And we agreed not to tell you beforehand. She wanted it to be a surprise."

"I'm surprised all right. Did she say you could sleep down here, too?"

"Oh, yes," she grinned, the smile breaking the tear streaks on her cheeks.

I smiled back—weakly. I sensed a personal disaster in the making. The wild seeds I had sown were germinating before my eyes in the basement. This was not working out as I had planned. While Susan and I had talked much of love in the back seat of my Cutlass, I had never seriously considered marrying Susan. She had been planning to attend the University of Michigan, while I had my sights fixed on the University of Maryland. I had thought September would come, and we would go our separate ways. We had even talked about this and agreed it would be all right to date others while we were apart.

Ironically, if Susan's father would have eased off and Mother would not have senselessly moved Susan in, the relationship would have ended with a natural death in September. So, it was with little enthusiasm that I began sharing my bedroom with Susan.

The story of our unusual romance eventually was reported nationwide, because during this period Mother was interviewed by writers for several major magazines—including *The Saturday Evening Post* and *Life*. By this time "Mad Murray," as Mother now referred to herself, had dealt with the media on almost a daily basis for nearly four years. She knew how to be quotable. The *Post* writer wrote that Madalyn was "a strange, immensely complicated woman, full of paradoxes, conflicts and challenges." He also said that Mother appeared to be a woman "who would say anything, do anything, believe anything as long as it was rebellious and antisocial." She proved this in the interview, telling him that if "people want to go to church and be crazy fools, that's their business. . . . They can believe in their virgin birth and the rest of their mumbo jumbo, as long as they don't interfere with me, my children, my home, my job, my money or my intellectual views."

In the same article Mother was quoted, "I want to be able to walk down any street in America and not see a cross or any other sign of religion. I won't stop till the Pope—or whoever the highest religious authority is—says atheists have a right to breathe in this world. . . ."

Of course, allowing atheists to breathe was okay with the Pope. It was my mother who did not want *him* to breathe. She has always hated Popes. Perhaps this is related to my father's Catholicism, which interfered with her desires for marriage.

Mother's closing comment in the *Post* story was, "I love a good fight. . . . I guess fighting God and God's spokesmen is sort of the ultimate, isn't it?"

The article in *Life* quoted her as saying, "Everything I learn makes me realize I don't know a thing. But compared to most cud-chewing, small talking, stupid American women, I'm a brain. We might as well admit it. I'm a genius." In this interview she labeled religious people as "cowards" because their God presented no problems and they did not have to face Him. She also called agnostics "atheists without guts" because "they're afraid to speak up."

For about two months after Susan moved in, not much happened. Her parents made some loud noises but with little effect. The last week of May I was looking forward to my eighteenth birthday when I would no longer be classified as a juvenile. My high school days were nearly over. I now had some hope that I could find a job and leave home, perhaps ditching Susan along the way. I was wrong. The light I thought was breaking on the horizon was not dawn, but rather the sunset before a long, dark night.

The morning of my birthday, May 25, 1964, I read the newspaper and received a jolt. A news story reported that an attorney for Susan's father had filed a complaint against me in criminal court. He was charging me with improperly enticing Susan to leave her home and abandon the Jewish religion for atheism. The attorney was relying on an old law that dated back a hundred and fifty years. It had been intended to preserve the state's Roman Catholics from assimiliation with non-Catholics through marriage.

The newspaper article went on to say that a show-cause hearing had been scheduled for the following Tuesday, June 2. That meant I would have to appear before the court and "show cause" why Susan shouldn't, as her parents were asking, be given into the care of her aunt and uncle, and why my mother and I shouldn't be restrained from having any contact with Susan—in person, by phone, or by letter—for an indefinite period of time.

I became indignant as I read. Enticing her away, indeed. She had fled. I remembered the meeting Susan and her father finally had had several weeks after she had moved in with us. Susan told me that he had become furious and struck her face so forcefully that he had broken a bone in his right hand. It was probably that and other similar incidents that had convinced him to name Susan's aunt and uncle as custodians. If he had named himself, Susan might have been able to show cause why she shouldn't be forced to live in his home.

I laid the newspaper down. I felt queasy and scared. The thought of going to jail for six months was terrifying.

That night Mother, Susan, and I gathered in the basement to plot. "What do you think is going to happen?" I asked Mother. She knew quite a bit about law.

"Well, first, you will have to be served with a summons, which has not happened yet. But, more than likely, you will go to jail, and Susan will wind up in some detention center for juveniles—if you don't do what her father wants."

"What can we do?" Susan pled frantically.

"Well, I suggest you get married and fast." Mother smiled.

"But how can we get married? Susan won't be eighteen for several months," I protested.

"There's always some loophole in the law. I'll look into it."

"I hope you're right," I said.

By the end of the week, no officer of the court had come to serve papers summoning us to appear on June 2.

"I don't get it," Mother shrugged as we discussed this in the living room on Friday night. "If they were going to serve us, they would have done it by now. They're supposed to give us enough time to prepare a defense. Who knows? Those newspaper reporters can foul things up."

"So, should we go to court on Tuesday?" I asked.

"No! Why should we? There's been no summons. Let's sit tight and see what happens. This could be a false alarm."

"Or a trap," Susan offered.

"That's true, but if it is, you two have a little contingency plan. I told you there'd be some loophole," she chuckled.

It wasn't exactly a loophole. Mother had discovered that marriage laws in Maryland vary from county to county. Just to the south of us, in Montgomery County, the legal age of consent for a woman was fourteen to seventeen, depending on circumstances.

Tuesday came and went, as far as we were concerned

uneventfully. But next morning's newspaper revealed how eventful the day had actually been. The court had heard the case in spite of our absence and granted Susan's father's petition. It was now possible that authorities would show up at our door and escort Susan right out of my life.

I was cornered and I knew it. Later that afternoon I "popped the question."

"Well," I said to Susan, "I'm in favor of a little drive down to Montgomery County to see the judge. How about it? Do you want to come along?"

"Is this your proposal?"

"I'm afraid so. You know we're kissing off college by doing this."

"Well, I have some other news for you, Bill. I missed my last period."

I was speechless. She gave me the details. Her news made it even more urgent in my mind that we get married. I was a bastard and so was my brother. I didn't want to have another one in the family. Besides, I did not want to begin my legal adulthood in jail.

The next day Susan and I drove to the county seat at Rockville, a suburb of Washington, D.C. We went alone. Dragging members of my family along might have drawn unwanted attention to us, something we were eager to avoid. We found the clerk's office, obtained the license, then located a judge. His bailiff served as our witness and, without much further ado, we were married. I slipped on Susan's left finger a simple gold band I had purchased at a pawn shop only hours before the ceremony. The deed done, we embraced each other mechanically, shook hands all around, then drove to spend the night in my basement room on Baltimore's Winford Road.

Although our marriage should have settled the matter, we thought it might be wise to leave Baltimore for a few days until the furor subsided. We decided to "honeymoon" in New York City. Mother had a friend there named Paul Krassner, and he had offered his apartment as a place to stay.

The first morning of my married life Mother was full of

ideas at the breakfast table. "You shouldn't leave until late tonight," she said.

"Why not?" I demanded.

"Look, stupid, they're after you. If you move around in broad daylight, you're asking for trouble."

"I can't believe this," I complained.

"And Susan, you've got to dye your hair black." Susan groaned, running her hand through her bright reddish-brown locks.

"In fact," Mother continued, "I think I'll drive you two up to Krassner's place in my car tonight. The police will be looking for your car, Bill."

We left about midnight, with Mother at the wheel. "The plan," she explained, "is for you two to lie low in New York. I'll get in touch with the court somehow and inform them that you're married. After that, maybe we can persuade Susan's family to drop the charges."

"I bet they won't," said Susan.

"Well, we'll just have to wait and see," I added.

We met Mr. Krassner, who at the time was editor of a magazine called *The Realist*. This publication printed shocking, controversial material, including an accusation that Lyndon Johnson had committed necrophilia with John Kennedy's body. In 1963 it had printed a story on Mother. In the interview she had bared her soul, commenting at one point that if she could not "come through the [prayer] case the same offensive, unlovable, bull headed, defiant, aggressive slob that I was when I started it, then I'll give up. . . . My own identity is more important to me. They can keep their g—— prayers in the public schools, in public outhouses, in public H-bomb shelters and in public whorehouses."

Although Krassner and Mother were kindred spirits, Susan and I soon found that we weren't really welcome at the man's apartment. We took a cab downtown and began looking for a cheap hotel. In the middle of our search we entered the lobby of an expensive hotel to rest for a few minutes. I told Susan to watch our things while I went across the street to check the rates at a deteriorating hotel that looked to be in our price range. When I returned, Susan was frozen in place, her face pale.

"What happened?" I asked.

"It's gone."

"What's gone?"

"Your good camera and some of my things."

"What? How did it happen?"

"I went over to the bathroom. I was only gone two minutes."

Now I was angry. "You've got to be joking. You let my camera sit unattended in a hotel lobby in New York?"

"We can ask the clerk. . ."

"It's no use," I cut her off. "He probably took it." I was furious. Thanks to this woman, I had lost my home and would probably be deprived of my education. Now even my prized 35mm camera was gone. I was beginning to wonder if she and my mother were working together to drive me out of my mind.

I forced myself to stop fretting. I needed to call my mother. I had found nothing in the New York papers about what was happening to our case in Baltimore. I found a phone booth and called collect.

"What's going on?" I asked.

"Susan's father found out the two of you were in New York and convinced the judge to cite you both for contempt. Thank G_, they couldn't slap me with that since I was essentially in compliance with the order now that Susan's not living here."

"Lucky you."

"Look, how long can you hold out up there?"

"I found a hotel. Things with Krassner were no good. I guess we could stretch it over to the end of next week."

"That's good. Maybe things will have cooled down a bit by then."

"I hope so. I'm almost out of money and I need my car."

"I'll have Irv bring your car up. He can ride back on the bus."

"Good, thanks. I'll talk to you later."

Susan, standing by me, sobbed, "Oh, Bill, how did we ever get into this mess?"

I wrapped my arm around her. "It all started that first night I told you about the foam I had ordered for Jennifer." I laughed, a bit of my bitterness showing through.

We left New York on Saturday morning, June 20. Traffic was light, and we made good time down the Jersey Turnpike, across the Delaware Memorial Bridge, and over the remaining sixty or seventy miles from there to Baltimore. We arrived around noon. Mother, Grandmother, and Uncle Irv were all at home.

Susan and I carried the suitcases to the basement and were unpacking when Mother called out, "Oh no! Bill, get up here right away!"

The urgency in her voice made me suspicious. "Susan, stay down here," I snapped, then bounded up the steps and through the kitchen. I found Mother in the front room looking out the window. I ran to her side and gasped. Three police cars were parked bumper to bumper in front of our house.

"There're two more in the alley," Mother said grimly.

"How did they find out so quickly that we're home?"

"They have lots of ways. Probably the neighbors called them."

Finally, two officers climbed from a patrol car and walked up to the front porch.

Mother cursed softly. "Come on," she said to me and walked to the door. I followed her out to the porch. The policemen stopped at the foot of the stairs and peered up at us. "What do you want?" Mother asked.

The older of the two men told us they were there to pick up Susan.

"Do you have a warrant?" Mother demanded.

"Look, lady, don't give me a lot of trouble. You know d___ well there's a court order out on her."

"Without a warrant you're not coming in here."

He scowled and walked back to the car to talk with his partner.

Mother whispered to me, "Bill, stay here and keep that guy distracted. I'm going to grab Susan and get her out of here before any more cops show up!" With that she disappeared into the house.

I sized up the situation. Mother's car was parked across the street. She and Susan would have to run across the lawn, past the police car, and across the street. I realized I would have to do some pretty serious "distracting" in order to give Susan and Mother the time they needed.

I sauntered down the walk and out into the street to where the police cars were double-parked. On my way I noticed that neighborhood kids and adults were gathering in small groups on either side of the house to see what was happening. As I walked up to the car the older officer turned around.

"Whadya want?" he grunted.

"Look, officers, Susan and I were married, just over two weeks ago in Montgomery County. That has to nullify the court order."

"It's not my job to figure stuff like that out, kid. Tell it to the judge," he replied.

"I thought you were supposed to enforce the law. The law says she's my wife now. Any fool should know that takes precedence in a situation like this," I persisted.

"Don't get smart with me, boy! . . ." Suddenly he looked up over my shoulder. "Hey there! Where are you two going?"

I didn't have to look to know that Mom and Susan were making their break.

"Get out of the way," the officer said, stepping in my direction and reaching to push me if necessary.

I didn't reply, nor did I move.

"Why you punk!" the officer yelled. He pulled out his billy club from his belt and shoved it near my face. I pushed him back knocking him slightly off balance. He swore, and as he struggled to stay on his feet, he swung at me. I blocked the club and punched him in the nose. Now I had real trouble on my hands. The policeman's partner jumped from the car, and he along with three others came to help subdue me. Seconds later they threw me on the ground and began kicking me. In the background I could hear my mother screaming, "You can't do that! You don't have a warrant!"

I could do little to protect myself. Blow after blow landed on my back and legs. They knew where and how to hit me with their sticks, so that when I went before a judge in a day or two, it would not appear I had been brutalized. My knees suffered the most from the beating—enough, I learned later, to do permanent damage.

After they had thrust me, handcuffed, into the back of a van, they went after Mother and Susan, who had not made their getaway. Mother also resisted efforts to subdue her and got roughed up. During the melee the crowd of bystanders swelled to over a hundred. Some of them must have greatly enjoyed seeing the "godless atheists" getting their lumps because I heard several shouts of "Hit her again!" "Kill them!" and "Get that b____." At the height of the punching, cursing, and yelling, Grandmother stepped out on the porch and promptly fainted. Uncle Irv lugged her back inside.

Shortly thereafter, Susan, Mother, and I were hauled to the Pine Street Police station. I was booked on suspicion of assaulting a police officer. After bail was set, I was led to an empty cell. I sat there, rubbing my bruises, steaming about the treatment I'd received. I swore to myself that one day I would do something to right this injustice. Whereas once I had wanted to run far away, change my name, and never again be associated with the name of Madalyn Murray, now I wanted revenge.

As the hours passed and I had plenty of time to think, I became convinced that I was being persecuted. I was regarded by the entire community as a close accomplice of Madalyn Murray—who was already called "the most hated woman in America." We had offended the public mores, assaulted their hallowed political assumptions, blasphemed their God and, because of Mother's involvement in the Fair

Play for Cuba Committee, maybe even indirectly helped to assassinate their president. Much of this was purely imaginary. Nevertheless, we had become intolerable villains who represented the most monstrous evil. I believed this mood of hate and frustration had led to the fury I had experienced that afternoon in front of our home in Northeast Baltimore.

"William Murray!" My angry reflections were suddenly halted. I looked up and saw a guard holding a key in his hand.

"That's me," I muttered.

The guard unlocked the door and pulled it open. "Come with me."

I struggled to my feet and limped after him down the corridor. Eventually we found our way to the front desk where I was handed a paper to sign. My mother and Leonard Kerpelman were waiting for me across the room. The lawyer had sprung us both by posting bond. The sergeant handed me my wallet and watch, and I walked away.

"Bill, are you okay?" Mother asked.

"I've felt better."

"Let's get out of here," Kerpelman suggested. "We can talk in my car."

As soon as we got outside, I asked about Susan.

"She's okay. They took her to a different jail close to her parents' home. We can go get her now," he explained. Then he looked at me strangely, "You're limping. Tell me what they did to you."

On our way to pick up Susan we compared notes and injuries derived from the afternoon's frolic. Kerpelman said that between us we faced ten criminal assault charges. When Susan joined us, she said the police had forced her to undergo a physical examination to confirm that she was pregnant. I seethed.

Back at home, Grandmother was waiting for us. We learned her dramatic fainting spell had been an act. She had hoped to distract the police from redesigning my body.

As the others continued to talk excitedly, I led Susan by the hand to the basement. Very sore and tired, I wanted only a hot shower and then some sleep. I sat down heavily on the bed and unlaced my shoes. When I pulled my shirt and trousers off, Susan gasped. "Oh, Bill, I've never seen bruises like that!" She started to weep, "I'm sorry, I'm sorry—please forgive me."

"What the h___? What are you saying that for?"

"If it hadn't been for me, this would never have happened to you."

"Oh, quiet down. It's not your fault. It's a conspiracy of sorts, like I've said before."

Susan whimpered and blew her nose in a tissue.

"We have to get out of here," I went on, "but I don't know how. Mother has all the money, and she's calling the shots."

Susan smiled, then embraced and kissed me. "I'll bet I can make you feel better," she purred. She did.

The next morning I struggled to climb from bed. Covered with multicolored bruises, I felt like a giant toothache. I creaked stiffly up the stairs and eased myself into a chair at the dining room table. It was Sunday morning, and I noted with disgust that the unusual events of yesterday had not altered a weekly tradition at our house. Each Sunday, while most of our neighbors were on their way to church, Grandmother served up pancakes—dry, rubbery pancakes that we tried to improve with copious amounts of cheap syrup. Those pancakes alone could have turned me into a churchgoer.

"If we show up in court tomorrow morning, they'll crucify us," my mother said, diverting my mental grumbling. "Bill, the judge could throw us in the clinker for a hundred years on those assault charges."

Susan gasped, "What are you going to do?"

"There's only one thing to do, and that's to get out of here," she announced. "The only real question is where. We could get out of the country altogether—like to Canada or Australia or England."

"I don't want to leave the country," I said firmly. "Why

don't we move as far away as possible, but stay inside the U.S.?"

"Wait a minute!" Mother's eyes brightened. "I know someone who can help us. . . . Maybe even help us get into Cuba."

"Cuba!" I gasped. "They're not going to want this bunch any more than Russia did."

"Shut up, punk! This is all your f____ fault anyway. Your hot pants got us into all this trouble."

With that, she walked to the phone and called a woman she knew named Betty Washington. Washington was a black "freedom fighter" with an organization called New Africa. At the time of the call, she was out on bail from a kidnapping charge in Alabama. She owed Mother a favor because Mother had purchased a handgun for her from a local sporting goods store. Buying such a weapon in her own name would have violated her parole.

Overcome by curiosity, I ran downstairs and picked up the extension phone. I heard Washington telling Mother, "Go to Hawaii until the coast is clear and you can get into Cuba. It will take time to get the Great One [Fidel Castro] to let you in. He's hard to get to these days."

"Why Hawaii?" asked Mother.

"Because it's half Buddhist. Half the people there will be on your side against the Christians back here in Maryland."

I almost dropped the phone in disbelief.

Washington and Mother went on talking. Washington agreed to camp out in our house until it was sold. This, I reflected, would not thrill our neighbors. No blacks lived in the neighborhood; one family had tried to move in, but they had been run off.

After hanging up the phone, Mother quickly gathered the household and announced her plan. "We're leaving in twenty-four hours for Hawaii. Irv, you don't have to come, but if you don't, you'll have to learn to cook and make your own bed." Irv left the room to go pack.

Susan and I went to the basement and talked over the plan. "You know, if we don't go along, she'll probably turn us in," I said.

"You're right," Susan said faintly. "I didn't understand the day I called her, but now I do. She didn't invite me to live here with you either for my sake or for yours. She did it for herself. She needs conflict that badly, and she wanted the same kind of conflict with you that she had with your grandfather."

"Oh, Susan, that's a bunch of s____."

"No, your grandmother told me. She said that when you wouldn't fight with Madalyn the way your grandfather did, Madalyn turned more against society. Face it, Bill, it makes sense. She studied law. She knew what could happen if she let me come to live here. She knew it would cause an explosion. She could have told me no, but she didn't because she relishes a fight more than anything."

Maybe she was right, but I said nothing in reply. We began to sort through our things. It was interesting to see what items each person chose to take. Mother carefully sealed her mailing list in a large envelope. Susan, of course, had only the clothes she had brought with her the day she had moved in. Grandmother made sure the family picture albums were in her suitcase. Uncle Irv packed up his dozen watches and his girlie magazines. I lovingly wrapped up Grandfather's 1908 Luger pistol.

I was already mourning what I feared would be the permanent loss of my car which, ironically, was the one thing that had seemed to guarantee a little independence.

"What will we do with the cars?" I asked Mother in the midst of that Sunday afternoon's frenzy.

"G__, I nearly forgot about them!" She paused. "Let me think."

"Seems to me you've got three alternatives: sell them, store them, or ship them," I volunteered.

"I'll call Betty and ask her to arrange for temporary storage. After we get settled in Hawaii, I'll see if we can have them shipped to us."

I was delighted. Maybe this move wouldn't be a total loss after all. I continued my packing with a lighter heart.

Final arrangements were completed on Monday, and on Tuesday, June 23, we arrived at Dulles International Airport in Washington, our fifteen pieces of luggage making the scene look like the beginning of a safari. Mother had elected to launch us from D.C. where we might not be as readily spotted. Some melancholy thoughts of our trip to Paris came back to me as we checked in. This time our traveling party numbered seven, if you counted the child in Susan's womb. Mother had booked us on a TWA flight to Los Angeles under her mother's maiden name. In Los Angeles we would transfer to a Pan Am flight that would carry us on to Honolulu.

A lucky reporter caught sight of us at the gate, and Mother gave him a quote or two. She said that we were fleeing to Hawaii because people were more tolerant there—"80 percent of the Hawaiians are Buddhist, and Buddhists are absolute atheists," she said. Reports of this erroneous remark arrived in Hawaii before we did.

We boarded the plane without incident, and as we sped westward, I gazed down at the terrain far beneath me. My preceding eighteen years on the planet passed before my eyes, and I sunk into a depressed state of self-pity. I had been kind to no avail. I had been tolerant to no gain. I had been helpful but had received no help. I looked at Susan who was dozing, her head against my shoulder. She was no beauty queen. The child she carried had no future as far as I could see. How would I support this new person who was about to join us? I knew I couldn't depend on my mother. College was out of the question. I would have to find a job without a degree.

By the time we landed in Los Angeles, I wanted nothing other than a chance to catch the next plane back to Baltimore. A jail cell awaited me there, but on the whole, that seemed preferable to the dismal prospects I envisioned in Honolulu. As our Pan Am clipper soared above the Pacific Ocean, my depression deepened. When we arrived in Honolulu, I was in such bad shape that I could barely function. Like the others, I followed Mother's orders like a robot.

Unlike me, Mother was in high spirits. She had foiled the authorities and had made her great escape. We learned that her underground contact in Hawaii was a local minister in the Unitarian church. He invited us to stay in his church for a few days until we could find a more permanent residence. Mother had somehow managed to get thousands of dollars out of the bank on the day before, which made her doubly exultant.

We drove to the church, and as Mother looked over our living quarters, I sat elsewhere in the building, staring out a window. Below the window flowed a lovely little stream. It reminded me of the brook into which I had poured our tropical fish the day before in Baltimore. My life was being wrenched apart, and I hated it. In my mind, my mother and Susan were responsible for this. I retrieved Grandfather's Luger pistol from my case and began to toy with it. What would it be like, I wondered, to blow my mother and Susan away with it?

"What are you doing with that?" Susan demanded, abruptly interrupting my thoughts.

"Thinking of blowing my nose! Why?" I yelled, irritated at being bothered.

"Don't scream at me!"

"Then don't intrude on my thoughts."

"Your mother said she's heard from somebody in the Communist party. They think they may have a place for us to live."

"The party, the party. I'm sick to death of the g——— party. I want a job and my own place to live and some peace."

"Bill, please, think about the baby."

"I'll give you the baby!" I reached out and knocked her to the floor. "That's for you, you little Jew b——! Now, leave me alone!" I was shaking with anger. Susan stood up warily and ran from the room, tears pouring from her eyes.

The next day I looked but could not find Grandfather's Luger. I learned that Susan had told my mother about the fight and my ugly mood. To punish me—or to protect themselves—they had turned the weapon in to a local police station. To me that pistol had represented my grandfather's manhood; it was the only such token he had left behind. Now it was gone.

When no housing could be found quickly, the Unitarian

minister moved us into a large room over the church sanctuary. There we camped for several more days.

A number of local dissident groups, it turned out, sympathized with my Mother's causes and came to our aid. She had managed to convince enough people that we were refugees seeking asylum from the oppressive and hateful regime in Catholic Baltimore. Consequently, we received help in the form of meals and offers of one sort of accommodation or another.

Before too long, Mother found a place to live—the first floor of an enormous old home on Spencer Street, near the top of Punchbowl, an extinct volcano crater between downtown Honolulu and Waikiki. Not far from the house was the National Memorial Cemetery of the Pacific, where thousands of World War II and Korean War soldiers were buried.

Our new living quarters were large, with as much space on one floor as there had been in our entire house in Baltimore. Having no choice, Susan and I moved in with the others, but we continued to search for an apartment of our own. Mother insisted that both of us enroll at the University of Hawaii. She would pay our tuition and other expenses, she promised, as long as we continued to live with her. So we applied and were accepted for the fall semester.

I was broke, so I found a job as a construction worker. I saved as much of my wages as I could, hoping to be able to afford an apartment before too long.

We soon learned that Hawaii was not quite the Shangri-la we had hoped for. We found out when we arrived that the local Buddhists did not appreciate being called atheists. In fact, they believed in a higher being. And Buddhists were not the majority anyway. That distinction belonged to a group we knew intimately: Roman Catholics. Worst of all, the court in Baltimore had been outraged at our "finger-in-the-eye" exit. Our actions had goaded people there to new heights of outrage. And comments about Baltimore and its citizens in the *Life* magazine article, which was published the week before our escape, had not helped. Mother had been quoted as saying that in Baltimore row houses bred row minds. "All anyone cares about [there], besides maybe religion, is the g⎯⎯ Orioles. Marx was wrong; it's baseball that's the opiate of the masses."

Although our alleged offenses in Maryland were certainly minor compared to robbery or murder, for example, the court had decided to pursue us to the bitter end and had filed orders for extradition. The governor of Hawaii, who happened to be a Roman Catholic, agreed to this request in August, but Mother filed an appeal.

By September I had saved enough money to rent an apartment. Susan and I moved just as school was starting. It was a small, one-bedroom affair, not three blocks from the police station on South Berritania Street. Not long after, I obtained a job at the Honolulu Book Shop, the largest store in the city at that time.

A routine developed. My days were occupied almost entirely between going to school and working at the bookstore. I still had no car, so I walked or rode the bus. I was busy and had little time to think. But when I did, I still longed to be far away from Madalyn Murray, free from her domination and the foul controversies that swirled about her. I often wondered if there would ever be a time when I could just be Bill Murray—not Bill Murray, son of the most hated woman in America.

"**Y**ou what?" I asked Mother in anger and disbelief. "I put your car in a safe place," she replied.

"You can't do that!"

"I can't? Try me. I'm the one who paid to have the cars shipped here."

"So? Why are you hiding my car and not Irv's?"

"Irv didn't desert the ship like you did."

"So that's it! You can't stand to have me out from under your thumb. Well, you can store that car as long as you like. I'm not coming back!" I turned and headed for the door.

"We'll see!" Mother yelled as the door slammed.

Disgusted about not having a car for three months, I had visited Mother to learn when she would ship the vehicles from Baltimore. When told they had already arrived, I was stunned. Now she was hiding *my* car. I burned.

Mother, Grandmother, and Uncle Irv were still living on Spencer Street, while Susan and I were hanging on to our small apartment. With both of us in school, we didn't see much of each other. I was carrying eighteen units at school and working nights at the bookstore. It was just as well. I remained sullen and angry about the course my life was taking, and Susan was a convenient target for my frustration. Her pregnancy was now showing, and sometimes I slapped her for getting pregnant in the first place (as if she had managed that on her own).

This dismal monotony of work, classes, and fights with Susan was strangely interrupted one day. The telephone rang—it was Mother.

"Bill, I want you to meet someone."

"Who?"

"Linus Pauling."

"You're kidding."

"Not exactly. You see it's his son, Linus Pauling, Jr."

"Is he a physicist too?"

"No, he's a . . . a doctor"

"Why do you want me to meet him?"

"Oh, I thought you two might enjoy talking with each other."

"Okay, what gives? What kind of doctor is he?"

"Well, he's a psychiatrist."

"What!"

"Don't get upset. I thought it would be nice if you two got acquainted."

"The h__ it would. What makes you think . . ."

"Just calm down. There's something in it for you if you go."

"What?"

"Fifty dollars each trip."

"Why, you . . ."

"Think it over, Bill. I know you and the Jew b__ could use the money." She hung up.

As usual Mother had me fuming. I knew she had trickery in the works, but what?

I told Susan what Mother had proposed, and she suggested I try to find out more from Uncle Irv. It took some scheming, but I did contact him privately. He told me that Mother was desperately seeking some way to avoid extradition to Baltimore. The strategy was to convince the judge that I was crazy. Then he might agree that it would be best for us to stay in Hawaii.

"D__ her!" I said to Irv.

He laughed and shrugged his shoulders.

The humiliating part of it was that I did need the money. I subdued my pride and made an appointment with Dr. Pauling. This visit added another bizarre experience to my abnormal life. Dr. Pauling interviewed me for several minutes, but we spent most of the session talking about cars. For this session I received fifty dollars, which probably made me the only person on earth who was paid to be "crazy." I went back several more times, but grew tired of wasting my time in this way and stopped going.

Accepting money from Mother in such a way was embarrassing, but in a way I felt I deserved it. I knew Mother was hauling in a lot of cash from her mailing list by crying out regularly to supporters about my financial needs, especially those related to the forthcoming birth of our child. But except for my wages received for acting insane, none of the funds were ever channeled to me.

Instead, this money was used for Mother's pet projects—old and new. In September when Jon Garth had enrolled in a public elementary school, she learned that in Hawaii students recited the pledge of allegiance containing the hated phrase "one nation under God." The previous spring Mother had tried to get the school officials in Baltimore to delete the same phrase, saying it violated "our freedom of conscience because we're atheists." Not surprisingly, her plea there had been ignored. In Hawaii she had taken a more serious step by filing suit on the same issue against the principal of Jon Garth's school as well as the state superintendent of instruction. These actions disgusted me. I did not understand why we could not just live our own lives and let people say their prayers and do their religious things.

During the fall, a political issue also enticed Mother. Protests against United States involvement in Viet Nam became popular, and Mother joined in. I'm reasonably certain that, in conjunction with these anti-war activities, Gus Hall (chairman, Communist Party of the U.S.) visited Hawaii that year. While there, he conferred with Mother at length.

However, Mother was always on the lookout for causes that could be uniquely her own. This she found in a Hawaiian institution known as the Kamehameha Schools/Bernice Pauahi Bishop Estate. It seems that late in the last century, Mrs. Bishop (the great granddaughter of Kamehameha I, who had united the kingdom of Hawaii) deeded her vast estate in such a way as to provide free education for children of Hawaiian or partly Hawaiian descent. Mother was able to detect inequity in this generosity and attacked the Kamehameha Schools, because in her opinion they should have been open to everyone, not just native Hawaiians. Since the schools were not supported by public funds and since my mother's stay in Hawaii was brief, nothing came of this.

"Hello, Bill?" It was another phone call from Mother.

"What do you want?" I asked. *What would she say this time that would inflame me?* I wondered.

"A fantastic opportunity has come up."

Sure, I thought.

"Bill, I want you to cooperate and help me get this thing going," Mother went on.

"What is it this time, Mother?"

"I've gotten in touch with a psychic from Seattle. He's here in Honolulu and has excellent credentials. He used to be at Duke University."

"What does he do?"

"He conducts seances and predicts the future."

"Is he for real?"

"Sure thing. And I want you to help me arrange his meetings. You know, take care of the administration and groundwork."

"I don't know." I pondered her proposal a moment. I was busy with school and work at the bookstore. "I think I better pass on this one," I said.

"You better give it some thought before you say no." She went on to tell me that it seemed likely we would lose our appeal to avoid extradition to Maryland. This psychic deal could raise some money in case we needed to flee again. She implied that if I didn't help her with this latest scheme, I might be left holding our legal baggage in Honolulu. She finally changed my mind, though, when she offered to return my car if I helped. I agreed warily, uncertain of what new indignities might befall me.

As it turned out, the fortune-telling business was spooky enough to hold my interest. It was a welcome change from the boredom I had endured when involved in Mother's political and social causes. And all kinds of leading citizens, I was amused to discover, were involved in the project, among them a Unitarian minister and a city councilman. It was fun.

In the predawn hours of February 16, 1965, Susan excitedly woke me up. Her labor had started. I drove her to the Kapiolani Maternity Hospital for the delivery, which proceeded normally. Our daughter, whom we named Robin Ilene, was born that afternoon. Only minutes after the birth, when I was still flushed with excitement, a nurse invited me to a small room for a visit with the doctor.

"Your wife is doing fine," the doctor explained, "but I'm afraid the baby is having trouble breathing. I think she has fluid in one lung from the sound of it."

"Will she be okay?" I asked, a sense of dread building in my chest.

"Yes, I think so, but we'll need to keep her here with us for a few days, maybe a week."

"How much will that cost?"

"Don't you have insurance?"

"No."

"Well, it won't be cheap, but I'm sure the hospital can arrange some terms with you. And I assure you I'll be willing to wait for my fee."

My heart sank. I knew the only person who could loan me money was Mother. I hated the idea, but there was no other choice. Susan came home from the hospital after just two days, but Robin remained for a week. The bill was way above anything I could afford.

Mother agreed to help pay, but she refused to give me the money to do it. Instead, she wrote out a check directly to the hospital. Her lack of trust irritated me. As usual I released my anger and discontent on Susan, although she was still weak from the childbirth. Now I slapped her for failing to give birth to a healthy baby. My behavior was childish.

We brought Robin home, and thereafter my sleep was interrupted almost nightly by her pleading cries. It was another strain on an already overburdened marriage. I was increasingly glad for the demands of my work that kept me out of the apartment and away from the messy diapers and late-night feedings. I had dropped out of school after the first semester, knowing I could not support my family with a part-time job.

My final undoing in Hawaii, though, was the legal mess in Maryland that was still not resolved. Not long after Robin's birth, our appeal to reverse the extradition order was turned down by the Hawaii court. The heat was on, and neither Mother nor I wanted to take our chances on receiving justice in Maryland. Mother decided to make a run for Mexico, hoping that nation would grant her at least temporary asylum. She asked me to go with her—minus my wife and daughter. I was not an enthusiastic husband and father, but even to me this seemed a low-down thing to do. Mother was insistent, though, and I gave in. I knew it was rotten to leave Susan and Robin behind, but I figured I would have to leave no matter what—either I would be returned as a prisoner to Maryland or I could run away a free man. I chose freedom.

I didn't look forward to breaking the news to Susan, because I knew she would not be pleased. I was right. I assured her that she could move in with Grandmother, Uncle Irv, and Jon Garth if necessary, as they were staying behind. The thought of this only made her more hysterical. Finally, I just told her bluntly that I was leaving, and she was wasting effort trying to stop me.

I booked a flight for San Francisco on May 9. I would travel alone. Mother would catch another plane to lessen our chances of being caught. I wasn't too worried because my face was not well known and the Honolulu Airport was one of the busiest in the world. I boarded without incident, and after an uneventful flight, I checked into a hotel in downtown San Francisco and waited for Mother to arrive. When we met the next day in the lobby, I almost failed to recognize her. She was wearing a wig and a large hat as a disguise.

"Excuse me, young man, can you tell me the way to San Leandro?" she said, trying to maintain the front.

"Oh, J____, hi Mother." I was too tired to play games.

"I beg your pardon, my name is Mary Jane O'Connor. Any resemblance to your mother is purely coincidental."

"Is this disguise really necessary?"

"I'll get rid of it on the bus. Just wanted to make sure I didn't run into any trouble in Honolulu."

Later, after we boarded the bus for San Leandro, Mother walked to a seat in the rear. She removed the hat and wig and set them beside her. Then, after allowing several minutes to pass, she discreetly took the seat next to mine.

Almost immediately a stranger approached. "Excuse me, ma'am," he smiled down at her pleasantly, "I think you forgot these." In his hand were the hat and wig.

"Oh, thank you."

A short while later she tried the same thing in another part of the bus, but again some helpful soul rescued them for her.

San Leandro was across the bay from San Francisco, just south of Oakland. Mother informed me that one of her supporters there, Wanda Higgins, had secured a car for the drive to Mexico.

Wanda Higgins, I soon learned, was an unusual woman. She had married an Air Force fighter pilot during World War II. During the Korean War, his plane had been shot down behind enemy lines only a few months before the UN cease-fire. During the following months Wanda had received several suspicious letters from him in which he extolled the North Koreans for their wonderful hospitality. Then, after the war when the prisoners of war were exchanged, Wanda's husband never turned up. The North Koreans denied that he had ever been a prisoner. And, since our Defense Department had no positive evidence of his death, he was still listed as missing in action.

The whole experience had embittered Wanda over the years because she had not been free to remarry. Had she done so, the Air Force would have ceased paying her benefits as the wife of an MIA. She lived alone with her daughter Sandra, aged twenty, except for a gentleman friend who lived with Wanda on weekends.

Sandra had acquired her mother's bitterness. She was a full-fledged member of the counter-culture, active in drug-running and paired off with a man named Jim Hardlick.

Hardlick had founded a drug operation front called Blake College in Valle de Bravo, a little resort town in the mountains west of Mexico City. Through the halls of Blake College passed some of the finest marijuana in the Western Hemisphere. But its chief attraction to my mother was that it promised a possible means of getting into Cuba. She had convinced herself that Fidel Castro owed her something for all the work she had done for the Fair Play for Cuba Committee, and although I was unaware of it at the time, she had already established some preliminary contact with the Castro government.

In the meantime, Mother needed transportation from San Leandro to Valle de Bravo, and that was where Wanda Higgins planned to help. Her boyfriend bought and traded cars and was making arrangements to get us one.

The next day, Mother and I drove to Berkeley to obtain a driver's license under her new name, Mary Jane O'Connor. With that in hand, we drove to the motor vehicle office in San Leandro where I took the test for my license. I was now Patrick O'Connor. Mother used her new license to identify herself to them and then vouched for my identity as my mother.

After that we went to pick up the car Wanda's boyfriend had found for us. It was a weather-beaten, light green 1953 Plymouth that appeared to be near death. I could hardly believe my eyes. *Some judge of cars Wanda's boyfriend must be,* I thought. Still, the gasping Plymouth would beat riding the bus. We drove it to Wanda's house and packed for our trip south. Sandra was going to accompany us. She needed to get back to Hardlick and her drug supply in Valle de Bravo.

We must have looked ridiculous rolling along the interstate highway in that old car. All the other cars zooming by us were of the long and low variety of the sixties. Our car, however, rode a good two feet higher than most of them.

But, if we looked ridiculous, we felt even worse. The old car had no air conditioning, and the late spring heat was almost unbearable. We reached Los Angeles just in time for the afternoon rush hour. As we creeped along, we were deprived of the wind that had given us some comfort while moving at higher speeds. The thermometer stood at ninety-five degrees.

Finally, after the engine nearly overheated several times, we left Los Angeles behind and headed on to San Diego. Daylight persisted well into the evening, so it was just dusk when we arrived at the border station in Tijuana. The guard was not cooperative.

"I'm sorry, Señor," he said, "but I cannot let you pass, not without insurance papers. It's the law. Please use that area over there to turn around and go back into your country." I grunted but did as he said.

"Bill, don't make any trouble," Sandra cautioned as I turned the car back north. "If you do, they'll look us over carefully. If they do that, they'll probably recognize me from my drug convictions. Then it'll be impossible for me to get across the border."

"What can we do?" Mother asked wearily from a near prone position in the backseat.

"We'll have to drive along the border and try to cross at one of the little stations where they don't watch things so carefully," Sandra answered.

We drove about an hour and approached the border at a small post.

"*Certificado?*" the guard asked.

I cursed under my breath. He, too, was about to turn us back for lack of an insurance certificate.

"Give him twenty dollars," Sandra suggested.

"Mother?" I looked over at her.

"Just a minute." She pulled her wallet out of her purse. "Here you go."

I handed the twenty-dollar bill to the guard and tried out my Spanish, "*Aquí, está el certificado.*"

He smiled: "*Gracias, está bueno.*"

A few minutes later we pulled up in front of a small hotel. We were still within sight of the border, but the car was smoking and I was dead tired after driving all day. We checked in and collapsed.

The next morning I took a good look at the little town we were in. What I saw was really depressing. I had never before seen such poverty. My mood fell further when I discovered that the car wouldn't start. I walked to the only auto repair shop in town.

"I'm sorry, señor," the owner explained. "Your engine is gone. There is nothing I can do for it."

"Swell, what do I do now?" I groaned.

"I would like to buy your car from you," the man said.

"You mean just like it is, with the engine shot?"

"Yes, señor. My brother and I own the border cab service. We own just one car, a 1952 Plymouth very much like this one."

"How much, Juan?" I figured the heap was worth maybe fifty dollars.

"Two hundred and fifty American dollars, señor." He quickly added, "A new engine would cost you nearly five hundred."

"It doesn't have papers," I explained, as I recalled with relish that my mother had paid only one hundred and fifty dollars for the old car in San Leandro.

I went back into the hotel to explain our predicament and Juan's offer to Sandra and my mother. "We don't have a choice. He'll give us the money and a ride to the bus station with all our junk. There we can take a bus to the nearest rail link. Juan thinks the total fare to Mexico City should run us between sixty and a hundred dollars. It's that or walk back to the other side." I pointed toward the border station. The ladies accepted my reasoning.

We caught the bus and by that evening were aboard a southbound train. Sandra and I got high as a kite, filling our lungs full with her rich grass while standing on the platforms between the cars. After midnight, we were sitting near the bar in the smoking car, drinking and listening to a debate between the conductor, who was a Communist, and the bartender, who was a Nazi. The Spanish was too fast for me, but not for Sandra. She was truly fluent and kept me abreast of the heated argument, even entering into it herself occasionally. The bartender was pouring free booze to anyone who expressed sympathy for his side of the argument. I saw his point immediately.

Finally, around two o'clock, Sandra and I tired of the politics and walked back to the sleeper car. "I'm supposed to be in the bunk over your mother's," Sandra whispered as we walked into the car.

"She snores a lot," I remarked. "Let's sit in mine and have another joint."

"Okay." She smiled.

I smiled back and parted the curtains for her. We crawled in, lit up and exchanged drags silently until the cigarette was gone. She undressed.

"You like me?" she asked coyly.

"I like."

At Mexico City we left the train and boarded a bus for the trip into the hills and Valle de Bravo. Blake College consisted of a large old home, having about fifteen rooms and a courtyard. The curriculum consisted of dope, dope, and more dope. Just five miles from the college, on the edge of an artificial lake, stood the largest and finest country club in all of Mexico. On visits there I noted that on any given weekend the limousines of the Soviet, Polish, and American ambassadors to Mexico could be found, parked side by side in perfect harmony and peace.

Thirty balmy summer days passed uneventfully as I biked in the mountains or hobnobbed at the country club. The evenings were inevitably devoted to smoking the exceptionally fine grass available at Blake. And I often enjoyed Sandra's company.

The setting was pleasant, but I found myself growing restless. And unsettling things began to happen. Jim Hardlick returned to Valle de Bravo, and after conversations with my mother in which she hinted about how much she knew of his dope trafficking, he began to pressure us to leave.

In addition, a letter had come from Susan telling of how she and a mutual friend of ours, Bruce Tong, had been

Row houses in Baltimore. (Reprinted by permission of *The News American*)

The picture which appeared with the first story about the protest over prayer and Bible reading, October, 1960. (Clarence B. Garrett, courtesy the Baltimore Sunpapers)

Mother sending me off to school on October 28, 1960, the day I ended my absence in protest of the opening exercises.
(Reprinted by permission of *The News American*)

Mother folding materials for another mailing. (McCardell, courtesy the Baltimore Sunpapers)

Mother, Jon Garth, and I at the house on Winford Road. (Clarence B. Garrett, courtesy the Baltimore Sunpapers)

Mother with attorney Leonard Kerpelman. (Reprinted by permission of *The News American*)

Our day at the Supreme Court, February, 1963. (United Press International Photo)

Mother and I commenting to the press after the Supreme Court decision was announced. (Reprinted by permission of *The News American*)

The Murray-Mays clan in Honolulu, several days after we fled from Baltimore. Standing (L to R) Grandmother and Uncle Irv. Sitting (L to R) Jon Garth, me, Susan, and Mother. (United Press International Photo)

Police detectives and I arrive in Baltimore after I was arrested in West Virginia, September, 1965. (Reprinted by permission of *The News American*)

Richard O'Hair and
Madalyn, 1969. (United
Press International Photo)

Bob Harrington and Madalyn compare notes prior to a debate in Chattanooga, Tennessee, August, 1977. Looking on is Harry Thornton, local television personality. (Delmont Wilson, Chattanooga *Free Press*)

Mother and Jon Garth working on a legal case, 1978. (Larry Murphy, *Austin American Statesman*)

Mother participating in a demonstration
at the White House, April, 1982.
(Photo courtesy of Revival Fires Ministries)

A speaking engagement after I committed my life to God.

Daughter Jade and I fishing for crabs. (David Nance/PEOPLE Weekly/© 1980 Time Inc.)

arrested for shoplifting at the GEM department store in Honolulu. Bruce had taken the blame so Susan was let off the hook, but this was troubling news. In the same letter she had asked me to meet a friend of hers at the Mexico City airport. The friend was in some trouble and needed help.

So on July 6 I dutifully traveled through the mountains to the city in a car I had managed to rent using my expired temporary driver's permit from California. When the passengers debarked the plane, it was not Susan's friend I saw coming toward me but Susan herself, with baby Robin in her arms. I felt my stomach drop.

"What are you doing here?" I demanded. "Where is your friend?"

"Bill, I didn't want to tell you I was coming. I was pretty sure you'd tell me not to come."

"You're right. That's exactly what I would have done."

"But I had to come. So the only question left is, now what?"

"*Now what* is right, Susan. There's no way I can take you and that child back to Valle de Bravo. Robin would die in that stink hole!"

I drove the three of us to the Hilton Hotel in downtown Mexico City. Susan had brought everything but the kitchen sink with her. She even had Robin's playpen. There was so much that I had to tie some things to the roof of the car.

When I checked us into the Hilton and learned what the rates were, I realized I had only enough money to last for two days. I called Mother to tell her what had happened. She caught the next bus to the city and checked into another room at the Hilton.

She was furious at Susan. "You left my little boy there alone with his grandmother? You b___, why didn't you bring him with you? That f_____ old b___ of a mother of mine will ruin him. We have to get him down here with us!"

She ran to the phone and reached Uncle Irv in Honolulu.

"Irv," my mother yelled over the transoceanic line, "you get that kid on an airplane right now! With Susan and Robin gone, we can be traced too easily."

I was listening on an extension as Irv replied, "I don't have the money to do that. Your people are not supporting you anymore. The money just isn't coming in."

I left the phone to check out a loud noise in the hallway. When I came back in and and was closing the door behind me, I heard Mother telling Irv, "We'll have to sell the cars to get Garth down here."

After she hung up, I said, "You'll have to sell them anyway."

"Why?" she demanded.

"The hotel just posted two guards at the door. With the phone bill, they say we owe them over five hundred dollars. They're not going to let us out until we pay."

"Oh, no!" Susan began to weep, which only added to the bedlam because the baby had been crying already for some time.

Mother's eyes narrowed at me, "You see the trouble your hot pants got us into now? Now she's down here," she said, pointing to Susan, "and we're really in a spot."

Desperately I began to try to think of ways to raise the money. That's when it occurred to me that I might be able to strike some sort of deal with the U.S. Embassy. I called and finally talked a military attaché into coming over to see me about information I might be able to gather on Cuba and the Castro regime.

The man from the embassy arrived about an hour later. "Tell me about your idea, Bill," he said. He leaned back on the couch across from me.

"I'm willing to go into Cuba with my mother if you guys will get my wife and daughter out of here and back into the States." The attache was impassive. I went on. "Once we're in Cuba, my mother's contacts will lead us to the Great One himself, and I'll be able to supply American intelligence with all kinds of information. Then, whenever I get back out of Cuba, I'd like your help to get rid of the charges against me in Baltimore."

"Seems to me you've got a more immediate problem," he answered. "How do you plan to get out of this hotel?"

"You can't help?"

"We can't help people who can't help themselves. You get some money together. Sell a car or something," he smiled, knowingly. "Then you'll need to get ahold of one of these local attorneys to help you get out of Mexico, since you're here with no visa or other documents." He paused and smiled again. "No, I'm afraid we can't help you, but I have a friend who might be able to offer you a lot of help. Do you want me to ask him to give you a call?"

I nodded affirmatively.

He rose to leave and said, "Just one other thing. You'd better get yourself down to the embassy and apply for a passport once you get out of this hotel."

Only seconds after he left, I placed a call to Uncle Irv in Honolulu. I told him to sell my 1963 Cutlass immediately for whatever he could get and to wire me the money. Within twenty-four hours the local telegraph office called and said money had arrived. The two hotel guards escorted me to the telegraph office and then to the bank. There I cashed the check and then peeled off $700—half of what Irv had wired— to pay the hotel bill.

When I returned to the hotel, Mac, the friend of the American military attaché, had already called and was waiting in the lobby with Susan and Robin. Mac had contacted me by phone the day before.

"So, you got yourself out of this bit of trouble, eh?" he quipped with a crisp British accent. Mac claimed to be an ex-British intelligence agent. I would learn in the two months I knew him that he was also a con artist and horse trainer who was a "friend" of the U.S. Embassy.

He and I led the others upstairs to locate Mother. She had just hung up the phone as we entered the room. "Mother," I announced, "this is Mac, a new friend of mine."

She ignored us. "I just got off the phone with Irv," she said excitedly.

I persisted, "Mac knows how to get us out of Mexico."

"Irv put Garth on a plane at noon," she was bound to have her news heard first.

"You're kidding!"

Mac interrupted us and said that we better leave the hotel

before they stuck us with another bill. He had brought a truck with him. We loaded our luggage and Robin's gear into the truck and drove away from the American sector. During the move Mother filled me in on what had happened. Unknown to me, she had asked Irv to wire me only half the actual proceeds from the sale of my car. Irv had kept the other half to finance Garth's trip to Mexico. This had proved more costly than anticipated. Garth was only eleven, and the airlines would not allow him to change planes unaccompanied by an adult. Consequently, Uncle Irv had flown with Garth as far as Los Angeles in order to see him safely on the plane to Mexico City. Irv was now on his way back to Honolulu.

Mac stopped the truck at the door of what appeared to be a cheap hotel. We went to the desk and found that no one spoke English. Mac took charge, making our arrangements using faultless Spanish. While we were lugging the baggage into the hotel, I saw Mac looking at Robin. He motioned for me to come over and said in a low voice, "How old is this other kid that's coming?"

"Eleven," I replied.

"This isn't an expedition, it's a bloomin' circus. I would suggest, son. . . . Let's go sit down and have a beer or two."

In minutes we were seated at a table in a little cafe. I ordered two beers and looked Mac in the eye. "What is it you want to say to me?"

"First, you've got too many d____ people. They're going to get in our way," he said.

"What do you mean?" I asked.

He took a pull on his beer, rolled the liquid in his mouth, then swallowed with obvious pleasure. "Look, Bill, there's money to make on any expedition, but the people with that money look for one thing before they shell it out—and that's results. But you can't get results with this traveling circus on your back."

I looked up as the barkeeper cleared our empty bottles. I was already getting a faint buzz from the beer, and my bravery was on the rise. "Sí, Señor," I said to Mac with a knowing smile—even though I hadn't a clue as to what he was talking about.

"That wife of yours is a loser. Your mother needs a man to keep her busy between the sheets. And you need to get out of the mess you're in."

"Hmmm." Now he was making some sense.

"We'll pick your little brother up at the airport and then take the whole gang of them over to that college in Valle. I know an old smuggler there named O'Hair. He's an ex-FBI informer."

"I know Richard O'Hair. I think he wants to sleep with my mother."

"We can use him. He'll play macho man watching over the women and children while we get this thing financed. Let your mom work on her Cuban thing. We can always sell the contact names. *Dos mas*," he called to the bartender, who brought us another round.

"And stay off that dope they use up there. You'll get raped. You're too young to handle those hardcore types. You don't know your a_ from an eight ball when it comes to real crime."

"Are you going to teach me?"

He snorted. "Shut up, and let's get your brother. Better yet, I'll get him. You'll wind up getting yourself arrested."

After a final round of beers, Mac went to pick up Garth. I teetered back to the hotel, more sober with each step as I reconsidered the wild schemes bubbling inside Mac's head.

N ot long after all of us returned to Valle de Bravo, I found out that one of Mac's fund-raising ideas involved cock fights. He enlisted me as his aide, and one warm night in July, we gathered some cash and headed for the local cock fight arena. We entered the steaming, smelly frame building, and after finding seats, Mac excused himself. He returned on the run, obviously excited.

"Get all the money down you can on the red one," he instructed me, impatiently.

"How do you know he'll win?"

"How do I know he'll win?" he whispered. "Cause I drugged the other one. Now get it down!" I did as he said. The cock fight only lasted about fifteen seconds. The big black rooster—the one Mac had drugged—strutted out with shiney blades locked onto his legs. But he was no match for the red one. One blow, then another fell as the red rooster leaped high in the air and descended on the other's neck. Nearly decapitated, the black rooster rolled over and died.

I hurried away to collect my winnings, my stomach churning from the odors of sweating bodies and chicken blood. I was tucking the peso notes into my billfold when I heard angry voices. Sensing that the shouting in Spanish had something to do with me, I jumped down behind the bleachers and crawled out of the building through two bro-ken planks. I ran to Mac's jeep and turned the key. The engine turned over but didn't catch. The battery started to weaken. I could hear the mob yelling inside the building. Some of the spectators were streaming out a door. I turned the key again and at last the engine roared to life. I blew the horn and headed toward the entrance door.

Mac came out on the run. Blood was flowing heavily from one of his arms. He put one leg in and pulled himself aboard as I hit the gas. The forward thrust almost broke Mac's grip, and he nearly lost his hold. Ten or fifteen men chased the jeep and several shots rang out.

Once we were safely away from the arena, I slowed the jeep a little. Mac frowned as he examined his arm. "I gave that rooster too d__ much. He didn't put up any fight. That's what made 'em figure it out," he said with disgust.

"I don't know why I get involved in this s__ with you," I muttered.

"Because you've got nothing better to do than sit around and smoke dope."

We both were silent for a while. Then Mac looked over at me. "How's your mother coming on the Cuban deal? I'm getting pretty tired of this petty stuff. You know," he said as he ran his forefinger symbolically under his chin and from ear to ear, "we could make a bundle if we could get close enough."

"You mean, kill Castro?"

"We could both retire, boy."

I thought about that as we drove along the curving, hilly road to Valle. For the time being I was somewhat taken by the exotic life I was leading, but I hardly wanted to make a career out of it. I liked Mac, but basically he was nuts.

We arrived back at the college. Susan had taken up dope, too, and was high. Mother was lecturing Richard O'Hair on how the Mexican government should be overthrown. As usual, Mac and I decided to get drunk.

Two nights later Mac and I were again engaging in our favorite sport. Mac opened another beer and said, "Ever seen a gunfight, Bill?"

"We came close enough the other day."

"No, a real gunfight. The reds are going to shoot up the police barracks tomorrow night."

"How do you know that?"

"Because they shoot it up every Saturday night." He laughed uproariously. I laughed, too. With several bottles of beer bubbling in my stomach, my courage was high.

The next night we drove to an area near Valle I had not visited before. It turned out that Mac was not particularly a lover of gunfights. This was just another opportunity to make some money. In the confusion of the usual Saturday night melee, it was possible to grab some weapons that would bring a handsome price on the black market.

"I thought you were kidding," I said. "What's the name of this town? I want to know where I'm going to be buried."

Mac chuckled and pulled a .45 automatic pistol from his belt. He flipped off the safety. "Here," he said, "I want you to cover me with this. I'll move in that way and see what I can find while they're shooting at you. Whatever we get tonight, we sell back to the reds tomorrow. Automatic weapons bring the highest prices."

"But the reds'll know we stole the guns from them—and that we were shooting at them," I protested.

"Of course," Mac shrugged. "Maybe next time they'll get us. But this is this time. Remember to wait until the garrison fires back before you duck behind that building. Now, cover me!"

Mac ran toward the position occupied by the guerrilla point man. Meanwhile I laid fire over the main body of the guerrillas and briefly pinned them down. Quickly, however, they started firing in my direction. That was my signal to pull back behind the adjacent building where the jeep was parked. Mac was waiting at the jeep when I got there.

"While one of them was shooting at you, I belted him over the head," Mac said. "Never had to kill one yet. We got a Colt and a Russian assault rifle. I'll get three hundred dollars for them easy."

"Mac, you're crazy!"

"I'm crazy? You're the one nuts enough to draw their fire."

That shut my mouth, and I thought about it a good while. I had risked my life for a paltry sum of money. Why had I done that?

Back at the school I lit up a joint of grass and popped the lid off a bottle of beer. "Do you think I hit anybody, Mac?"

"I doubt if you hit the planet. And, I keep telling you, you'll never make it in my business if you keep smoking that s___. You'll wind up just another dead soldier."

It was difficult to take Mac seriously, because as he was bestowing his fatherly advice, he almost inhaled a half-pint of brandy. When he put the bottle down, he began again. "We've got over a thousand in the pot each," Mac said. "Your mother doesn't have her act together. I'm headed south for the winter, maybe Rio."

He paused and eyed his bottle but did not take another drink.

"You're welcome to come along if you like," Mac went on. "You should do that or get yourself and your wife and kid the h___ out of here. Take 'em back to the States. You shouldn't stay here, because your mother and her boyfriend are getting on the wrong side of the dopers. They're going to wind up dead and you with them."

This got my attention. Mac was one strange, wild fellow, but he did recognize the scent of trouble.

At dawn the next morning we loaded our luggage and childrearing gear on the top of a taxi. Susan, Robin, Mac, and I had decided to head for Mexico City. The taxi would get us there for fifty dollars. My mother, I knew, would not be pleased by our departure. She wanted Susan and, especially, Robin under her thumb. She felt there was no danger of losing that control because she assumed, wrongly, that Mac and I had drunk up all our money. What funds were available had to be in her hands.

The noise we made loading the cab apparently awakened my mother. We were just pulling away when she ran out into the street, clad only in a bathrobe. "They have no money, no *dinero,"* she screamed over and over. "Come back, I want you here!" She actually ran up the street after us.

Once we were outside of town, Susan asked, "Why didn't we take the jeep?"

"It was hot, honey," Mac replied.

"Hot?" asked Susan.

"Stolen," I explained.

"Oh."

When we got to Mexico City, we checked into a nice hotel. This time we could afford it. After we were settled in, Mac took me aside. "Made up your mind?" he asked.

"Yes," I replied. "I'm going to take them back."

"You'll get caught," he warned.

"I know, but I'll have fun. I'm going to try for Canada."

"Well, then, here's what you have to do. Get passport photos taken of yourselves this afternoon and then go to your country's embassy first thing in the morning. They'll issue you passports the same afternoon, around four o'clock."

"But they know who I am."

"They don't care, son."

We got the photos that day and went to the embassy at eight o'clock the next morning. "Where are you going?" the clerk inquired.

"Where?" I asked.

"Yes, we have to have a reason to issue these here. You don't need one in Mexico," she said very pleasantly.

"Oh, Israel," I said. "My wife has family there."

"You don't need one for Israel either." She smiled.

"We'll be coming back by way of Japan," I quickly improvised.

"Okay, Japan it is. Come back here around four o'clock. They should be ready for you by then."

Mac was waiting for us outside the embassy. "Things okay?" He said with a knowing smile.

"So far, so good," I said, "but I don't have any document authorizing me to be in Mexico. Susan's got a tourist card for her and the baby, but I don't."

"Get a hundred silver dollars and put them in a brown paper bag. Take them with you to the Mexican government offices and ask for an appointment with a man named Manuel Herrera. When you get in to talk to him, just set the bag on the floor. Plead your case to him, but say nothing about the money. Simply ask for an exit permit. He'll play with his pen and say, 'I see your problem.' That's when you do it."

"Do what?" I asked.

"You say, 'Pardon me, Señor Secretary, but it seems you have left your bag on the floor containing a hundred silver U.S. dollars. Someone dishonest might take it.'" Mac looked me sharply in the eye. "Got it?"

"Got it."

I sat for two hours that afternoon in Manuel Herrera's waiting room. Finally, it was my turn. I told him my story, and when I was done, he tapped his pencil on the desk and said, "I see your problem."

I took the cue and said the lines Mac had taught me.

"Oh, my wife's present," Señor Herrera said mechanically. "How could I have left it there? I will put it away after you leave. Wait outside. My secretary will prepare an exit letter for my signature."

"Thank you," I said, bowing slightly.

The next day Mac drove us in a rented car to the airport. Susan was wearing a new leather coat that Mac had wangled from a storekeeper. She was happy to be leaving Mexico. Robin whimpered now and again. My mood was closer to hers, because I knew I would miss Mac. He had almost gotten me killed a few times, but I cherished anyone's friendship highly since I found it so seldom. After we unloaded the luggage, I grasped Mac's hand firmly and said good-bye.

"Bye, sport." He winked, then turned and walked away. I've not seen nor heard from him since.

In the airport my exit letter did the trick, and we got on the plane without mishap. The flight was scheduled to touch down in San Antonio for a customs and immigration check, then continue on to New York City. Thus we arrived in New York that Friday evening, August 13, 1965, and checked into a hotel. Our funds were exhausted. All I had left of value were shares of life insurance stock I had managed to keep. The stock had been given to me by the atheist-nudist farmer in Kansas as a birthday present.

I decided to sell the shares, from which I hoped to pocket about six thousand dollars. With that I could buy a car and rent a place to live. Then I would try to find a job. I knew this would be difficult because I would not be able to give any references. I would have to use my phony I.D. from California and hope for the best. If caught I would be put on the next train to the Baltimore city jail. I told Susan of my plans, and she listened halfheartedly. After being married to me for only fourteen months and being involved in one crazy event after another, she had adopted a wait-and-see attitude.

I called in the sales order on the insurance stock on Monday morning. Around noon the three of us visited the stockbroker's office, and with the money in hand I promptly went and bought a used Volvo. Then I found a small furnished apartment in the Bronx. It was really a hotel-apartment, and its biggest advantage was that it required no lease. I found a job selling encyclopedias. This was night work, so I had the opportunity to look for regular work during the day.

After two weeks I had sold only two sets of books with a total commission of less than $250. And I had been unable to find daytime employment. All of the good jobs required references. To further depress my mood, Robin fell and cut her nose. We carried her to a hospital emergency room where the doctor stitched the cut. Knowing how expensive everything was in New York, I wondered if this small disaster would wipe out our cash. I was surprised and pleased when I found out there was no charge. Since we were city residents, our first visit to a community hospital was free.

Back at the apartment, Susan and I discussed our dim prospects. "Look," I said, "maybe you should take Robin back to Hawaii. I'm going to wind up getting caught here, sooner or later. I want to go to Canada."

"Okay, we'll go up there with you."

So, on September 1, less than three weeks after arriving

in the city, we packed and headed north. But things weren't much different there. I still needed references and didn't have any. Susan grew insistent about our needs as a family, complaining that Robin needed a permanent home because she was starting to walk. She wanted to go back to the States, so I decided to head for Detroit. Maybe a factory job could be found there.

The Volvo's engine had been sputtering badly during the two weeks in Canada. I wondered if it would make it to Detroit. It didn't. When I found out repairs would cost $1,500, I junked the car and had a serious talk with Susan.

"I'll give you a choice between Baltimore and Honolulu," I told her. "We're out of money, and I'll have to write a bad check to get you to either place, but you've got to go."

"What are you going to do?" she asked.

"Rob banks."

"I'll go to Honolulu."

The next day I put Susan and Robin on a United Airlines flight. I gave them each a kiss and a squeeze. It was the last I would see of them for some time. I was tired of running. I decided to head for Baltimore and turn myself in.

Nearly broke, I hitched some rides with truck drivers and earned some food money by helping them load and unload freight. After several days on the trucks I made it to Wheeling, West Virginia, on Saturday, September 18. I rented a room in a downtown hotel and called Uncle Irv collect in Honolulu. I asked him to sell what possessions I had and to wire me the money. I knew I would need money for a lawyer back in Baltimore.

Only a few hours later, a knock on the door woke me. It was the police. I believe now that someone had tapped Irv's phone in Hawaii. When I called in, the police found out where I was. I was taken to jail, and when the authorities in Baltimore heard I had been caught, they pressed for my extradition. I knew I would lose anyway, so on Monday I waived an extradition hearing. The next day two officers from Baltimore's fugitive squad flew me back to Baltimore. Once there, I was taken in a squad car to police headquarters where detectives interviewed me for forty minutes. Then, shortly before six o'clock that evening, sheriff's deputies took me over to the city jail to begin serving the six months to which I had been sentenced after being convicted *in absentia* for contempt of court in regard to the allegations brought against me by Susan's father. I had been tried and convicted and now was to spend time in jail without having my day in court. On top of that, I still had to face the assault charges.

A court date was set for Friday, September 24. While I stewed in jail, the newspapers reported that Madalyn and Richard O'Hair had announced marriage plans in Valle de Bravo. I wondered why Mother was now so interested in the vows of matrimony, something she criticized as being unnecessary and actually harmful. On Friday, I appeared before Judge Dulany Foster in criminal court. Speaking on my behalf was Leonard Kerpelman, who had volunteered to help me. He entered a plea of innocent to the assault charges and requested that I be tried by a jury. I now wanted a fight.

After this arraignment hearing, I was escorted to a tile-walled detention cell in the courthouse and given a dry cheese sandwich. Several reporters gathered around, and I was interviewed at length. Kerpelman hung around to be sure I didn't tighten the noose any tighter around my tender neck. The next day a long article by Nicholas Horrock appeared in the *Evening Sun*. With the article was an old photo of Mother, Susan, and myself. Horrock's story made it sound as though I were a sincere young man who only wanted to clean up his life and return to the arms of his lovely wife and child. I don't recall having those desires, but it's possible, I suppose, that I did reveal in the jail cell that afternoon a tender and vulnerable part of my personality which, in subsequent years, I supressed more and more thoroughly to protect myself from pain.

Two days after my arraignment, Mother's name once again bedecked the pages of the Baltimore *Sun*. In the Sunday morning edition, a one-column headline said, "Police Hold Mrs. Murray In Texas City." The article explained that she had been expelled from Mexico the previous day and that authorities in San Antonio had taken her into immediate custody to await extradition to Baltimore. Her only companion on the flight from Mexico City was a boy who, according to the report, was about nine or ten years old. This was Garth, of course. She had identified herself to police as Madalyn Evelyn Mays.

Mexican authorities had picked Mother up at Valle de Bravo on Friday and taken her to Mexico City. Late on Saturday, for reasons not noted in the article, they had ordered her to leave the country. She had caught the next available plane to San Antonio.

The more complete story, as I later learned it from Mother and Richard O'Hair, was a bit more interesting. Mother had become nervous when she realized that her residency in Valle de Bravo was one of the worst kept secrets in North America. Consequently, she had applied for permanent residency and, in an effort to ingratiate herself to the Mexican authorities, had turned in the operators of the drug smuggling ring headquartered at Blake.

Contrary to her expectations, the Mexican bureaucrats did not welcome the hot tip and actually took a dim view of her own involvement with the operation at Blake. They had decided to expel her from the country.

When Mother was taken into custody in San Antonio, Jon Garth was placed in a childcare facility for about ten hours. Mother spent about half that time herself in jail. She quickly found a sympathetic attorney who bailed her out and rented her a house he owned in Austin, Texas.

On Monday morning, the Baltimore deputy state's attorney filed papers asking Maryland's governor to have Madalyn extradited from Texas. He complied the next day by sending the request via air mail to Governor John Connally of Texas. The same day Mother wrote a letter to Governor Connally pleading for mercy. She released to the media a copy of the letter. In my jail cell I read a portion of it in the local newspaper. She begged Connally, "Please do not let them take me back to Maryland. I do not want to be murdered." Later she would claim her fate in Baltimore would be worse "than that of a Negro being extradited to the state of Mississippi."

On September 30, two other attorneys, Charles C. G. Evans and Joseph H. Kaplan, at the request of the president of the Maryland Bar Association, were added to my defense team. The next day the state's attorney who had been prosecuting my case announced that he was dropping the charges against me for assault and disorderly conduct. As reasons he cited my youthful age and the fact that my mother had been the "moving party in the entire incident." The state's attorney also said that he was not dropping the same charges against Madalyn because the flight from justice had been open and notorious, not like the usual fugitive who steals away in the night.

I was relieved but still had over five months to serve on the contempt charge. My new attorneys, who had by now completely taken over the case from Leonard Kerpelman, filed a writ of habeus corpus to challenge the validity of my sentence.

In the ensuing days, Mother loudly announced that she was considering waiving her extradition hearing but wanted advice from "my man" Richard O'Hair. O'Hair, who was still in Mexico, decided to test her sincerity by wiring a request to her for money to pay his fare to San Antonio.

How Mother was able to obtain funds I am not sure, but she did send him enough for a one-way bus ticket. He was important to her case, for she had told the press that their marriage would cure all of her problems. Years later, one time when Richard was drunk, he told me that on this bus ride a homosexual had bothered him. The incident had happened while Richard was intoxicated and had so alarmed him that he had taken this as a sign that he ought to marry my mother and remain in the United States.

Apparently unswayed by Mother's dramatic pleas, Governor Connally ordered her extradition to Maryland on October 11. At her hearing Mother said she would consider killing herself if she had to return. The governor, ultimately, was unmoved. Mother, true to form, filed an appeal with a state district court.

On October 13, my attorneys argued the merits of my contempt sentence before Judge Joseph R. Byrnes in Baltimore City Court. The judge heard the arguments and then retired to his chambers to think the matter through. I had no idea how long it would be before he ruled. I returned to the city jail.

Judge Byrnes took six days to make his decision. He ruled in a five-page opinion that the Baltimore Criminal Court had been without jurisdiction in issuing the order that had restrained me from having any contact with Susan. Therefore, he reasoned, the contempt conviction based on that order must also be reversed. At last the court system had admitted their severe error in not serving the summons for that hearing in June 1964. I had thought in the clamor over the "larger" issues, another matter—some 1964 traffic violations—might be overlooked. No such luck. After saying good-bye to my cohorts at the jail, I was hustled to traffic court where my attorney paid my overdue fine for driving with an expired license. Then I was told I still had a speeding ticket and bond to resolve. The court could not hear my case, so two hours after I had been freed, I was back in jail again. I spent the night, much to the merriment of the other prisoners.

The next morning, my attorneys and I went to the court. My defenders argued that I had already suffered an unlawful thirty-one-day jail sentence at the state's hands. In other words, the state of Maryland owed me one. The judges agreed, and after paying a minor fine, I was released. This time I was out for good.

The same day, October 20, Fred Weisgal, the ACLU attorney who had briefly helped Mother with the prayer and Bible-reading case, filed a motion in criminal court asking that all charges against Mother be dropped. The reason was very ironic—even for the American justice system. The Maryland Court of Appeals had just declared that members of grand juries need not affirm that they believed in God, a statement which the swearing-in oath had long contained. Furthermore, the appeals court had ruled that actions taken by grand juries sworn in by this oath could be overturned.

Sure enough, the grand jury that had indicted Mother had been sworn in by such an oath. The court resolved that my mother and others like her had been denied equal protection under the law. The timing of this series of events should have made even Mother believe an angel was watching over her affairs. On October 26, all charges against her were dropped. And the state's attorney decided not to try to reindict Mrs. O'Hair. (Mother and Richard had married on October 18).

My flickering faith in the justice system, which had been rekindled by the handling of my case, once again diminished. I was bitter that Mother had escaped punishment again while I had been forced to sit in jail for a month. The day of my own release from jail I had told a reporter that I no longer had hard feelings, because "justice works in America; it's just that, sometimes, it takes a while." I felt like calling him and demanding a retraction.

After the legal hassles were over, I had little to do. I moved back into the old family home at 1526 Winford Road. I had no money. The water and power had been turned off for over a year. Likewise, the gas for the furnace was disconnected, and winter was near. Happily, a new family had moved in next door who had not been around until after our family had departed. The man took pity on me and paid the past due bill and deposit so that I could have heat.

Mother's friend Betty Washington had done an abysmal job of watching the house. The televison and most of the household appliances were gone. So was all the art work that had decked the walls. And my mother's vast, and mostly unread, library had vanished. Still, there were enough items left that I could hock in order to have the phone reconnected. After it was installed, I dialed a call to Hawaii.

"Susan, how's it going out there?"

"Bill, do you have any money? I have to get away from these crazy relatives of yours. I can't take it anymore."

"Sorry, I'm broke."

"That life insurance company sent you more shares—a split from before you sold the other stuff."

"Send them to me."

"No."

"What?"

"I said no. Robin and I have needs, too. If I send those shares to you, you'll stay put in Baltimore. And I can't leave here. I'm reenrolled in the university."

"I'm getting the s___ kicked out of me while you play tea time at the university! And now you tell me you're going to hold my money in balmy Honolulu while I freeze my rear off in Baltimore?"

"That's not what I want, Bill. If you'll come here, I can pay your fare. I know the only way Robin and I will get some of that money is if you sell the stock here in Hawaii."

"Thanks a lot. By the way, your mother was here yesterday." I was so furious I had to change the subject.

"At your house?"

"Yes, I gave her a picture of Robin and a vase."

"A vase?"

"Right, a vase. She said your father's heart was beginning to soften."

"Hmmm." Susan was taken aback by the news.

"Well, I'd better get off the line. This call is expensive," I said.

"Okay, I'm going to buy you a plane ticket to Honolulu, right?"

"Yeah, I suppose so. Send it to me and I'll call you when it gets here."

"Right, good-bye Bill."

A week passed. It was lonely in the house on Winford Road. An eerie stillness contrasted so sharply with the bedlam that had prevailed there for so many years. The plane ticket came in the mail. On my last day in Baltimore I packed a few belongings, then made myself a cup of coffee and sat down in my grandfather's chair in the kitchen. I stared about. Even though most of the furniture was still in place, the house seemed empty.

As I sat there I could see and hear the violent fights that had so often occurred in this room. I thought of the mounds of perverted sex literature that my uncle kept secreted away in his upstairs room under lock and key. The steady thump of my brother's head against the side of the crib seemed to throb in my head.

Snow covered the ground outside. I stared into the whiteness and thought about the thirty-one days I had spent behind bars. I pulled a pack of cigarettes from my pocket. I had smoked my first conventional cigarette in my cell in West Virginia. Smoking had helped pass the time in jail. Now it was a habit. I finished the cigarette and rubbed it out in Grandfather's ashtray.

I decided to call Grandmother to ask if there were some things she'd like me to bring from the house. Oddly, the thing she wanted most was a little black book in which Grandfather had kept his records. I found it and thumbed through the pages. It included a record of his Social Security checks and for what they had been spent. Almost all of them had gone to make the mortgage payments on the house at 1526 Winford Road. I was glad Grandfather could not know that it was unlikely anyone in his family would ever live there again.

awaii's flower-fragrant air greeted me anew when I stepped off the Boeing 707 at Honolulu International Airport. I had not known what to expect, so I was surprised and pleased by the collection of people who had come to welcome me. Susan and Robin were there, conspicuously accompanied by Bruce Tong, as well as Uncle Irv and several of the friends I had made during my brief stay at the University of Hawaii. Among them were Jim Smythe and his longtime companion, Sandra Jenkins.

Susan and I exchanged a quick, polite kiss, and I reached to take Robin from her arms. She turned away and burst into tears. I was a stranger to her. Instead of wanting me, she clambered toward Bruce Tong, who nearly blushed with embarrassment. He reached out to shake my hand but couldn't look me in the eye. I glared at Susan.

Jim Smythe broke in to ease the tension. "Bill, I bet you could use a joint of that good Kona grass. Long flight, right?" He clutched a large brown bag of grass in his hand.

"Sure was, Jim. But let's wait till we get to the car," I replied.

Jim smiled, looked furitively around, and then slipped the stash back into his guitar case.

Susan handed Robin to Bruce and kissed me again lightly on the cheek. "It's been too long, Bill."

"I know, Susan, I know." I looked at Bruce.

Uncle Irv couldn't wait any longer. "I hope you brought money, nephew," he said, "cause your grandmother's sick.

Those suckers of your mother's aren't coming through, now that she's back stateside."

"Bill." Sandra caught my attention as Jim looked elsewhere. "I think I have Jim talked into making it with me," she smiled and went on without waiting for me to respond. "And guess who's in the Army? Gregg. You gonna tell us about Mexico? What was it like?" She paused a moment to catch her breath.

"That's great. Good for you, Sandy," I inserted.

"Bill, your wife said something about stock," Irv tapped my shoulder. "You know how hard I've worked here. The old lady has Medicare, but that won't pay for food."

I threw up my hands and shouted, "Everybody hold it!" That seemed to shut them up. My head was beginning to throb. Someone needed to organize this strange bunch. "Bruce, take Susan and the kid up to Irv's place. Irv, just go home. Jim, roll one of those things. Sandy, we'll take your car and pick up some beer."

Sandy drove while Jim sat in the back seat playing "Tangerine Man" on his guitar. I took a deep drag off the joint and passed it to Sandy. Before she took a drag, she asked, "What are you going to do, man?"

"Blow my brains out with pot," I replied.

"Besides that?"

"I don't know."

We stopped at Long's Drugs. I went in and bought a case of beer. Then Jim took the receipt back in and picked up another case. It was a busy place—easy to walk out with just about anything, but the receipt was a good trick just in case someone stopped you on your way out.

"One of these days they'll catch you guys at that," Sandra protested with a smile. We all laughed.

We drove on, and at last there was a period of silence. I admired again the green beauty of Oahu. I began to think about the way my life had changed in just eighteen months. Only a year and a half before this I had celebrated my eighteenth birthday in Baltimore. Since then I had fled the law to Hawaii and, in turn, to Mexico. I had learned to drink alcohol, smoke pot, and steal. I had even been involved in a rigged cock fight and a gun battle. How starkly all of this contrasted to my previous life. Back in Baltimore, my old friends and I had been absorbed in drive-in movies and radio equipment. My new friends had introduced me to a radically different lifestyle. I was young and eager to try whatever life seemed to offer. I loved what was happening to me.

We stopped outside of the Spencer Street house. Before Jim and Sandy drove away, we made plans for a huge party, to take place in a couple of weeks. I waved as they sped off.

Inside I said hello to Grandmother, who was now in her mid-seventies. She looked ill. I told her and Irv that the party would be in the large vacant house behind ours. It was, as they well knew, owned by a person who was very sympathetic to Mother's causes. It was readily available to my crowd.

I excused myself and led Susan into one of the bedrooms. We crawled onto the bed for a talk. "You know," I said, "this marriage isn't going to work. Too much has happened to us, just too much—more in two years than happens in an entire lifetime for most people."

Susan stared at the ceiling. "I know, Bill. It just seems as though it was condemned from the start. I feel so sorry for Robin. Why did she have to have us for parents? With someone else she might have a chance."

"I know."

"You aren't going to stay, are you?"

"I don't know. I just don't know," I muttered.

I'd been thinking a lot on my plane trip about what Susan was now asking. I was without a car, mine having been sold. Irv had even managed to sell Mother's. The only car left for the family was my grandmother's 1965 Buick Skylark. I would need a car to hold a job, or would I? I had thought that I might be able to support us by reviving the *Free Humanist* magazine and thereby milking the mailing list for some donations. The money from the stock that Susan had been holding would be enough to revive the magazine or to buy a car. But which should I do? Exhausted by the tension of these choices and my long flight, I fell into a deep sleep.

The phone rang first thing the next morning. It was

another old friend nicknamed the "Fox." He came by later, and together we planned a scheme for setting up a fake auto accident injury so we could bilk an insurance company. With this business completed, at about 11:00 A.M. we headed for an apartment on Waikiki that supposedly contained the finest cache of drugs in the area. There was no response when we knocked on the door. Fox tried the knob, and the door opened. Stale marijuana smoke hung thickly in the air. The window shades were pulled; it was hard to see anything. When my eyes adjusted I saw that about ten people were scattered on the floor, each rolled in a blanket. It was a one-room apartment with a kitchenette and bathroom. Just as we walked in, one of them stood up, glanced at us, and walked into the bathroom.

"There she is," Fox whispered as he walked over to one of the still-bundled figures on the floor. "Linda, wake up!"

"What?" a bleary voice emerged from inside the blanket.

"Steve's worried about you. He called me last night."

"Steve who?"

"Steve Blake, your husband."

"Oh," she crawled from under the blanket, fully clothed, and headed for the kitchen. She looked at me as she passed. It was a friendly look.

Linda came out of the kitchen holding a glass of water in one hand and a pill in the other. She took the pill and looked at me, "It's my cousin." She pointed to another girl on the floor. "She's sick in the brain. I had to stay with her last night. She wanted to waste herself."

"You need a ride out of here, don't you?" I observed.

"Yeah, but let me give this water to my cousin."

Her nursing done, we got in the car and headed toward the exclusive Wailai-kahala area where Steve and Linda lived with her parents. Just past the Kahala Shopping Center we turned toward the mountains. Linda's home was almost on a cliff. During the ride Linda and I sat comfortably close. She was a striking girl. It seemed we were becoming friends although we had scarcely spoken and had not yet been alone. Fox and I dropped Linda off at the top of the driveway.

As I was letting her out of the car, I told her about my party and asked her to come.

"Okay if I bring my husband?" she asked.

"Sure, bring anybody you like."

Fox frowned when I got back in the car. "Both of you will wind up sorry."

"Nothing has happened yet, Fox."

"No, not yet."

The day of the party, after picking up some booze and groceries, I drove across the Manoa campus of the University of Hawaii. Pleasant memories came back to me. Fox, Jim, Sandy, and I—and the rest of the gang—had enjoyed some good times together there during those early weeks of the fall semester the year before. We had all been entering freshmen. One by one each of us had dropped out. Jim lacked money; Sandy wanted to stick close to Jim; Fox for a reason that was never clear to me. And I had had to work to pay for Robin's delivery.

Back at Spencer Street, I turned the car and some money over to Jim. I spent the rest of the day readying the vacant house for the party. I called Linda. She told me she and her husband planned to bring several friends, some booze, and two chairs. Bruce Tong and I moved some of the furniture from our house into the big house. Early in the evening, the guests began arriving. One friend brought enough food to feed a regiment. It promised to be a wild evening, just the type of entertainment I enjoyed these days.

The party began to roll an hour ahead of schedule. I had learned that the man who intends to score doesn't get drunk. Therefore, I carefully sipped at a beer and stepped outside only for an occasional toke.

Bruce Tong had volunteered to tend bar. He was testing a concoction containing several gallons of Vodka. He had mixed batches of the brew in the blender. Everyone seemed to like it and kept coming back for more. The party was happening on all three floors of the old house. As the host I made a point of visiting on each floor for about fifteen minutes. Susan hung out near the bar with Bruce. My grand-mother didn't aprove of such parties and was happy to have the job of babysitting Robin at home next door.

Finally, Steve and Linda Blake arrived. They were greeted by applause, much to Steve's bewilderment. He didn't realize it, but Linda was known to be bringing a heavy stash of marijuana. Everybody had been waiting for it.

I spent nearly an hour after that watching Linda. I was strongly attracted to her, and I was gratified to observe that she didn't seem to be close to her husband at all. She seemed to dance with a different guy every five minutes, but never with Steve. I decided to make my move. "You want to dance or go outside?" I asked.

"Outside," she replied without a moment's hesitation.

We walked behind the house, and she was the first to speak: "I thought you were going to ignore me." She caught her finger on the neckline of her blouse and pulled it nearly to her navel.

"You can't be ignored," I said, enjoying the view. "Doesn't your husband care about you? He hasn't been with you since you got here."

"He cares about his fish. He's an oceanographer. Besides, he has someone to talk to in there."

"And now you have someone to talk to out here," I said, smiling.

She smiled back. "Let's get a couple of drinks and go somewhere private."

"I can't drink too much. It makes me sick. How about if you roll me one instead?" I was firmly resolved not to do any serious drinking.

"You bet."

We went back inside, then announced some pretext for leaving the party. Soon we were in my grandmother's Sky-lark, headed down the road. We drove to a popular romantic overlook, the Pale, and parked. Near us were darkened cars containing teen-agers doing the same things we hoped to accomplish as soon as possible. But, to my disappointment, Linda had to talk first. It was as though she wanted us to know each other before we became intimate. She did have quite a story.

"I got pregnant by Steve when I was sixteen," she began. "He and his parents insisted I get an abortion. It hurt me. I got real sick. Girls don't know how terrible it feels to have a baby ripped out until it happens. So, I married Steve to take revenge."

"What do you mean?"

"His parents hated me. I got pregnant twice after that abortion, and both times I miscarried. I can't have any children now. Being married to Steve is my way of getting even with them for that."

She paused. I looked at the moon and its reflection mirrored in the water far below.

"Bill, does it make any difference to you that I can't bear children?"

"No, Linda, I have a kid already. Robin is a year old."

"I wish she were mine."

I didn't know what to do with that remark, so I changed the subject. Before long we stopped talking and let our feelings take over.

When we returned to the party three hours later, we were no longer strangers. In fact, we knew each other very well.

The frolic of the party behind me, I turned my attention to more mundane matters—like finding a job. I didn't want work to interfere too much with my dope use, so I started driving a cab. The flexible hours and relative freedom suited my needs perfectly.

Susan and I shared her room at the house on Spencer Street, but we didn't see much of each other. She was busy at the university, and I spent much of my spare time with the drug crowd—Linda in particular. Susan and I were finished.

I made a lame attempt to start a new atheist magazine, but my heart wasn't in it. After publishing one issue, I cancelled out.

Since Mother was no longer a fugitive, she and Richard must have decided to settle in the good ole United States and forget about relocating to Cuba. They chose to stay in Austin, Texas. We no longer heard from Mother very often, although I had picked up a copy of the October 1965 *Playboy* in which an interview with her appeared. She was at her quotable best, and the less stringent editorial policy of the magazine allowed her outrageous ideas to be said with four-letter bluntness. The interview had actually been conducted before Mother and I had fled from Hawaii, so some of the information was badly dated. I chuckled when I read Mother's castigation of marriage, but most of the interview was a rehash of Mother's standard line that I had heard at the dinner table for as long as I could remember.

In December, I finally tired of the exotic but purposeless life I was leading on the island. Driving a cab was not exactly my idea of a dream career. I was also tired of trying to act the role of husband and father. The time seemed right to leave. One afternoon I just decided to take off. I was packing my suitcase when Grandmother walked in. "Are you moving out?" she asked.

"Yes, I'm going back to the mainland."

"Your magazine deal for those atheists of your mother's didn't work out, did it."

"No, Grandma, it didn't."

"I knew it wouldn't. You don't have enough of her in you. Bill, you're too good for that atheist and Communist stuff. Get a job and take care of your kid."

I had nothing to say about this. I was still only nineteen years old and had no desire to be shoved into the "daddy" mold.

"I may not see you again, Grandma," I said, changing the subject.

"You'll be back here next fall. I'll see you one last time before I meet the Maker," she said, a small smile curling her lips.

My farewell conversation with Susan went more easily than I had expected. "I'm leaving tonight," I announced.

"With Linda?" she asked matter-of-factly.

"Yes, with Linda."

"That's what Bruce said you'd probably do. Will you send money for Robin?"

"I'll try. I'll only have a hundred bucks to my name when I land in California. No stocks or bonds or cars to fall back on this time. All I have left are these hands and this head."

I kissed Robin good-bye and bid farewell to the others. Linda met me at the airport, and we boarded Pan Am's flight two, bound for San Francisco. In our wake we left two spouses, a one-year-old child, and assorted relatives and obligations. I now cared only about feeding my own appetites. Although I was blinded to it, I represented the same picture of deceit and selfishness that I cursed my mother for. I too was climbing down into the pit where there is no light, and hope cannot be glimpsed but in dreams.

Linda had many friends in Berkeley, and so we found a small apartment there. Through an employment agency, I was hired as an installer with the E. D. Jones Co. in San Francisco. This company sold private phone, intercom, and TV systems. One of my first assignments with the company was the installation of a complete private phone system at a local NASA installation. The work was simple for me, since I had both my general class amateur radio and second class commercial radio phone licenses. An added job benefit was a company-owned truck which I was allowed to drive home at night and on weekends. Thus Linda and I had a vehicle.

For a long time I had wanted to sue the Baltimore newspapers and public officials for what I believed were personal damages resulting from reports of the prayer and Bible reading case and subsequent events. I contacted the offices of noted attorney F. Lee Bailey, but he would not take the case without a sizeable advance, which I did not have. He did suggest, however, that I avoid any connection with my mother. That was not hard to do. I had not heard from her in months.

In February I read in a magazine that Mother's case advocating taxing the churches had been dismissed by the Maryland Court of Appeals. In May she and others appealed this decision to the U.S. Supreme Court. I was quite content to have her in Texas and me in California, although I constantly feared someone would identify me as her son.

While installing equipment for E. D. Jones I contacted many companies about better employment. To me, "better" meant "white collar" employment.

Advertising and public relations had always intrigued me. The opportunity to enter the field came to me in a strange way, as a result of some after-dinner conversation one night in February.

"How did your hunt for a job go today, Linda?" I asked. I now realized that Linda was quite skilled at looking for work but quite poor at actually taking a job.

"I'm having trouble, Bill. If I like the job, the boss doesn't like me. If I don't like the job, he loves me!"

"What do you have for tomorrow? I'm off and I can drive you. You won't need to take the bus."

"The employment agency gave me one I'm not even going to. They want an assistant to the president of some company that sells calenders and pens with junk messages on them."

"How much does it pay?"

"Oh, eight hundred dollars a month I think."

"That's about what I'm making installing these phones. If I took that I wouldn't have to climb poles anymore. I'll go see the guy."

Early the next morning I called Carl Rosenfeld, the president of the Walter W. Cribbins Company in San Francisco. I told him I was interested in the job. We met that afternoon.

"Good day," said Mr. Rosenfeld, a short, stocky man, with a heavy German accent. "I'll tell you about the company and myself, then you tell me about Bill Murray."

I liked Carl Rosenfeld from that moment on. He had graduated from law school in Germany just months before Adolf Hitler passed a law barring Jews from practicing law. After that he had married a beautiful young woman whose family owned a saw mill. He had managed the mill until the Nazis took that too. He and his wife then had left Germany for America with only their tickets, some clothes, and a wristwatch.

During their ocean voyage to America, Mr. Rosenfeld had taught himself English by reading a novel. In the United States he had been hired by Walter W. Cribbins to sell a little metal cricket given by businesses to kids. An advertising message appeared on it. At that time, the Cribbins company consisted of Mr. Cribbins and one or two other employees.

Rosenfeld had proved to be a hardworking employee, and he had eventually become chief executive of the company, which now had about forty employees and a large clientele that included the Bank of America and Kaiser industries.

In turn I told Carl Rosenfeld about myself, omitting any information about my mother and the thirty-one days I had spent in jail. He seemed impressed with the fact that I could type and use the English language well. He hired me. At last I had that "better" job.

For about six months I was a dutiful employee who showed up for work on time and did what I was paid for. Linda gave up looking for work, but I was so satisfied with my situation I didn't care. A day-to-day predictable pattern developed. Then Linda surprised me one afternoon in September.

"I'm pregnant," she told me, the tears streaming down her face.

"You told me you couldn't get pregnant."

"Well, I am. I'll have to get another abortion."

"No, no, I can't let you do that. I spent eighteen years listening to Mother tell me she wished she would have aborted me. I don't believe in it."

But the solution was not that simple. Both Linda and I were still married, but not to each other. I had not given much thought to Susan or Robin lately, other than to send a small check when I could. Now I had to think. I was caught in the middle—unable to return to them yet not free from them either. I decided to call Susan.

"Sue, I am going to have to get a divorce. I'm not coming back."

"I didn't think you would be. It's okay with me, but you're going to have to pay for the divorce. I've got no funds other than the student loans for my tuition. This school means my life now, and I can't drop out."

"That's fair. I'll call someone and get it started."

On October 20, 1966, I flew to Honolulu for the divorce court proceedings. The Cribbins Company paid part of the expenses, as I was to contact several of our customers while there. Susan and I had hired one attorney to represent both of us.

We had agreed to the simple terms of the divorce. Susan was to retain legal custody of Robin, but I was to take temporary charge of Robin until Susan graduated from college. At this time, custody would return to Susan. During the summers when Susan was not in school, Robin would live with her mother. When Robin was in Susan's care, I would send support payments.

At the hearing all the documentation had been presented when the judge suddenly lashed out at our lawyer.

"I don't ever want to see you in this court again representing both sides in a matter such as this," he said.

"But, your honor," the attorney objected, "both parties were in full agreement."

"Not when custody of a child is at stake," the judge responded. "In this case the infant stands almost without legal representation. I will grant the motion; however, there will be a one year waiting period from this date. If I am not notified of reconciliation, the decree will be final."

Outside the courtroom, I could think only of the problem facing me. The divorce would not be final for one year. In the meantime, Linda would give birth to a bastard like myself. Susan interrupted my thoughts.

"Well, Bill," she said, "you have the divorce you wanted. I hope it makes you happy. I hope it makes Linda happy. I hope she will take care of Robin."

"I guess she will," I said without much confidence.

"Bill, whatever you do, don't ever let Madalyn get ahold of Robin. I'll have you killed if you do!"

"Don't worry, I don't want that either."

On October 22, Robin and I flew to San Francisco, where

Linda met us at the arrival gate. She took Robin in her arms and kissed her. "What a sweet little girl," she said.

We walked to the car, a 1958 English-built Hillman I had bought some months before. As we drove away I saw tears in Linda's eyes. "What's wrong?" I asked.

"Oh, Bill! Do you think people will think she is ours?"

"What's wrong, Linda?"

"I didn't call you because you couldn't have helped anyway."

"What is it?"

"I lost the baby while you were in Hawaii. I just started bleeding, and by the time I got to the doctor, it was gone."

I was actually relieved, but sincerely sorry for Linda. That first abortion years ago was going to haunt her for life. "I'll try to make it up to you," I said.

Back at work the next day, I realized my position with the Cribbins Company might not last much longer. For some unknown reason, Uncle Irv had given the details of the divorce to the Honolulu *Advertiser*. Associated Press had picked up the story, and it had been run by the San Francisco *Chronicle*. The headline had read, "Atheist's son divorces wife, brings daughter to San Francisco Bay Area." I was destroyed. Carl Rosenfeld said nothing, but the coolness from the other officers in the company was evident.

In November other problems arose. As is true with most Bay Area middle class apartments, no children were allowed in ours. Linda and I didn't think a one-year-old would bother anyone. But we lived on the second floor, and within ten days after Robin moved in, twenty complaints were filed by a downstairs tenant who said Robin woke her up by playing on the floor. She claimed she could hear Robin running. I confronted the woman.

"Do you hear me walk, too? You can hear a twenty-five pound child run, but you cannot hear a two hundred-pound man walk?"

"The place says no kids," she replied. "I'll have you kicked out."

True to her word, I received a letter from the apartment

management. It warned me that I had three days to get rid of Robin or move out.

"Oh, Bill, what are you going to do? Susan won't take her back right now will she?" Linda said with a moan.

"She can't, Linda. She is in the same situation we are. When I called, she said it could take months for her to find a place that takes kids. It's harder there than here. Worse, we do not have the money to move. I doubt if I have $200 in the bank. A new place would be first and last months' rent, plus security because of a child. That new building down the street would run about eight hundred dollars just to move in."

"Could your mom take her until we can get another place?"

"I don't think I can do that to Robin."

"You could give her that old *Humanist* mailing list as a gesture of friendship."

"Let's see how bad it gets first."

Seventy-two hours later the situation was very bad. An eviction notice had been taped to the door. I started to panic. *Suffer it out*, I told myself. *Don't sell out a little girl for a place to live. Remember your promise to Susan.*

But the little integrity I had was engulfed by my desire to rid myself of another problem I blamed on others. I picked up the phone and dialed Mother's number in Austin.

"I need help with Robin. I have her here, and I'm being kicked out of my apartment because of it." Mother and I had already exchanged short, caustic pleasantries. Now we were at the heart of the matter.

"Sounds like a problem to me. What are you going to do?" Mother asked.

"I need someone to keep her until I can find a new job and a house."

"Why a new job?"

"They found out at work who my mother is, Mother. People don't like me all that much once they know who you are."

"You have to fight them Bill, that is what life is about. You've got to make them do it your way."

"You mean your way. Listen, I called to ask for help not a lecture. I'll throw the old *Free Humanist* mailing list in with the deal."

"You don't have it!"

"I sure do. I have all your old three-by-five cards. I wanted to start a humanist group here, but I don't care to now. All I want is to make a living."

"I'll ask O'Hair."

"O'Hair?"

"Don't you remember him from Valle de Bravo?"

"Sure, Mother. I'm just surprised you need him to help make decisions."

"We got married."

"What for? I read in the papers that you'd said you two were following Margaret Sanger's advice and living together."

"We had to get married to get a loan for this house. Besides, he and his FBI experience saved my a__."

"What about Robin?"

"I'll call you back tomorrow." She hung up.

The next morning I promised the landlord that either Robin would be moved or I would be out in three days. I desperately looked for an apartment that would allow children. Those that would, I could not afford. And Robin's novelty was wearing thin with Linda. Robin made her get up in the morning. Aside from that, my work was being adversely affected by the strain. I began to argue with those I worked with and with customers.

By the time Mother agreed to take Robin, I didn't have the money for the fare to Austin. I wrote a bad check for it. Robin and I boarded the plane for Texas alone. We landed, and as I walked from the ramp, there was Mother. I had not seen her for nearly a year and a half.

"I can only do this for a year," she said after we greeted. "Taking her has nothing to do with that mailing list either. I'm doing this out of motherly love."

"You're surprising me, Mother."

She glowered at me. "Well, Robin may grow up okay. She's pretty. As long as she doesn't know she's half Jew, she'll be okay. You didn't tell that Jew b__ ex-wife of yours you were bringing her here, did you?"

"No, she would have hired someone to bump me off."

Mother glared at me again, then her face softened. "Where's that old mailing list, Bill?"

"In one of the boxes with Robin's things. Why?" I smiled.

"Oh, it's not important. Not worth anything to me. I just wondered if you brought it along."

We went to the O'Hairs' home where Richard was waiting. He was a barrel-chested man, completely bald, with bushy eyebrows and a small moustache. I soon learned that he enjoyed his booze. At this point his drinking was confined to evenings. It would be several more years before he drank morning and night. I liked to party, too, but could not understand why anyone would drink the night before going to work the next morning. Dick assured me that an awareness of the benefits of such behavior came with experience.

The day I was to return to San Francisco, Dick and I ate lunch alone in a Mexican restaurant. We downed a few beers, which loosened Dick's tongue.

"I agreed to raise that half-breed brother of yours when I married your mother, but not that grandkid. I'm in my fifties! When you get my age, you want to be left alone with the finer things in life." He pointed to his beer glass and patted it fondly.

"If your mother hadn't begged me, that kid of yours wouldn't be here. It's a compromise. She needs those old cards to make money, and you need money for your kid. I guess the swap is okay." He drained half of his glass in large gulps.

I pushed my beer away in disgust. "Can we hit the airport?" I asked.

"Yeah, first I want you to have this." He handed me ten twenty-dollar bills.

"What's this for?"

"Because you need it and have to take it." He poured yet another beer. "Now you owe me one. I'll ask for it one day."

I needed the money, so I took it.

"Look at this s___," he said. I turned to see two young men holding hands outside the restaurant window. "They used to hang fags in this part of the country. Now they are everywhere, even make passes at you.

"Let's get another beer and we'll go. I can't be in the sun much. I got a metal plate in my head. Jap machine gun shell. They didn't have that plastic in the Big One. I was in Tripler Hospital in Hawaii. You know that place?"

I nodded, looking at his bald head.

"They put the plate in there. Temperature in the operating room was about 75 degrees. Now, if its colder or hotter than that, the thing shrinks up or expands. Either way it hurts. I don't believe in pain killers though," he said, draining his fifth beer. He paid the check and we left.

At the airport, Dick pointed to a jet and continued what had become a monologue. "I know you don't believe in God so you don't care, but there is no good reason for those things to fly."

"Do you believe in God?"

"Wouldn't matter. When you have killed as many men as I have, you are going to hell no matter what you believe. I may as well go with your mother as anyone else. We have some great fights."

"Right. Dick, thanks for the money."

"All right. Want a cigarette to take with you?"

"I have a pack, Dick. Good-bye."

On the flight back to San Francisco I reflected on my mother's situation and my own. For the second time in her life she was married. Both times the husband had been a U.S. Marine. She had borne no children from the two men she had married, but she still had two children. Now, I was living with a woman who was on again, off again pregnant. I had a wife (divorce not yet final) in Hawaii and a child in Austin. I had not forsaken our family traditions.

Two months later I resigned as assistant to the president at Walter Cribbins Company. The pressure to do so had not come from Carl Rosenfeld but rather from my fellow employees and from within myself. After the *Chronicle* published the article about me, I had ceased to be William J. Murray, assistant to the president. Once again I had become *the son of the atheist*.

I had no specific plans when I left Cribbins. For a while I thought I might return full time to college. I had been monitoring night courses in economics and transportation at the University of California. The leftist community in Berkeley was planning a "Free University." I thought maybe that would be the place to study.

Not long after I quit work, Jim Smythe and Sandy showed up unexpectedly at my door. At first I was pleasantly surprised, but the pleasure faded quickly.

"Bill, now I know you have an extra room," was the first thing Jim said to me when I saw his face. "Sandy and I need a place until I can get my Gibson fixed. We can sleep on the floor. We don't mind."

"Your Gibson?"

"My guitar. The neck got a crack in it on the trip over. I can't make a living without it. Times are hard. My grandmother cut off the money supply when I dropped out of U.H."

"Come on in, Jim."

"You got cigarettes? We've been broke."

"Here, they're menthol."

"I'll show you something great I learned. It's called a Denver Kool," Jim said as he opened his guitar case and removed the remains of what had been a lid of grass. He took out a toothpick and carefully removed two-thirds of the tobacco from one of the Kool cigarettes. Jim then refilled it with stems and other pieces normally called "harsh." He repacked the cigarette and lit it, took a long drag, and passed it to me. I inhaled deeply.

"That's really great. It's a mentholated joint. You know, I think this is the first smoke of this I've had in a year."

"You're kidding?"

"No, I haven't even had any beer since I took Robin to Texas. Age limit here is twenty-one. I'm still just twenty."

"Bill, you've been too tied up in that square job. Those things will screw up your mind. All of a sudden," he paused to take a drag, "you'll want to get married again and buy one of those funny little boxes setting on the hills. Hey, that reminds me," he pulled his guitar from the case. "Hope it will hold the key, d— airlines." With that, he began to sing "Little Boxes."

Linda, Jim, and Sandy found an older house for rent closer to the action at the University at half the cost of the apartment we were in. So we all moved over there. Like any good Californian, I had filed for unemployment. I was penalized two weeks, because I had left my job with Cribbins. The pay for being unemployed was eighty-six dollars a week. Once a week I drove to the unemployment office and turned in a form stating I had looked for work. I had looked . . . for names of employers advertising in the want ads. I never contacted them but put their names on the form.

In April 1967, I read in the newspaper that Grandmother had died. I learned soon thereafter that Irv was broke and had been unable to ship her body back to Baltimore so she could lie next to Grandfather. Her burial had been handled by the welfare department. I wouldn't have been able to help either, as I was nearly broke myself. After reading the news, I found some of Linda's grass and got good and high.

My unemployment lark had lasted thirteen weeks. Finally, hanging around the campus during the day and smoking grass at night became a bore. On a couple of occasions Jim and Linda used some acid. I didn't join them. I refused to take something so strong that I could not maintain control of it.

I decided to find another job. American Airlines had advertised some openings, and by devious means I obtained an interview. I learned during this first contact that there were eight slots available for agents at the airport and that over three hundred applicants would be screened and tested. After a battery of tests and a physical, five days later I was informed that I was one of those chosen. For the most part, aviation was to be my career for the next fifteen years.

At the time American Airlines had perhaps the best agent training program in the industry. The complete training program was six weeks for a post-departure agent, the actual position I had been hired for. I entered into the new challenge eagerly.

By now I was fed up with Linda, but when I told her of my feelings, she threatened to tell American Airlines that I was related to "Mad Murray." When she proposed this blackmail, I slapped her face so hard my hand hurt. She and Jim continued to stay at home and get high.

Later in April Mother called. She was coming to San Francisco for a television show and wanted to stay with us. This gave me an excuse to move Jim out for a few days. He balked at the idea and tried to divert me with another of his dope-inspired plans.

"Bill, look, I really have something lined up," Jim said. "You know crazy Joe, the prophet?"

"Yes, Jim." He was a guy who used so much acid he thought he was Christ. He went barefoot and wore a big cross. He also tried to run for city council.

"Yeah, well, he's agreed to be crucified this Easter."

"What?"

"See, we are going to do a movie of it. We'll pound the nails right through his hands. He wants it that way. Bill, we can live off the film."

I shook my head. These people were just too strange. "Jim, you've got to move out a couple of days."

"Well, okay."

Linda wasn't excited about entertaining either. "Why does your mother have to stay here, anyway?" she asked. "Won't they put her in a hotel?"

"She *is* my mother, and she's taking care of my child right now, even if I am sending her money for it. That's how it's going to be."

During Mother's stay, an article about her appeared in the *Chronicle*. The reporter wrote a short history of how prayer had been removed from the schools. My name appeared six times.

Mother left, but the publicity she stirred doomed me again. One of my fellow agents asked me if I were the same Bill Murray. This and other comments soured my mood so thoroughly that the next day I got into a silly argument with my supervisor and quit.

This was the end as far as I was concerned. What was the use of trying to lead a semi-normal life? I packed my most valuable possessions and then boxed up some more stuff, which I hauled to a storage company. When Linda returned to an almost empty house after a two-day stay with a friend across the Bay, she was surprised.

"Bill, where's our stuff? What are you doing?" she asked, almost hysterically.

"I'm going across country. First to Texas, then I don't know where. Maybe I'll stay there."

"What about me?"

"I don't know 'What about you?' If you can stay straight long enough to pack, you can go. Otherwise stay," I said, pointedly.

"Where is our stuff?"

"*My* things, those I can't get in my car, are at Bekins Storage. *Your* things are still around here."

"What are you taking?"

"My clothes and my typewriter."

"Not the stereo?"

"There's no room for it. All I'm taking will have to fit in the car. If I decide to stay in Austin, I'll send for the rest."

"Austin, a little junky town in Texas? What will we do there?" Linda moaned.

"*I* am going to spend time with my daughter. Remember her, Robin Murray? Then I'll see what I'm going to do. I don't know what *we* will do, but that's what *I'm* going to do. From there, I may go to Canada."

"Oh, Bill, why Canada? It's cold there."

"Look at this," I handed her a letter I'd received from the Selective Service. "They want to know when my divorce will be final. They are going to get me and put me on the front lines and kill me because of the prayer case in Baltimore."

"Wow."

"You have until morning to pack and say good-bye to your friends." Then I added, "And sell what grass you have to them. You'll need the money."

The next day we drove south toward Los Angeles. At Bakersfield we stopped and stayed at a Holiday Inn.

"This costs too much. I only have a few hundred bucks. We can't afford motels," I said.

"What do we do, sleep in the car?"

"No, in the National Park System. Tomorrow we'll go to an army surplus store and get bags and a tent."

"Bags?" she looked puzzled.

"Sleeping bags, you dumb broad."

"Bill, we'll be in Austin in a couple of days."

"The route I'm taking, it may take weeks."

The next morning we found a surplus store. The two heavy bags I bought were on sale for $7.95 each. The small tent cost only $19.95. The cooking equipment and lantern added only another $20.00. I had expected to spend $75.00 or more. That is when I spotted it. There in a rack was the cleanest, sharpest looking rifle I had ever seen. I asked the clerk to hand it to me from behind the counter. Immediately I could feel its perfect craftsmanship. I could literally balance it on one finger. The weapon was a Ruger .22 caliber long rifle with a rotary chamber that held nine shells. I was in love with it. The total cost with cleaning equipment was $85.00. I took it.

"Do you know how to use that gun?" Linda asked when we returned to the car.

"If you only knew," I said. The memory of the gunfight Mac and I had had in Mexico flashed through my mind.

"Well, if you want to play with guns, why don't you join the army and go shoot up those little innocent people in Viet Nam."

I reached over and slapped her hard across the face. "Look slut," I said angrily, "you are a hanger. You know what that is?" She cringed. "You suck off of others. You don't work, you don't clean house. All you know how to do is make a man feel good in bed. For that you get your food and your highs. That's why I let you come on this trip. Just remember that."

Linda didn't make a sound until we reached a park late that afternoon. "In case you're wondering, I'm stopping early so I'll have light to put up the tent. I have to read the directions. Take the car and get some food and some ice for the cooler." I put a ten dollar bill in her hand.

An hour later when she returned the tent was up. She kept her back to me. Finally, I reached out and forcibly turned her toward me.

"Listen, you can stop this . . ." Then I saw what I had done.

"Oh, Linda. I didn't mean to hit you that hard." Her eye was half closed and black and blue.

"Bill, you just don't realize how big you are. You're strong. It really hurts."

"Linda, I'm sorry. I just have problems with my temper," I said.

"Did your dad do that too?"

"I don't know," I said, pulling her into my arms. "I only met him once or twice."

I made an ice pack for her and then cooked a typical sportsman's dinner—Spam and eggs. We ate in silence and then entered our small tent.

The trip to Austin took three weeks, since we stopped in nearly every campground on the way. We spent a week at the Grand Canyon.

As we crossed New Mexico and the deserted stretches of West Texas, I laid out the entire trip's route in my head. From Austin I would travel north to Montreal to the World's Fair. From there to Boston. In Boston it would be my turn to leech off Jim Smythe. Jim and Sandra had drifted east and had rented an old place on Lake Boone, some thirty miles outside of the city. My final goal had become that house. Jim, Sandra, and I had talked by telephone about making the house the center of a new, vibrant commune. But first, there must be the stop in Austin. Robin was now two and had been living with Madalyn and Richard for nearly six months. It seemed unlikely I would be able to take her back anytime soon.

As the little Hillman whined down the flat highway, I stuck my head partly out the window. Maybe the hot air rushing against my head would drive away the accusation hurling out of my conscience: *You are letting what happened to you happen to Robin.*

W e arrived in Austin. When Linda and I walked in the front door, Robin ran excitedly to meet us. Garth, now twelve years old, asked me one question after another about San Francisco. Mother was in another room on the telephone. Dick wanted to know when I'd be leaving town.

The first night Linda and I slept in our sleeping bags on the living room floor. During the early morning hours we were startled awake by sounds of a loud crash. I got up and looked outside, but saw nothing. Later, in the morning daylight I saw what had happened. Some drunk, unable to maneuver the sharp curve in the road in front of the O'Hairs' house, had slammed into the rear end of my little Hillman Minx. The bumper was caved in at least eight inches, and the trunk lid smashed and popped half open.

Dick walked out to inspect the damage with a shooter of vodka in his hand. It was 7:00 A.M. Mother trotted out in her bathrobe and began to scream and holler about the "S.O.B. Christians."

"Mother," I said, "I seriously doubt that the drunk who did this knew whose car it was."

"That's what you think. I know what persecution is like. You don't know what I go through because of who I am."

"No, Mom, I don't. I only know what *I* go through because of who you are," I answered.

"Well, I'd be sick and in tears if that happened to my car," she said angrily.

"That's the difference between us, Mother. To me this car

is not an end, it's a means. It doesn't matter to me if it's mine, only if it works. If this one doesn't work, somehow I'll get another one. I'd have to replace it someday anyway."

"You don't care about your possessions; that's why you don't really have anything, Bill," Mother said, accusingly.

"Mom, you raised me to be a good Marxist." When I said that, Dick turned and glared at me.

"You taught me that the desire to own private property was at the heart of all evil in the world," I went on.

"That's before I met Dick."

"Oh, G__," I moaned.

"He has *nothing* to do with it," she said with a smile, pleased with her little joke.

I stalked away and began a more careful study of my wounded car. Fortunately, the damage didn't affect the gas tank or exhaust system, and the car still ran.

My first confrontation with Dick occurred the next day. By four in the afternoon, he was blind drunk, wandering around the house. I realized by now that he was an alcoholic. He went into the kitchen, banged some plates around, then confronted me in the living room, angrily accusing me of eating a can of tuna fish he had opened.

"Dick, I really don't know what happened to your tuna fish."

"You are just like your d__ brother and mother. Always sneaking around. Never ask, just take."

"Dick, I didn't eat your tuna fish. If I had, I'd tell you."

He charged over to me and I stood up. "You ate the g—— tuna."

"Dick, if it will make you happy, I'll tell you I ate the tuna."

"See, I knew you were a d__ liar like your mother." As he said this he pushed me backward. I grabbed him by the arms and shoved him back against a wall.

"Look old man, I don't want to hurt you, not in your own house, but you're not going to push me around. You're not going to touch me again. You do, and I'll break your f__ neck."

With that I let him go. Then I added the ultimate masculine insult. I turned my back on him to let him know I could whip him even if he jumped me from behind. He stormed out of the house.

Later that day, I tried to talk to my brother.

"I wish you'd get Robin out of here," he said.

"Why, Garth?"

"Cause of what goes on here."

"What goes on here?"

"I can't tell."

Try as I might, he would not tell me what he was talking about. I already sensed that Garth was taking most of the responsibility for raising my daughter while my mother and stepfather fought. Trying to figure out what Garth was so mysterious about, my imagination went to work and came up with all sorts of horrid ideas, all of them involving harm to Robin. I desperately wanted to take Robin out of this insane environment, but I couldn't see how. I had perhaps a hundred dollars on me and no job. My possessions now included my clothes and a wrecked car. So again I slammed the door in the face of my accusing conscience.

The next morning I found myself alone with Dick again. He was in a friendlier mood.

"Let's shake and forget it, Bill," he said. "I was p____ at your mother yesterday and took it out on you."

"Dick, I didn't do anything."

"Well, in a way you did. Madalyn says she can divorce me now that you're back. She said you do better work on the printing press."

"Oh, h__, Dick, I'm not staying here! You couldn't pay me to stay here. I'm even sorry I brought Robin here. I know she's in your way. If I could take her I would."

"You leaving?" He perked up.

"Tomorrow, as soon as I can hock my typewriter for gas money. I'm going to Canada for a while."

"You don't have to do that," he said reaching in his pocket for a roll of bills. "Here's two hundred. That's what you'd get for it. Just don't tell Madalyn I gave it to you."

"Dick, I don't want your money. Spend it on Robin."

"Take it or I'll go blow it on a whore and give your mom V.D." He grinned.

I took the bills, carefully folded them, and stuck them in my wallet.

On the third day of our visit, while my mother and Linda went shopping, I packed and loaded up the car. When they came back, I was ready to leave.

"Where are you going? You can't leave!" Mother yelled.

"We're going to Canada for the winter. I want to see the fair."

"You're crazy! You don't have money; you'll starve. You have to stay here. I have plans. I've decided . . ."

"Not now, Mother, maybe later."

Mother turned to Linda and grabbed her arm. "You're his woman, you stay and he'll stay. You can't go. I need you."

"We're going," I said firmly.

"That S.O.B. gave you money to go. I'll kill him." She charged into the house after Dick. I waved to Robin, and she began to cry. Linda and I hurried into the car and drove off.

We headed north on Interstate 35. As always, I had with me a list of leftist contacts I had assembled over the years. It included names of the stronger members of the S.D.S. and the Communist party. If we ran out of money or had trouble, I thought one of them would be able to help.

Five days later, about the time we crossed into Canada, the trouble came. The brakes began to fade so badly on the Hillman that I could barely stop the car. Finally, at a rest area I removed a front wheel and discovered that the brake shoes were wearing unevenly. One was almost useless, the other looked new. I reversed their positions, and we drove on.

Linda had a brochure saying there were not enough hotels in Montreal and that many local residents were renting rooms in their homes at reasonable rates. Once inside the city we bought a newspaper and checked the want ads for rooms. One ad listed a place to stay for ten dollars a night, so we went there.

As we walked from the car to the rooming house someone called out to me—"Hey, your car's on fire." I turned quickly. Sure enough, smoke was pouring from the front wheels. The brake shoes I had reversed must have been rubbing for the last one hundred miles. When the smoke cleared, I couldn't even get the wheel cover off. The whole wheel assembly had welded itself together. Linda and I now had a broken-down car and no funds to fix it—in a foreign country. A further complication was the public transportation strike, which we had read about in the newspaper.

After we checked into our room, I had the car towed to a shop. The mechanic gave me two estimates: The first for $300 to do the job right; the second for $120 to break open the wheels and replace the shoes. I told him not to go over $120.

I called a contact at the Canadian Broadcasting Company (CBC) and told him the situation.

"Bill, I can't help you personally, but I could put you on a talk show. You can promote atheism or something. It will pay you $185."

"I'll do anything, thanks." We set up a time for the interview. For once, being a notorious atheist was beneficial. The next morning I made my appearance at the Montreal studios of CBC. After the make-up was applied, a local news-type briefed me on the interview.

"Just tell them who you are and that you're here to organize whatever it is you're organizing," he said. "If you don't mind, voice some mild displeasure at the transit strike." He winked at me. "Nothing blunt, we don't want to upset the workers you know!"

"Three, two, one, air" came the background voice.

"Today, we have William J. Murray with us, son of the U.S. atheist and antiwar activist Madalyn Murray O'Hair. Besides being avid spokesmen concerning the Viet Nam war, the Murray-O'Hair family is well known for stopping the recitation of prayers in U.S. public schools. Tell me, Mr. Murray, what are you doing in Montreal."

"Well [I could not remember the man's name], first off to see the splendid exposition that we are calling a World's Fair in the U.S. and then to organize local support."

"So the atheist movement is going forth throughout the world."

"Oh, yes, it seems there are atheists everywhere."

"Tell me Mr. Murray, being from an activist family, what do you think of the current transit situation in Montreal?"

"Well [I still could not recall his name], I think it will discourage some tourism and take dollars from the community. But, I can understand the position of the working man as well."

"Thank you, Mr. William Murray of the United States."

"Clear sound, clear graphics. You're off," came that voice again.

"That was really good, Mr. Murray. They will have your check ready at the cashier's office. Give our mutual friends my best."

We shook hands, I picked up the check, and Linda and I headed for the fair.

The local citizens were providing volunteer transportation in private cars on the main streets to the fair. Cabs were charging by the head to get as far as the main bridge heading to Exposition Island. The walk over the bridge and to the first exhibit was almost a mile.

I was astonished to find how commercial the exposition was. Everyone was selling everything. The only exhibit that didn't smack of commercialism was the geodesic dome put up by the United States. The Communist countries had the most overt commercial displays and the most aggressive salesmen. I will never forget the U.S. exhibit, which was free and featured a space capsule and other items from American life.

There was a long line in front of the Soviet exhibit. When Linda and I reached the "thirty minutes from this point" sign, we learned there was an admission charge.

"Linda, I really believed this would be the other way around," I said.

"What?"

"Oh that the United States exhibit would be selling all

kinds of junk and that the socialist countries would be showing off their development."

"It's the way you were raised."

"Right, I almost wound up in Russia," I reflected.

Just then a light rain began to fall. Within seconds I heard
the shout.

"Genuine Soviet rain coats, handmade by the Russian
Working Class."

"Oh, my G__." Linda said.

"Hockers, g____ hockers. I don't believe it." I was
shocked.

"Don't ruin your clothes. Buy your genuine Soviet rain
coats with caps now," a man continued to chant.

"So much for Soviet anticommercialism." Linda laughed.

"I don't think it's funny," I said in anger. "They hold out
hope to poor countries, but all they really want is a buck."

"Going to buy one?" she teased.

"I'll drown first."

Inside the exhibit, I found more that disgusted me. The
arena was one big sales showroom, and no matter where I
stopped, someone tried to sell me something.

"Clean engineered turbine, is it not?"

"Ah, yeah."

"Well, this turbine is adaptable to any configuration and
ready for immediate delivery."

"Excuse me."

We found a door marked "exit." We passed through it
only to find a jewelry store.

"How do we get out?" I asked a comrade behind the
counter.

"By the other end of the showroom. Sir! All watches are
half price today only."

"Right," and then to myself I thought, *and yesterday and
tomorrow!*

"Linda, let's get out of here." She was laughing, amused
by my reactions.

We were walking back over the bridge when I spotted a

small crowd ahead. Then I heard the comments of others passing in the opposite direction.

"She must have been drunk."

"There isn't a sidewalk, why isn't there a sidewalk?"

"Walking on the bridge wasn't allowed until the strike."

By the time I reached the group, I was curious. My eyes widened. A woman's leg was lying in the middle of the bridge, having been ripped off at the hip. I could not see what had hit her. The woman's body was by the rail.

"The unions s___," I heard someone say.

"Where's the ambulance," another said. "It's been fifteen minutes."

"Probably on strike, g____ unions."

"Don't need one anyway. She's dead as a mackerel."

"Bill, I'm going to be sick," Linda said.

"Let's go," I muttered.

As we walked to the car, Linda kept talking about the woman. I thought about what I had seen and heard in the hours just past. I concluded that my love for unionism and Marxism, which had been instilled in me at home over the years, had died this very afternoon.

The car's brakes had been repaired, so we left Montreal immediately and reentered the United States at Niagara Falls. At our campsite in a state park, I was cooking dinner when Linda came back from a shopping trip.

"Bill, I found them."

"Found who?"

"Jim and Sandy."

"You're kidding, where?" I looked around expecting to see them.

"I called them. They're at Lake Boone, like they said they would be. They have a fifteen-room house on the lake. They want us to come. I got the directions," she said enthusiastically.

I was less excited. We were nearly broke. I didn't know if we could make it, but the next morning we headed east.

When we arrived at Lake Boone early the following day,

we saw that Jim and Sandy had not exaggerated the size of the house.

"You're only paying seventy-five dollars a month?" I asked in disbelief.

"Yeah, and it's furnished. Even dishes," Jim bragged a little. "But we have to buy fuel oil. It runs maybe seventy-five dollars more a month."

"Look at that lake. Is there a boat?" Linda asked.

Jim ignored her question. "Bill, our car is in the shop. We blew the engine. I don't have a dime left. Sandy hasn't found a job yet."

"What about you?"

"You know I don't fit into a working environment. I have to be free." As he talked, he rolled a joint. "We don't even have food. Just a couple cans of corn."

"Let's eat fish."

"I got no money to buy fish, and neither do you."

"Tomorrow I'll hock my gun or typewriter, and we'll have money. Right now I'm hungry, and we'll eat fish. This guy you rent from must have gear."

Sure enough, twenty minutes later we had found it in the attic. As I assembled a rod I could still not believe the situation.

"Jim, why are these people renting this place to you for this price?"

"This is a summer place. They leave here every September for their home in Florida. They only rent it so someone will be in it and it won't be robbed."

Florida, I thought.

About an hour later we had eight fish in two frying pans. As I fried the fish, I realized something. This was communal living—the overwelming drive of the masses to do nothing. Jim would have to go without food for days before the thought of working would cross his mind. Tomorrow, I would hock the typewriter I still had, thanks to Richard O'Hair's generosity. Then I would pick up a newspaper and find a job.

The next morning I drove to Boston and placed the Royal

typewriter I enjoyed so much in a pawn shop. Then I went to a coffee shop. I sat there with coffee cup and newspaper in hand. In the front section was a story on rising unemployment. It went into great detail on the difficulty of finding work locally. In the back section were the want ads. There were several pages listing available jobs.

I scanned the pages. "Professional?" No, I wasn't looking for a career job. "Skilled?" No, I didn't want any manual labor. I wanted something that paid weekly and paid well. I wanted to get enough money fast to get out of the communal situation at Lake Boone. Then I saw it: "Private Investigator, undercover work, $260.00 per week."

"That's me," I said to myself and headed for the pay phone. I made an appointment for an interview that afternoon.

This started my ninety-day career as an industrial undercover agent and "shopper." For the first week I worked as a "shopper" while awaiting my first undercover assignment. The company, Merit Protective Services, specialized in stopping employee-caused shrinkage: We helped identify embezzlers and in-house thieves. My supervisor worked hard teaching me how to steal so I could recognize someone else doing it. A "shopping" crew normally consisted of a four-person crew: three shoppers and one licensed investigator.

The three shoppers would enter a store separately, pick up several items, and then go to one check-out position. The first in line would make an even money purchase, that is, present the proper change for an item before the checker could ring it up. This shopper would quickly walk out without a receipt. The second shopper then made a purchase that required change. This gave the checker an opportunity to steal. If she or he rang the purchase of the second shopper and not the first, a theft had been committed and the checker was caught.

Shopper two, apparently acting on impulse, then picked up a low ticket item near the counter and also made an exact change purchase, then walked out. This gave the checker a second chance to steal.

The third shopper was the final observer. The licensed investigator then entered the store and had the manager remove the cash register record tape. The evidence was presented to the clerk, and she or he was given the opportunity to sign a confession "for all the money they had ever stolen from the company."

Merit was not in business to jail clerks who took ten dollars a day. As part of Merit's program, if an individual signed a confession, the employer kept the employee. A reasonable amount was taken from the employee's wages to pay back the company. The employee also was made to understand that if Merit caught him or her stealing again, the signed confession would be used to put the person in jail. Our firm received fifty percent of all recovered funds.

My first undercover job was with a company called Automatic Radio. I was required to get myself hired as a truck driver by giving false references.

Automatic Radio knew that some of its warehouse men and drivers were delivering electronic components to underworld elements. My assignment was to act broke and make it look as if I had excessive personal vices. Hopefully, one of the gang would offer me a chance to earn easy money. I played the role well, borrowing between ten and fifty dollars from every driver and some of the warehouse men. I never talked about anything except girls and gambling.

There were other assignments, for the most part warehouse jobs. Merit made up the difference between what the company I was assigned to paid and my $260 weekly salary. Thus, my income was consistent.

During those first few weeks, I called my mother to check on Robin and to leave my address and phone number. Mother called me back and said that she had been asked to speak at the Harvard Student Union and at M.I.T. When she arrived, we lodged her in one of the many bedrooms at the Lake Boone house.

Mother seemed impressed with the place, as it was a beautiful time of year in New England. She had experienced little outdoor living in her life. The day she arrived, I showed her how to fish. Later, she caught her first fish there in Lake Boone. The next morning she arose at dawn and caught two limits of fish before I woke up. Despite her obvious pleasure, she found time to point out that "no individual should own a house this big."

Linda and I accompanied her to Harvard to hear her speech. The whole evening was an embarrassment. Mother's presentation was so vulgar several students left. Before the question-and-answer period, she made her pitch.

"Okay, fellows, this evening is free for you but not for me. You would have blown ten or twenty dollars on a date at a movie tonight. Surely, this show was worth a two-dollar movie ticket, so we're going to pass the basket." With that she passed around a small container for donations.

After the evening's escapade, we headed back to Lake Boone. Just outside Cambridge, the Hillman's carburetor jammed in a rich position and I could not get the car over thirty-five miles an hour. Mother was dozing in the back seat.

"What's wrong with the car?" Linda asked.

"Probably my mother being in it. Man, I could not believe what she said tonight."

"It sounded okay to me."

"Sure, it sounded okay to you. You were high as a kite. She said people didn't know babies came from intercourse until the nineteenth century and that the mystery of birth was what caused ancestor worship and then all religious beliefs."

"So?"

"Linda, if people didn't know intercourse caused babies, how were royal lines established?"

"Well . . ." Linda yawned and dropped off to sleep, too. I guided the creeping car the rest of the way in silence.

After my mother's departure, I continued working with Merit. At the commune I became increasingly vocal in suggesting that those who wanted to eat should also work. These announcements were not well-received. The last straw for me, though, came when I was accused of not sharing. I happened to be buying all of the food, gas, and grass. So what if I kept a few bucks? I never knew when we might need a can of beans after all the other money went up in smoke.

Finally, I told Jim and Sandy they could have their commune. Linda and I packed and left for Boston.

The next day Linda and I rented an apartment. It was a two-room flat in an older house. The owner, who lived with his family downstairs, told me he had chosen us as renters because we looked like a nice, quiet couple.

Now that Linda and I were alone again, the flaws in our relationship became evident. Linda stayed at home and did nothing. Each day I returned from work physically exhausted, only to find the apartment a disaster. Dishes were never washed, and whenever Linda took off her clothes, she left them in a heap on the floor.

Winter came, and it was severe. Snow stood three feet deep for weeks in some areas of the state. Driving a truck was tiresome and dangerous, and at the end of the day, I still had to prepare my reports for Merit. These strains led to vicious arguments between Linda and me.

One afternoon I wearily climbed the stairway and entered the apartment. I was tired and just wanted to sit down, but the place was so littered I was unable to locate a place to sit. Linda had passed out on the floor. I tried but could not wake her. Looking at her sprawled amid the rubble, I realized what I needed to do. The next day I told Linda she would have to find a job or leave. I was not about to support her lifestyle any longer. She became hysterical and began breaking dishes. I tried to restrain her, but her consuming fury was more than I could manage. She found a large butcher knife and slashed the upholstery and our clothing. The landlord heard the racket and called the police. When two patrolmen arrived and the landlord saw the carnage, he gave me the bad news in one word, "Out."

Several of Linda's new friends came and picked her up. I packed my clothes and stopped at the bank to withdraw all of my money. I parked the barely functioning Hillman in a tow zone and walked to the Trailways bus station. There I bought a ticket to Miami. I wanted to go far away from the cold weather and my leeching girlfriend. In Miami I hoped to find the same type of undercover work I had been doing. After I had saved some cash, I would cross the sunbelt back to Austin and visit Robin. But my stay in Miami was to be short. I never made it out of the bus station.

I arrived in Miami at almost 1:00 A.M. Not wanting to spend money on a hotel room, I decided to spend the last hours of the night in the terminal. I found a seat, stretched out my legs, and fell asleep. My dreams were interrupted by a police officer.

"Get on your feet and let's see your I.D.," he said.

At first I thought he was checking for bums. I handed the officer my wallet, money and all. Then I looked around. There were blue uniforms everywhere. As many as fifty officers were milling about in the waiting room.

"What's going on?" I asked.

"You'll see, let's go." The cop led me away.

When we entered a back room of the bus station, I saw about twenty men who matched my general description. Several plain clothes detectives were talking to some of them. One of them soon approached me.

"O'Conner, Treasury Department. I need your full name, address, and Social Security number."

"William J. Murray, 80 Beacon Street, Boston. What's going on here?"

"Social Security number?"

I gave it to him. "What's up?"

"Where you headed, Bill?"

"Here for now, why?"

"Where after here?"

"Austin."

"Austin?" The man was startled. He immediately called over two other men. He handed one of them the slip of paper with the information about me on it.

"This one's headed for Austin; let's do him next, Harris."

"What do you mean, 'do' me?"

"We just want you to read a statement to see if someone recognizes your voice. If they don't, you can move on. Okay with you, isn't it?" O'Conner asked.

"Yeah, sure," I said.

He picked up a phone and said, "Here's number seven," then handed me the phone and a piece of paper. "Read this to the guy on the phone."

"Okay," I said and began to read. "A group of heavily armed men are on their way from Miami to kill President Lyndon. . ." I stopped. "Wait, I don't even want to say this stuff." I handed O'Conner the phone.

He took it eagerly, "Well?" He listened, "Yeah, looks young, too." He turned to me, "Sit over there." I sat down on a folding chair.

Then the thought hit me. *These people think someone here wants to kill the President. When they find out who my mother is, they'll arrest me and let the guilty guy go.*

I walked over to O'Conner. "Look, I really want out of here. I'm sure the man you talked to told you that he didn't recognize my voice."

"You're that atheist woman's boy and probably a ring leader. You better sit down and shut up."

I was devastated. I sat in a corner for the next several hours. Finally, O'Connor came over and sat next to me.

"Here," he handed me an envelope. "It's a ticket for Austin."

"You found the right guy?"

"Let's say we're going to let everyone we stopped here go."

"I want to stay in Miami for a while."

"Everyone who stays will be under some suspicion. What

was supposed to happen was supposed to happen here. Still want to stay?"

I shook my head. Within an hour I boarded the bus for Austin. When I arrived, a real surprise was waiting at the O'Hairs' home—Linda. She had sold everything in Boston and had rushed to Austin, where she knew I would show up eventually.

I looked at her and realized that even with all our problems, she was all I had. If I had to choose between Linda and my mother, it would have to be Linda.

"Linda, tell you what" I said, when we were alone. "Let's go back to Hawaii for a while. Both of us can go back to school. I'll get a simple job driving a cab or something." She nodded. We had a short visit with Robin, and within twenty-four hours we were on our way to Hawaii.

On the islands again, I first worked for QANTAS as a load and balance agent, then with Pan American as a passenger service representative. But I allowed one of my old friends to talk me into a fifty percent deal on a cab.

During the next six months I was able to become an independent operator, and I assembled my own "fleet" of four cars. Because of my success I was able to quit my job with the airlines.

I bought a condominium with the profits, and Linda and I moved in. Linda had straightened up her act and had become a talented tour guide during the day. Each morning she would find an elderly tourist couple and talk them into a private tour of the island for $200.

Considering my past experience, I should have known that this success could only be temporary. But for several months, life was calm and basically trouble free. My ex-wife apparently had moved. No one seemed to know where she was, and I was not eager to find her anyway—I had no desire to explain what had happened to Robin.

Then my carefree life was interrupted by a letter from my draft board. I had been selected to offer my body for military causes of the U.S. government.

I sat down with Linda for a long talk. I told her I was going back to Texas to see Robin and Garth. After that I would try to join the Air Force or Navy. "I'm not going to walk around in rice paddies looking for little men with guns," I said.

"What about the cab company and our condo?" Linda asked.

"If you need money, sell the condo."

I left the next day. After spending some time with Robin in Austin, I tried to join the Air Force but found out everyone else had the same idea and there was a waiting list. The recruiter gave me an idea. Supposedly, the Army needed pilots. Sure enough they did. I went to Dallas and signed up.

During my fourth week in the Army, a letter came that made me smile. My draft board had reported me a draft-dodger. I was to be arrested, tried, and jailed. I wrote and told them not to worry; I already had my green suit.

After basic training, I received orders for flight training school at Fort Walters, Texas. I was assigned to Orange Company, one of eight training units. Each company consisted of four flights each with forty WOCs (Warrant Officer Cadets). Although all WOCs had the same E-5 rating, two were picked by the actual officer in charge as the student commanders. The chief student commander was called Flight Commander, the second in charge was called First Sergeant. I was the First Sergeant of my flight.

Surprising as it may seem, I enjoyed those first months in the military. No one cared about my past, or so I thought, and I was just another guy with a short haircut in combat fatigues. I had stopped drinking and smoking marijuana. I stayed straight because I didn't want anything to block my becoming a warrant officer and helicopter pilot.

On my first day in the military I registered the fact that I had a daughter living with my mother. Because of this the paymaster sent a check each month to my mother for Robin's support.

My marks in ground school and actual flight training

were good. Then the demons in my past paid a visit. One afternoon after a practice flight, a civilian instructor motioned me aside.

"Murray, you got an unsatisfactory today," he said

"Unsatisfactory?" I blurted out.

"That's what it says."

"But. . . ." I started to complain but was interrupted.

"Be careful, you're in the Army," came the warning.

My head swam as I stood in the Texas sun waiting for the others in my flight. *I can't fail,* I thought, *it was a good training mission. I did nothing wrong.*

I formed up the flight after the last cadet returned and called the cadence as we marched back to the barracks. When we arrived, I was called into the company headquarters office. There an officer gave me a pass and sent me to base headquarters.

As I walked toward the base H.Q., my mind summoned up all that could be wrong. At first I thought something had happened to Robin. Or maybe they were going over that incident at the bus depot in Miami.

"Cadet Murray, this is Captain Redford, military intelligence. He would like to ask you some questions," said the company commander.

"Some questions" lasted nearly five hours, until 6:00 P.M. I was informed to report back at 8:00 A.M. There was no need, I was told, to report for training until certain issues were resolved. Of course I would receive an "unsatisfactory" mark for each class missed.

I soon discovered that the primary object of the questioning was to obtain information about my mother and her activities. Even lines of questioning that did not begin with her ended with her. This interrogation continued for three days. I'll never forget that last hour with Redford.

"So," the captain put down his cup of coffee, "you say you have renounced the Marxist doctrine you were raised with, correct?"

"Yes, sir!"

"Why, again?"

"First, the Marxist economic system does not in practice work. Second, their methods stink, sir."

"How's that, Bill?"

"Like Viet Nam, sir."

"Your mother is still an outspoken opponent of the war and a supporting member of several pro-North Viet Nam groups, is that correct?"

"Yes, sir, but I don't support her in it."

"Cadet Murray, I see here that you have designated your mother, Madalyn Murray O'Hair, as the recipient of your child's monthly benefits."

"My daughter lives with her, sir."

"You said you don't support her?"

"Yes, sir."

"She controls the well-being of your child and collaborates with the enemy. Do you think that should affect your secret clearance?" He narrowed his eyes as he asked the question.

"I'll do anything, I'll sign anything. Please, I just don't want to be punished for my mother anymore." I began to cry.

" Anymore . . . what?"

"Anymore, sir." I was sobbing. I was broken, and he knew it.

"You have received several unsatisfactory flight reports. It would probably be in your best interest to resign at a formal review of your performance," he continued. "You will also have to handwrite the answers to many of the same questions I have asked as to your loyalty. By the way, you mentioned God. Do you believe in God?"

"I don't know, sir. I've never met him, sir."

After three weeks of doing nothing, I finally found myself in the review room. The tape recorder took down every word.

"Cadet Murray, you received three unsatisfactory flight reports. This warranted a special check ride. During that check ride, you did nothing to indicate that those unsatisfactory marks should be anything but that. As a result you are hereby given the opportunity to honorably resign from this program. Do you choose to do so?"

I had no fire left. I had been beaten: "Yes, sir."

"Please sign this in triplicate."

"Yes, sir."

Three days later I received new orders for, of all things, military police school at Fort Gordon, Georgia. Once there I volunteered and was accepted for advanced leadership training. By this time though, I was mentally and physically weak. During a three-mile run I collapsed.

I was rushed to the intensive care unit at the post hospital. One lung had collapsed. After a one-day stay I was moved to a respiratory ward for a week. The doctor said my lung had failed for no apparent reason. When discharged from the hospital I left on a ten-day leave to visit Robin.

When I arrived in Austin the last week in September, 1969, no one was thrilled to see me. The first thing Mother said was, "Well, you failed again. I presume I will get less to take care of Robin now."

Mother was busy and preoccupied with more of her publicity stunts. Unbelievably, just a few weeks before, she had filed a suit in Federal District Court against NASA calling for a halt to any praying or Bible reading by astronauts on space missions. The previous Christmas Eve, while orbiting the moon, Colonel Frank Borman had said a "prayer for peace." Later the same day, Borman, Major William Anders, and Captain James Lovell had read the first ten verses from the first chapter of Genesis.

Mother also objected that a small disc with a prayer by Pope Paul VI had been left on the moon by Neil Armstrong and Edwin Aldrin, Jr. It seemed that not even outer space was safe from the outlandish causes Mother dredged up. I thought all of this was ridiculous. No wonder I could not lead a normal life.

After Mother's condemning remarks on my failure at helicopter school, I really wanted to kill her and then leave the country. I decided instead just to leave the country. I thought about the beautiful lakes I had driven by during my trip to the World's Fair just two summers before. Why did the Army want me in the military police anyway? My leave ended, but rather than return to Fort Gordon, I boarded a bus for Canada. I was a deserter for four months.

My escape from Army duty ended at Tripler Army hospital in Honolulu, where I eventually had returned. I had received a bad concussion in an automobile accident several days before but had walked away not realizing the extent of the injuries. A friend had talked me into going to the army hospital. He rightly believed that I was in such poor physical and mental health from my army ordeal that nothing would be said about my extended absence. I really didn't care. I was tired and ill.

There was much more to it than that. During the previous months, I had managed to cross over the United States-Canadian border twenty times with everything from hot cameras to dope. That's how I had lived—and lived well in all the finer hotels along the border. I had come to Hawaii to pick up "hot" money to run back to Canada to "wash." I now knew more law breakers than law abiders.

An army major asked to see me. I sat in a pair of hospital pajamas across from him. He spoke first.

"It has come to my attention that by the time you recover completely you will have served out your two years." He droned on. "Aside from this absentee problem, probably caused by your injuries, your record is clean. I don't think a court martial would be in order."

Of course not, I thought. *A court martial would be public. They would have to talk about all the questioning and bad grades I got unfairly.*

"Therefore, Private Murray, your old company commander has dropped all charges. As you don't have enough time left in your enlistment for retraining, we will give you the option to accept an honorable discharge at the earliest possible date."

Two months later, in March 1970, I walked out of the Oakland Army Depot a free man. I not only received an honorable discharge but also a letter from General Westmoreland thanking me for the service I had performed. Since

I had actually joined the army in Texas, I was given a travel order with a one-way ticket to Dallas.

A free ticket to Texas was good enough reason to go to Austin and see how the family was doing. When I got there, Mother told me that I could get over one hundred dollars per week in unemployment with my honorable discharge, which I did. I also learned that during my AWOL, Mother had gained custody of Robin. To reverse that action would have required legal action. I did not have the money to hire a lawyer and—to be honest—at the time I wasn't all that interested in becoming responsible for my daughter anyway.

I tried to help my mother with her work, but I lacked interest. Since I had been gone, Mother and Richard had started an organization called Poor Richard's Universal Life Church. The two of them had become ordained ministers by obtaining mail order divinity degrees from some outfit in California. Richard was listed as president, pastor, and prophet. Mother was the church's bishop. The whole matter was an attempt to qualify for religious organization tax exemptions and to gain publicity.

I readily saw that Mother and Dick were destroying the nationwide organization they were trying to build. Dick opened all the mail and confiscated any cash for booze. He now had a large pot belly. He and Mother were always fighting. I learned that one of their fights had prompted Mother to file aggravated assault charges against Dick in February. She had dropped them soon after. In April the U.S. Supreme Court dismissed Madalyn's suit against NASA.

In early summer I applied for a job with Braniff International Airlines. They had one slot open for a vacation relief agent. The station manager in Austin wanted someone with experience, which I had from working with QANTAS and Pan American in Honolulu as well as with American in San Francisco. I was hired and worked the next forty days straight before being laid off. Several days later, I was rehired and worked sixty days, almost without a break. The second span qualified me to join the Teamsters Union and pass probation. Braniff was a closed shop. All jobs other than management required union membership.

After being laid off again, I opted to transfer to a vacancy in New York at Kennedy Airport. In Austin I had rented a two-bedroom apartment for $225 per month, including utilities. The apartment complex had a game room with pool tables and a heated swimming pool. After this I was not prepared for New York City. A non-air-conditioned two-room flat infested with roaches cost me $450.00. To top that, the owner wanted three months rent in advance and a three-year lease. I knew New York was expensive, but I had not expected a cup of coffee to cost exactly twice what it did in Dallas.

For almost a year I manned a ticket counter in New York. For the most part I worked international flights to South America. I tried hard to turn down most of the bribes I was offered to accept excess baggage without charge or to ignore improper documents. Unfortunately, like most airline employees in a similar position, I did succumb to some of the larger bribes around the time each month's apartment rent was due. My base pay was only about eight hundred dollars per month.

In early 1971 a vacancy opened as a lead agent or supervisor. I heard several of the senior agents discuss who should or should not bid for the job among them. While these agents with many years of seniority were busy with their discussions, I sent in my bid for the position and received it. I became one of three lead agents at the international freight house.

While I was away from Texas, Mother and Richard adopted Robin, who was already of school age. It angered me that she was now permanently bound to Richard and Madalyn, but I lacked a strong inclination to do anything about it. I still tried to maintain at least a minimal relationship with Robin. Once I flew her and Jon Garth to New York for a visit. I took them sightseeing, including stops at the Empire State Building and the Statue of Liberty.

In late 1971, I was offered a position as assistant manager of ramp and operations at Braniff's hub station in Dallas. I didn't care that much for New York or the Teamsters. I was glad to get out of both. I packed and left for Texas.

N ow that I was back within the borders of Mother's adopted state, I sensed the grip of her reputation and influence closing in on me once again. Happily, I was able to visit Robin more often, but when Madalyn would see me, she would urge me to help with her atheist causes.

At first Mother's requests were minor. Once she asked me to fly to Florida to check on an estate that had been willed to her organization. For the fun of it, I did. And now and then she asked me to buy her discount airline tickets. Since she was an immediate relative, she was entitled to some fifty percent and seventy-five percent discount tickets, depending on the circumstances. However, these circumstances did not include travel for profit. I did what I could, though, and Mother seemed appreciative.

The warming trend in our relationship started to cool in 1972 when Mother asked for three round-trip, half-fare tickets to India, where an international atheists' conference was to be held. The tickets were to be used by herself, Robin, and Dick.

"Mom," I told her, "I just can't do it. You'll be in the newspapers. Somebody will spot you. Besides, Richard isn't my father. It's against the rules."

She didn't press me, so I forgot the matter. Then she called back a few days later.

"Apparently, Bill, you don't want your people at Braniff to know I'm your f____ mother. If you won't get me the tickets,

I'll call the chairman of the board, Harding Lawrence, and tell him exactly who you are."

She had me trapped. I could not risk losing my position with Braniff, so I surrendered to her demands. Late one night I instructed a ticket agent to write the tickets, which I paid for out of my own pocket. As he slid the three envelopes across the counter, I though to myself, *If there is a God, I hope he stops her from using these.* My stomach was queasy, sickened by what I was having to do to save my job.

At this time, eighty-five percent of my mother's income came from writing projects or speaking engagements where her main theme still was the Baltimore prayer and Bible-reading case. Over one fourth of her income was from the sale of the book *Bill Murray, the Bible and the Baltimore Board of Education.* Even in my absence I was the primary source of her income. But that was not enough. Now I was being forced to risk my livelihood and ultimately my independence from her. I was an adult with a job that involved considerable responsibility. At the same time I was at the mercy of my mother, whose reputation had ruined me in the past and could ruin me again in a moment. I carried within me an angry awareness that I was still a fly in Madalyn's sticky web.

I was walking through the airport one afternoon when my office reached me on my ever-present portable transceiver. I was told a woman claiming to be my mother was being barred from a flight to Austin because she was intoxicated. I walked hurriedly to the gate area, wondering if this would be the incident that would seal my fate with Braniff. There I found Mom, cursing up a storm. I grabbed her arm and hustled her away to the coffee shop. I discreetly chose a table in the corner.

"It's your f____ airline's fault. They fed me the booze on the flight from New York," she said loudly.

"Mom, please, I work here. Please keep your voice down, and I'll get you on the next flight." I glanced around nervously, afraid one of my employees might see me.

"You can have your g____ f____ tickets back. That

b_____ Gandhi won't let me in her f____ country because I don't believe in her f____ god.

"What are you talking about?"

"She turned down my visa application to India."

"It's their country. They don't have to let anyone in."

"Bill, it's not fair that people don't want me. I'm a f____ nice old grandma. The Russians didn't want me, Gandhi doesn't want me. You don't even want these Braniff f____ to know I am your mother. I'm just a sweet f____ old lady. I don't see why you all treat me this way." She laid her head on her arms and cried herself to sleep.

Three hours later I ushered her onto a flight to Austin. As the plane backed away from the gate, I realized what my true feelings toward her were: I neither hated nor loved her; what I felt was pure pity.

Later another strange incident threatened to bring about my doom. A Christian leader located me at Love Field while he was between flights. He told me he had followed my mother's activities since the Baltimore days. The man had contacted my mother and had asked her if I believed in God. She had told him to ask me and had explained where and how to find me.

I was furious! I wanted desperately to be disassociated from the miseries of the past. Now Mother had turned this Christian loose on me, as if I were an animal to be stalked.

"So how do you feel about God?" the man asked.

I was fuming inside, but I answered with a smile: "I have my own beliefs. I am not in the public arena."

He mistook my smile and vague answer and within a month published a story in his newsletter about his encounter with me.

Mother sent me a copy of the newsletter. When I saw it I had an intense desire to kill both of them. I believed she had used him to move me one step closer to the door marked "out" at Braniff and one step closer to her control.

I had managed to make many friends at Braniff, despite

my growing dislike for the Teamsters Union. To me the travelers signed our paychecks. However, businessmen and people on family emergencies suffered equally from frequent employee slowdowns over job rules. For reasons not apparent to passengers, many flights left hours late.

It was during a Teamster work stoppage that I befriended a senior line co-pilot named "Fitz," short for Fitzgerald. He had chosen not to sit in the lefthand seat at the time, because it would have interfered with his law practice and aircraft rental business. I was in his cockpit hiding from the complaining passengers, when in the middle of the conversation he asked me if I had a pilot's license. When I said no, he asked how I knew so much about the aircraft from a pilot's standpoint. One thing led to another and he agreed to teach me how to fly on one of the two Cherokees he owned.

That following Monday we met at the Addison Airport north of Dallas, and he introduced me to the single engine Piper Cherokee. The second time around the field and on an approach he said, "Take the controls." I did. I followed his instructions and did a "touch and go." That completed the first hour of instruction. Two weeks later in the middle of the third hour of instruction, Fitz told me to land. We pulled off the runway, and Fitz unlocked his belt and opened the door.

"Bill, you don't need me here. Do three touch and goes, and I'll sign you off."

"After only three hours? I thought you said it took seven."

"Not for you. Go." He slammed the door and walked to the terminal.

I released the brake and contacted the tower as I taxied out.

"Tower, Cherokee 37 Echo for some touch and goes."

"37 Echo taxi to one three and hold short."

"37 Echo," I confirmed.

"37 Echo taxi to position and hold."

These words reminded me of my experiences with the United States Army. They had decided I was a poor pilot. The memory prompted me to curse softly.

"37 Echo start your roll. I said clear for take off!" the air controller barked, jarring me out of my memories. I had not heard him the first time.

"37 Echo," I said and pushed the throttle to takeoff power. Less than twenty seconds later I pulled back the stick and lifted off. As I turned left into the pattern, I went through the post takeoff routine and turned on my downwind leg.

"37 Echo your traffic is the Cessna on final."

"37 Echo, I have him."

I cut power to idle on the crosswind and dropped the flaps. The landing was on the numbers. Flaps up and back to take-off power, I sped on down the runway. As I lifted up again, my mouth was no longer dry. *Poor pilot indeed!* I thought, smiling triumphantly. Twenty minutes later I was back at the hanger, and Fitz signed me off. I was qualified on the Cherokee.

Flying again had lifted my spirits, but my life was still generally on the downswing. I was deeply in debt, primarily because I was paying for my fun with credit. Linda and I were living together again and had taken trips to Europe, Hawaii, and South America. Although the plane tickets were free, the fine hotels and ground transportation were not. The arguments between Linda and me added to my woes. Our relationship was as rocky as ever, and I really wanted it to end. But I needed her because I could not stand to be alone. I dallied with several girls at Braniff, but these affairs could not break my bond to Linda. I realized I could not leave her unless someone else were waiting for me. I needed Linda, if for no other reason than she knew how to argue with me.

Three major goals came to dominate my life, all of which were negative. First, I wanted out of the intense relationship with Linda, but I didn't have the strength to leave. Second, I wanted to leave Braniff—I didn't like all of the overtime, but I could not afford this for financial reasons. Third, I wanted to go far enough away from Madalyn Murray O'Hair that no one could link me to her. This goal, too, seemed unreachable.

I tried to dispose of my problems with drinking but didn't even have enough time to do this right. Because of problems with the Teamsters, managers were working double shifts, six and seven days a week. During my average twenty-four hour day, I spent twelve hours at work, three hours arguing with Linda, three hours drinking, and less than six hours sleeping.

After months of this grueling schedule, I frantically sought some escape. I sold my home in Garland and moved into an apartment. That done, I tried to save money for my immigration to Australia or some other place where I could be anonymous.

Finally, late in 1973, just before Braniff moved to its facility at the new Dallas-Fort Worth airport, I worked twenty-one consecutive days. This was too much, and my frustration with the job peaked. My final day of goodwill at Braniff began at 6:00 A.M. That evening at 6:00 p.m. I was told I would be the evening "duty manager." This would require my presence at the field until about 2:00 A.M. I said "no thanks" and went home—fully aware that throwing such a wrench into the Braniff machinery would cost me my job. Sure enough, two weeks later I was told that union employees could refuse to work, but managers were not afforded the privilege, even if ill. Death, I was told, was the only excuse. I was dismissed.

I had planned to save money and leave the company the following May—on my birthday, as a gift to myself. Being fired drastically changed my timetable. At once I sold all of my remaining property, including furniture and my beloved amateur radio equipment. Cash in hand, and without saying good-bye to Mother, I flew via United to Honolulu. I truly believed this was my first step to leaving the United States for good. Once there I applied for and received a job with an air freight line as a load and balance officer. I would have been headquartered in Guam had I shown up for work, but I didn't. An old friend of mine talked me into buying a taxicab in partnership with him again. Thirty days later he signed onto a freighter, and I was stuck driving the cab.

Linda, who had joined me in Hawaii, had talked her

parents into financing a business venture. From the first it was shaky financially. Somehow I let Linda and her parents talk me into becoming the company's president, and they sweetened the deal with a fresh infusion of $20,000 more of their money. Ultimately, this didn't help, but we struggled on for several months. The nation was entering its worst post World War II recession. It was not the time to be establishing a new business.

During this period I finally broke up with Linda and she moved into her parents' home. I became a friend of Tom Peters, who was president of an advertising agency. His company was as financially troubled as the one Linda and I were trying to pull out of the red. We worked on some joint ventures to save the two firms, and on several occasions he asked me to join his firm as executive vice-president. However, I had promised to stick it through December with the job I had, which I did.

Meanwhile, Linda was busy firing every secretary I hired. She asked each one to leave because of some suspected sexual involvement with me. Finally, in despair and need, I told Linda to find a suitable secretary for me. She hired a very sweet nineteen-year-old girl by the name of Valerie Guellermo. This turned out to be the nicest thing Linda ever did for me.

When December came I quit my job and became business manager of Tom Peters's agency. Valerie joined us as my secretary. I soon learned the firm was near bankruptcy. Tom was not even aware of it because of his involvement in a new electronic media project and was distraught when I showed him the bleak figures. It was obvious his agency could not be saved. My advice was to spin off the electronic media company as a separate entity and move to the mainland with it. He agreed.

In February of 1975 the entire company, equipment and employees, boarded a United flight to California. The equipment we required was in the bin of the aircraft, and the executives, Tom and I, and our "staff," Valerie, sat next to each other in three seats.

Although we were small, our new venture on the mainland started well in spite of the recession. In fact, the dismal economy probably forced many merchants to use the inexpensive advertising that Tom and I provided. We leased a house that had a bedroom for each of us. Living in "company housing" not only cut expenses but increased the salaries we could pay ourselves. Valerie seemed to enjoy every minute of her new life on the mainland. That winter she went skiing for the first time. She had not seen snow before and tumbled in it like a small child. I liked Val and enjoyed making her happy.

In March 1975, after having no contact with my daughter or mother for over a year, I recalled that Madalyn's birthday-convention was to be held somewhere in the West in April. Late one night, feeling guilty about ignoring Robin, who was now ten years old, I made a telephone call. As usual, Mother answered.

"We decided you were killed in the Pacific," she said. Then off the phone I heard her say, "Garth, it's your long lost brother." Speaking again to me she asked, "Where are you?"

"In the West. I just got back from the islands a few months ago. How's Robin?"

"Fine, but Richard's out of the picture. We are getting a divorce. I caught the S.O.B. with my own secretary. There they were, f___ right in . . ."

"Mother," I interrupted, "I'm paying for the call. You can fill me in on the details of your love life later. I called to see where all of you would be so I could see Robin."

"We're right here!"

"No, for your birthday . . . I mean, your convention."

"It's Jefferson's birthday, that's why I have the convention then. He was our greatest atheist. It's only coincidental that I was born the same day."

"Right, Mom. Where's it going to be?"

"Hollywood."

She gave me all the details and told me Robin was on some school trip and I would have to wait until later to talk to her. But in the background I could hear Robin asking Mother where I was.

On Friday, April 11, I paused to say good-bye to Valerie. She started to cry and told me to be sure to come back. She said that she loved me. I was speechless for a moment. Then I mumbled that I only planned to be gone for the weekend and left. The tenderness in Val's face had made me remember that people could love and care for each other. I was quite moved.

At the Burbank Airport I rented a car and headed for Hollywood. I found the hotel, a seedy looking place that had seen better days. An astonishing collection of tramps and nuts showed up for the convention. For two days all I heard were lectures about atheism and acclaim for my mother. There were perhaps a dozen "normal" people there. The rest each had some "thing" they needed to prove beyond their atheism.

Present were some anti-Semites and a number of homosexuals, including two sets of lesbians. Missing were the Marxists. They had been replaced by racists and National Socialists. Finally alone with my mother, I popped the question: "What happened to all the commies, Mom?"

Her answer was swift. "They had to go. I've got them all out now. We are American atheists. There were too many fallacies in Marx's work. He didn't take into account the unions, for example."

"Or that new Cadillac you're driving?"

"Nothing to do with it. I deserve it because I risk my life daily for the cause."

"I see," I said.

I spent much of the weekend trying to reacquaint myself with Garth and Robin but without much success. Robin was distant, and I sensed something had to change or I would lose her permanently.

Sunday afternoon I boarded a flight for Seattle, where Tom and I now had two offices. On Monday we suddenly had a big problem. The bank informed me that checks given us for thousands of dollars of business were being returned. Our account would go into a five-digit overdraft. Tom and I argued briefly about the reasons and then agreed to break the firm into two divisions until the problems were settled. I was to take the printing division and all its equipment. That consisted of several metal tables, a modern printing press, a plate maker, and a composer.

That night I took Val out to dinner. "Still love me?" I asked. When she answered yes, I told her who my mother was and that I had a daughter. Then I informed her that I had not had a vacation in years and was about to take one.

When we had first arrived on the mainland, I had purchased a large pickup truck with a camper. Now I intended to load up the printing equipment and head out for unknown destinations and have fun until I used up the several thousand dollars I had in the bank. I told Valerie we could live in the National Parks until we settled down. We, that is, if she wanted to go with me. She did!

Less than a week later I pointed the big red truck toward Death Valley. For nearly a month we visited every sight worth seeing west of the Rockies. In Las Vegas we went to a dinner show and had our picture taken together. I asked Val that night if she wanted to marry me while we were there. I was twenty-nine and she only nineteen. She said not yet, and we drove on to the Grand Canyon.

We arrived at the rim of the canyon as the winter's final snow was drifting to the rocky ground. The tent we pitched in the campground was small but effective. That first night I cooked hamburgers on the Coleman gas stove as the snow flakes hissed and vanished in the flames.

The next day I rose before six and stood in line at a ranger station hoping to gain a cancelled spot in one of the campgrounds near the canyon's floor. I received one an hour later, and Val and I headed down the south wall toward Indian Springs. At mid-afternoon we crossed the Colorado River and set up our tent. We stayed near the river only one night. During the climb back up the next day my lungs ached badly. I had now been smoking cigarettes for over nine years and wanted to stop, but I didn't have the personal willpower to do it.

Five days later we left the Grand Canyon and headed for Denver where I had friends. After this three-week vacation my funds were getting low, and I only had about $2000 left. With it I needed to rent an apartment and an office so I could go back into business.

I had barely opened the doors of V & B Printing (which stood for Val and Bill) in southeast Denver when Tom Peters walked through the door.

"Need a salesman?" he asked.

"Tom, what happened and how did you find us?"

"Well, the bank took everything after you left. As to how I found you, I was sitting in an employment office and saw your card attached to your price list. I can take a $20,000 salary with an ad agency or give you a hand, partner!"

Nobody has ever been able to say no to Tom Peters. In a month he tripled our business. At this point everything would have been fine had it not been for a little greed on my part. First, I wanted both Valerie and Robin near me. Second, I remembered that during our visit in Hollywood Mother had said she used commercial printers. Thus, I called good old Mom to let her know I would help her out with printing anytime she was in a bind. Within days she called to tell me that she was going to be in Colorado on a speaking tour and would stop by Denver to see our operation.

In July her large grey Cadillac pulled up in front of our building. I stood up and walked outside. Garth, now twenty years old, was at the wheel with Mother beside him. I greeted them, "C'mon in. Tom and Valerie are in the back."

"Who are you doing work for?" Mother asked.

"Our biggest customer is the Homebuilders' Association. We've got contracts with several local government agencies and a number of private businesses."

"Sounds like you're busy," Garth commented.

"We are. That's Valerie over there. She's working on our IBM Composer, setting type for some job."

I don't think Garth heard what I said because he began to stare at the display of our work that covered the walls. "Wow, Bill, this stuff is really nice."

"Thanks. Tom comes up with the concepts, and Valerie has a knack for getting them onto paper. She's a good artist."

Meanwhile, Mother had gone to stand over Valerie's

shoulder and watch the composer work. Her eyes widened as Valerie sat back and punched the print button. The typing element of the Selectric composer sped across the sheet justifying and spacing the copy Valerie had just put into its memory.

When the composer stopped, Mother's first words to Valerie were, "How much does one of these cost?"

"Thousands I think. You'll have to ask Bill."

"Would you give me a little demonstration of how it works?"

Mother was full of questions that morning, which made me a little edgy. The last time somebody had been in the place asking those sorts of questions, he had turned out to be a competitor. We talked more at lunch.

"Richard is a drunk," Mother explained. "I'm putting him out to pasture. He came d___ close to destroying the Society of Separationists. We have published the *American Atheist* only a dozen times in the last five years despite the fact its supposed to be a monthly."

"Yeah," Garth added. "And we've had to farm out the monthly newsletter in spite of the fact that we own tens of thousands of dollars worth of printing equipment."

"What's the matter?" I asked.

"The equipment is ruined," he replied. "Dick let the ink sit on the presses hardening for months. Belts and gears on the folders and collators haven't been maintained and some are corroded together."

"And our mailing and addressing machines," Mother inserted, "are disassembled. The pieces are scattered between two different rooms in building two."

"You've got two buildings?"

"Yeah, the Society owns these two houses with just three rooms in each. That's where we keep the equipment," Garth answered. "And that's where Richard keeps Tusok."

"Tusok?"

"Several years ago Richard bought this large parrot and named him Tusok. He's pretty much had free run of the one office for the last year," Mother explained.

"A parrot in a print shop?"

"You guessed it, Bill," Garth chuckled. "Much of the machinery is literally covered with bird s___."

"Can it be salvaged?"

"I don't think so," Garth said, as Mother shook her head in agreement. "It'll probably have to be replaced."

"How do you plan to do that?"

"That's where you come in." My mother cleared her throat. "Bill, I'll pay for you to relocate your company to Austin. And you can use the two-room commercial building we own next to one of the houses."

"Where are you going to get the cash for a move like that?"

"Well, just because the day-to-day operation is shot to h__ doesn't mean we don't have money. We receive large estate bequests from members who die. We've been real lucky the last several years on the bequests of dead members."

"Let me be straight with you, Mother. We've built up a good business here in Denver. You could see that for yourself this morning. It'd cost a lot to leave that all behind."

"Don't worry about that. With the money I've got from this latest estate, I can cover losses with ease and make you a lot more."

I raised my eyebrows with interest.

"In fact," she continued, "in addition to letting you have the one building rent-free for an entire year, I'll also guarantee you at least two thousand dollars' worth of business from the Society every month. What do you say?"

I sighed deeply. I was suppressing the memory of my childhood and adolescence. I longed for a reunion with Robin and a chance to establish a solid relationship with her before she got much older. I think my mother had sensed that during my visit to her convention.

"Bill, I'm getting older. Dick's killing himself with booze," she looked at me imploringly. "And I can see you've got what it takes to make things happen. I'm not a real business woman. Won't you please help me?"

Before the day was over I had more or less made my decision. For years I had been plagued in business and in my personal life by being the son of Madalyn Murray O'Hair. Now I could at last profit from that relationship—or so I told myself.

The next day I talked with Tom and Valerie about the proposal. "Bill, this sounds great!" Tom exclaimed. "Your mother's well-known. We could turn that in our favor. Besides, if it doesn't work out, we still have the equipment."

I looked at Valerie.

"You know me, Bill," she said with a grin. "I'd love to see Texas. I've never been there before."

"How long do we need to fill our present contracts?" Tom asked.

"I looked over the job orders this morning. Looks like it would take us only a couple weeks to finish things up, if we don't accept any new business."

'Great! Let's go for it!'

"I don't know. I'm sort of torn."

"C'mon, Bill, this is the chance of a lifetime," Tom urged.

Valerie was full of questions, first about Texas, then about my mother. Finally she asked, "What is an atheist?"

"An atheist is a person who does not believe in God—any god, not even the old pagan gods. The basis of atheism is found in various materialistic philosophies. Jean-Paul Sartre led the materialistic view to existentialism. But the final outcome is nihilism, because the whole thing comes down to narcissistic self-gratification."

"Bill, what does all of that mean?"

"It means 'if it feels good do it' because you only have to answer to yourself." I paused and opened a beer. "Call it atheism or humanism or secularism or whatever you want, but it all boils down to the same philosophical junk that gave Plato an excuse to be a fag."

"Is that why you drink, because you're an atheist? Is that what you mean, Bill?"

I almost choked and put down the beer. "Val," I said, "I don't know for sure that there isn't some being greater than mankind. I just can't believe in a god who is petty. A god would be truly great, forgiving, good. I have never run into a god like that."

We left Denver on a very hot weekend late in July. All our printing equipment had been loaded onto two trucks. We had stayed in the city only about four months.

As usual these days, Valerie was near me in the first truck. Our affection for each other had grown steadily as we had worked together on projects. Now, as we pulled away from Denver, we joked about owning a mobile printing plant. Tom Peters followed in the other truck.

Printing presses are among the heaviest pieces of machinery made, so our two overloaded trucks creeped along, seldom exceeding fifty-five miles per hour. There was a lot of time to talk, and for three days I answered Valerie's questions about my mother, my brother, my daughter, and atheism. As I talked, I worked hard to convince myself that my fears were unjustified. *Great things just have to be in store for us*, I thought. I was disastrously wrong.

"**B**ill! Good to hear your voice," Mother said on the telephone. "C'mon down and I'll show you the building we have for you."

She sounded pleased that our caravan had arrived in Austin. An hour later, Tom, Valerie, and I were standing in front of a garage.

"This is the free-standing commercial building?" Tom murmured.

"It sounded a lot bigger and nicer over lunch in Denver," I remarked. "This place doesn't even have air-conditioning."

Later we got a look at the two houses Mother and Garth had told me about. One housed her office and library. The other was the scene of the disaster they had described to me, including the printing press covered with parrot droppings.

Within a few days I was aware that Mother didn't have even one full-time employee. Nor was the Society of Separationists generating enough monthly income to produce more than a fraction of the business my mother had promised us.

Tom, Valerie, and I rented a townhouse in the hills of northwest Austin. The business prospects were disappointing, but it was good to be near Robin at last. I wanted more than anything to win her trust and to establish a substantial relationship with her. I knew it would take time, but I was glad to see how readily she and Valerie became friends. This had something to do with the fact that they were closer in age than I wanted to admit.

Meanwhile, Tom and I had a lot of work to do. Tom

started prospecting while Val and I readied our equipment in the "office." Within a week Tom had secured printing jobs from the local home builder's association as well as from a number of other organizations and businesses in the city. That gave us a foundation to build on, and we also started moving Mother's publications right along. Within thirty days, the first edition of the *Amercian Atheist* to be printed in years was on the press. In short order the monthly newsletter was also in the mail on schedule. Income of the Society began to pick up again. We sold more than a thousand subscriptions to the magazine that second month, at fifteen dollars each. Donations increased significantly.

Mother, I discovered, had been producing fifteen-minute talks that were broadcast once a week on KLBJ, an Austin radio station owned by Lyndon Johnson. The tapes of old programs were gathering dust. I purchased a cassette duplicator and started making copies of them, which we offered for sale to Society members through the magazine and newsletter. They became extremely popular, even though I priced them at $8.95 for a set of four programs on two tapes.

For the first time in ten years, the Society of Separationists was earning income from sources other than corpses, and Mother had more money than she knew what to do with.

From the day I arrived in Austin, though, I was in the middle of a variety of family members' "personal" problems. In time, the foul, hate-filled environment we shared would help me refine my own vices. But at first I just watched in wonder the absurd behavior within my clan.

Richard O'Hair now drank alcohol day and night. His daily pattern seldom varied. He started in the morning between five and six o'clock with a couple of "shooters" of gin to straighten his nerves. When the local pubs opened an hour or so before noon, he would be among the early clientele, downing one beer after another while talking to the boys. In the late afternoon Richard settled in with a bottle of bourbon, which kept him company until he no longer could stay awake. Despite what Mother had told me earlier, she had not filed for divorce yet, and she and Richard still lived together and argued viciously. I could not understand why they continued to tolerate each other.

Mother spent hours in her office, dripping tears on her old Adler typewriter. At first I thought she might be crying because all of the office equipment was German-made and often out of service because parts were hard to get. But I learned that Madalyn's tears were caused primarily by her inability to maintain control over Dick and Garth. She suspected that Richard was seeing other women, and Garth didn't always heed her advice on every matter. It seemed that only Robin was a "good girl" because she knew her grandmother's importance, or so Mother told me.

Madalyn believed that Dick had chosen to philander because she could not control her weight and therefore was no longer attractive to him. I was forced to endure endless monologues about her glandular problem. She told me she could not lose weight even if she fasted. These conversations were often held at mealtimes when Mother gulped down a hearty lunch or dinner finished off with two pieces of pie or cake.

My brother, Garth, was another story. Like Mother, he had a compulsion to talk constantly. When the two of them were together, they would talk simultaneously, each being unable to hear the other out.

On several occasions after Garth had overrun my patience with a talking binge, I left my chair, hoping to find some moments of peace in the bathroom. Even this tactic didn't interrupt Garth. He followed along behind me, the words flowing unabated. Once, while Garth was collating some papers with his back to me, I left the room quietly and didn't return for fifteen minutes. When I slipped back in he was still involved in the "conversation," unaware that I had been gone.

It could be that Garth's difficulty with listening to others led to an incident that fall I'll never forget. One afternoon Garth barged into my office and announced triumphantly: "Bill, I think I've got $20,000 in the trunk of my car."

I smiled, but tried not to laugh.

"You won't believe what happened!" he continued.

"Garth, how much of the money was yours?" I asked.

"Well, I had to put up $2,000 of our money . . ."

I interrupted, "And they locked yours up with this old man's insurance claim payment of $20,000 in the trunk. Then they kept the key to make sure you didn't run off with it. Now you can't find them?"

"How did you know?" Garth asked, his enthusiasm now dampened by a touch of anxiety.

"Garth, congratulations. You have just fallen for a con game so old that the Arabs used it on rich Romans during the time of Christ."

Garth never was able to tell the whole truth of the con to Mother. His final story was that someone had followed him into the bank with a gun and forced him to withdraw the money.

Then there was Tusok the parrot, perhaps the major reason why Mother needed to bring me and my printing equipment to Austin. Richard had purchased his pet bird during one of his drunks. Unfortunately, he had failed to buy his feathered pal a cage. For over a year Tusok had spent half his time on a wooden perch and the other half atop the printing press. Shortly after Valerie and I arrived in Austin, we spent hours scraping Tusok's substantial output from the floors and the equipment.

We were still cleaning up after Tusok one morning in August when Garth called on the telephone. He had been driving with Mother to deliver a tape to the radio station when the two of them had begun to argue. At a traffic light halfway between our office and downtown, Madalyn had suddenly opened her door, stepped from the car, and walked into the woods. I told Garth there wasn't much we could do but wait. Hours later Mother called for a ride home. She insisted, though, that only Garth come to pick her up because "we know what it's like to be alone." I had no idea what she meant by that and did not bother to find out.

Not long after this incident, Mother's car was found one

day with the driver's door open and the engine running. Garth thought she had been kidnapped. We found her later in tears sitting on a bench in a public park. I could tell Mother had not overcome the rapid mood shifts I had observed while growing up. A few days later her spirits had brightened so much that she went on a spending binge.

After just a few weeks I was already convinced I had made a terrible mistake in returning to be near my family. I hated myself for my own stupidity. It had taken years for me to calm down after the antics in Baltimore. In fact, only since returning to the mainland just a year ago had I felt some degree of normalcy. Now the adrenalin surged constantly through my veins from the unending arguing and general insanity. Seeking relief, I began to refine my own abnormal behavior—alcohol abuse.

Since turning twenty-one I had enjoyed drinking for fun and escape. But my drinking had always had a happy ending, and I rarely even had a hangover. Suddenly alcohol turned sour for me. I started getting drunk frequently and became increasingly violent. Once I slapped Valerie across the face, and my agitated mood resulted in the end of my partnership with Tom. My anger was over the loss of our first and largest commercial account. Tom had brought the man to see the plant. Madalyn had showed up, and after she had informed him in no uncertain terms that her work always came first, he cancelled out.

My self-esteem was being dismantled on a daily basis, particularly by the Society. Since coming to Austin, I had been trying to purchase a particular office building about four blocks from one of Mother's offices. Her buildings, at two locations, were small World War II frame dwellings with three rooms each, plus a bath and kitchen. They were not adequate for a successful business. Finally, in October I managed to arrange financing and insurance for an office building on Medical Parkway, and it was purchased by the Society of Separationists. It cost $85,000 and was located in northwest Austin across the street from a Baptist church. Mother proudly hung a sign on the door. The media flocked in to tell the world of this latest omen of the coming triumph of atheism. Mother did her best to be quotable and told of her big plans for the organization, which included, according to her, a desire to start a summer camp "where an atheist young man can meet an atheist young girl."

Mother was less positive behind the scenes. The day we moved in, she berated me because she thought the 4,000 square foot building was too small. I couldn't take it and exploded.

"Mother, you have been here ten years, and all you had to show for it when I got here was a house full of bird s___ and a husband who f___ your only employee. I haven't been here six months and you have an office building with six employees. Give me a break!" I walked down the street to the Common Interest bar and got drunk.

By December, only five months after my reunion with the family, I resembled an alcoholic. Meanwhile, Mother had "removed" Dick from the board of directors and presidency of both her corporations. She also had filed for divorce naming her ex-secretary as his mistress in the suit.

I could not stand being made to feel like cow manure in a situation where I felt I was the only positive element. To lift my self-esteem and to prove to the community that I was more normal than my mother, I decided to run for the U.S. Congress. I paid my $1,000 fee to enter the Republican primary, scheduled for the following May. This caused so much family warfare that within a few weeks Valerie and I packed up and moved to Houston, leaving my printing equipment behind.

For a month or so I took the jobs that were available, including selling cars, to make money. But by February I once again had my own business. Valerie, I, and a new business partner ran my campaign for the House of Representatives from Houston, although the district I was running from was in Austin. I drove there almost weekly to campaign.

In March Madalyn made a little news splash by announcing that she was going to quit as the unofficial head of

American atheists. The next day she decided not to quit. I laughed when I heard of this. Mother would have died if her soapbox had been given to someone else.

By April I had calmed down somewhat and was willing to listen again to my mother. In a phone call she assured me that she had learned a great lesson. According to her, she had taken Richard's advice against mine too many times, and that had caused the arguing. Their divorce would soon be final, and I was needed back. She offered me the use of the office for my campaign. I wanted to win, so I accepted her offer.

My campaign themes were simple. I maintained that first, no man should be forced to join any organization, not even a union; second, the majority should rule with respect for minority opinions; and third, people who work harder to earn more should not be punished with higher taxes.

On election night in May, I watched the election returns on television with mixed feelings. I honestly believed I had not been able to overcome my mother's image and would be fortunate to get ten percent of the vote. I was astonished when I received forty-six percent and carried several precincts. It was an exhilarating evening.

Shortly after the election, Mother asked me to come back and take over as business manager of the Society of Separationists. Valerie was shocked that I would even consider the offer. Yet, my near victory in that election had given me a strong desire to return to Austin. I believed I now had a political and business base in the city. And there were other reasons. Valerie and I had decided to get married, and we wanted to bring Robin into our family and rescue her from the chaos she put up with. We thought at least she needed a place away from the five dogs my mother allowed to roam the house. Robin often had to wipe up dog excrement before she could walk into her own room.

And there was the violence. I was told that Madalyn and Richard's fights often reached epic proportions, and on several occasions, Robin became so alarmed that she slipped out and went to a neighbor's house to call the police. The cops came and restored the peace, but this was hardly a pleasant environment for an eleven-year-old girl.

I confided to Val that I wanted to return to Austin and to my mother's organization long enough to show Robin and Garth how even a halfway normal person lived. Once more I made the mistake of thinking that somehow I could change them. I was wrong again.

We returned to Austin in December of 1976 and rented a large three-bedroom house just east of town. As usual, Mother had a few causes boiling in the pot.

Like clockwork, almost every year Mother would find some event or issue that would outrage average citizens of American society and generate nice-sized newspaper headlines in the process. Near the time Val and I rejoined her, Mother announced that henceforth every Thursday would be the sabbath for American atheists. She encouraged all atheists to take each Thursday off, and if they met opposition, to seek protection from a recent U.S. Supreme Court ruling that ordered businesses to rearrange work schedules to accommodate anyone who observed a day other than Sunday as the Sabbath. Mother was quoted as saying that "Thursday is the day I led the children of atheism out of the wilderness of religion."

Then in December Mother staged "The First Annual Celebration of the Winter Solstice." Some reporters showed up and watched as Mother tumbled around, wishing everyone "Happy Solstice." She announced that when atheists became a majority, they would celebrate the holiday the way the ancient pagans did. "They all went out in the street and they sang and they drank and they fornicated," she said.

I observed all of this with a mixture of amusement and disgust. What bothered me most was that by now Robin was a firmly entrenched part of Madalyn's life and causes. My daily date with the bottle helped me to forget this, however.

About the time Valerie and I rejoined my mother late in 1976, Garth was dating a girl, whom I'll call Beverly, and soon after they announced marriage plans. One day I arrived at work and was stunned to see that furniture had been moved in to the small apartment over the Medical Parkway office. I recognized the pieces, since they were from Mother's bedroom.

I found Madalyn. "Mother," I asked, "what is going on? That's your bedroom furniture, isn't it?"

"I'm moving out so Garth can have that b___ move in my house."

I felt sorry for her. She was about to lose one of her prized possessions, Garth. I tried to cheer her up. "Look, Mom, Valerie and I have a marriage license. If you still have your minister's papers from the state, you can perform the wedding. If you want to."

She lit up like a Christmas tree. "I'll do it after I fix it with the newspapers," she said.

"Mom, please, just a quiet wedding. Just you and the family and some friends at our house. One other thing, when a male cub brings home a playmate, the tigress does not give up the lair!"

She thought about this for a moment. "Well, I needed all new furniture anyway."

"What?"

"You don't think I'm going to move that old stuff back in my room after it got all banged up bringing it up here, do you?"

"I guess not." I shook my head and headed for the Common Interest for a few noontime beers.

Valerie and I were married on January 25, 1977. Mother officiated the ceremony—which, of course, was atheistic. I was already losing the battle to control my alcohol use. Under these circumstances our marriage got off to a shaky start.

By this time Beverly and Garth's engagement was in its last throes because of Mother's opposition to it. Beverly was becoming desperate. When Valerie threw her bouquet at the wedding, Beverly knocked down two other girls and dived onto the floor trying to catch it. Even with that effort the flowers landed in someone else's grasp.

A few days later Beverly's parents stopped at the Medical Parkway office to meet who they thought might be their future in-laws. Mother responded to this social pleasantry by locking herself in her office and refusing to come out. A week later the engagement was called off.

I n spring the entire family traveled in a caravan to Chicago for the annual atheists' convention and checked into a two-level suite at the Hyatt Hotel near O'Hare Airport. I was not thrilled with the prospect of devoting four days listening to propaganda, so I quickly numbed myself at the nearest bar.

Valerie was pregnant, and of late I had refrained from excessive drinking. But the atheists debating and cavorting at the convention forced me to find an escape. A bottle provided one.

The second day in Chicago I got up in the middle of the night to go to the bathroom and fell headfirst down a spiral stairway to the lower level of the suite. I had been drinking heavily earlier in the evening, and had I been completely sober, I probably would have broken my neck. The next day I had to drink even harder to ease the aches and pain from the fall.

As always the highlight of the convention was to be the selection of the atheist and the religious hypocrite of the year. (The atheist of the year award normally went to the person who had contributed the most financially.) This year Mother was pushing hard to have a nun, who had become pregnant and had aborted her baby late in pregnancy, named the religious hypocrite. This announcement would of course be distributed to the news media. This irritated me, and I finally headed off the nomination. I really believed that by belittle-ing that poor nun my mother was actually belittling herself. She reluctantly changed her mind and selected Eldridge

Cleaver instead. With this, my only serious involvement with the convention ended.

Back in Austin, Mother immediately became involved in another newsworthy incident. One evening she went to hear Robin play in a band concert at Robin's junior high. The woman PTA president announced she would open the evening with prayer, and Mother stood up and walked to the front, objecting. As some in the crowd booed, a bit of shoving ensued, and Mother later charged the PTA president with assault. Robin must have been embarrassed.

During the summer of 1977 I negotiated the purchase for the Society of a brand new 10,000-square foot office building, which we named the American Atheist Center. Mother called a news conference and announced a new lineup of upcoming legal actions, including suits to remove "In God We Trust" from U.S. coins and to drop "under God" from the country's pledge of allegiance. Mother was quoted as saying that President Carter was a great aid to the atheist cause because "he keeps smiling and putting his foot in his mouth and quoting those idiocies, because the Bible is an idiotic book."

The more spacious quarters did not stop the family fights, though. Mother and Garth argued daily about his personal life, and the bickering between Mother and her brother escalated to the level of violence. During my absence in Houston my uncle Irv—John Mays—had been recruited by Mother to replace me. After Grandmother had died in Hawaii, Irv had moved to California where in 1975 he had been involved in an industrial accident in San Francisco. When his workman's compensation payments had expired, he had contacted my mother for help. She had refused, but Irv had threatened to tell the world about her attempted defection to the Soviet Union, among other things.

The deal they had finally struck was typical of an atheist family. Mother had promised Irv a job for life. In return he had agreed to sign a document confessing to fraud. If he ever would say anything "against" Mother, she would release the document. Irv also had agreed to hand over his final settlement money from his accident.

Irv worked in the mailroom at the Medical Parkway building. Madalyn had given him the privilege of sharing a small three-room house with her now estranged husband. Richard and Madalyn's divorce was to be finalized within a few months. He had sued for half the property, and she had settled his demand by giving him a "life trust" in one of the Society's old houses.

It was Irv who gave me the gruesome details of Dick's unattended illness in the summer of 1977.

"Bill, the old S.O.B. sits in the kitchen, working on those little trains he has. He is in so much pain he bought an old motor cycle innertube to sit on in that chair. He can't eat. The kitchen and his room stink to high h__. Bill, there is blood everywhere. He s__ blood. He doesn't want to see a doctor because they'll put him in the hospital."

"My G__ Irv. Madalyn knows about this, doesn't she?"

"Bill, I've told her a hundred times. The last two days he hasn't been out of bed. He drinks himself half unconscious and does his other business in the bed. Man, does that place stink. I gotta live here. You know, your mother hasn't paid me a dime since I got here. You got to get her to get him out of there so that place can be cleaned up."

I was nauseated just hearing about this. I quickly went to see Mother, and our conversation was not pleasant. I told her that Richard was on the Society's property, and if he died from lack of care, somebody was going to pay dearly in court. If his real children from a previous marriage didn't sue, there was always the possibility of a manslaughter charge.

That night Dick was removed by ambulance. The diagnosis didn't take long: cancer of the colon, and the disease had spread to other parts of his body.

The next day Mother called Garth and me to her office and told us of Dick's illness. But to my amazement that was not all she had on her mind.

"Boys, the divorce is off," she said. "We have to find some way to block the formal decree. I've been on the phone with the V.A. If the old f__ dies before the divorce is final, it's worth a fortune. Since Richard and I adopted Robin, the V.A. will pay her college expenses. Between his veteran's benefits and my widow's share from Social Security, I'll get as much as $800 a month tax free."

"G__, Mother," I said, "just let him die."

She gave me a sour look but said nothing.

Garth was directed to buy the best portable color TV available and take it to Richard's hospital room as a "peace offering." A letter also was sent out to the Society's larger contributors asking for sympathy and financial help with medical fees. No mention was made that the V.A. was paying the bills.

Money was a continuing source of problems. Mother's outrageous spending habits led to conflicts that involved nearly everyone at the Society. For example, just a few days prior to a payroll, she might make some lavish expenditure on Garth or herself. Then on payday she would call the staff together to announce that the payroll could not be met.

Most of the funds received from wills of dead members were squandered. In 1977 a Society check for nearly $20,000 was written to purchase my brother a new Cadillac Seville. That same week the payroll could not be met in its entirety.

In the middle of this madness I was introduced to Rev. Bob Harrington, the "chaplain of Bourbon Street" in New Orleans. Bob and my mother had met and debated on several occasions. For the most part these debates had been arranged by local radio personalities in Texas and Louisiana.

During one such debate in Dallas I had a conversation with Bob's business manager, Zonnya LaFerney, and the subject of commercializing the debates came up. We decided the prospect was worth pursuing, so two weeks later I flew to New Orleans to talk with Bob directly.

I was extremely impressed by his offices. The walls were covered with framed photographs of Bob with mayors, Bob with governors, and even Bob with presidents. His gold records were displayed in his private office. Bob's headquarters were about the same size as ours in Austin. There was a small print shop, a sound studio, and considerable computer equipment. The main difference was that Bob had a chapel. He explained to me that this place for worship must remain a secret because New Orleans had an ordinance prohibiting churches on Bourbon Street.

Bob and I agreed to a forty-five/fifty-five split after expenses of all income from the debates we were to hold between him and my mother. I agreed to allow him the fifty-five percent because I believed that eighty-five to ninety percent of the total revenue would come from people whom Bob attracted. We both felt that the average amount given by each person would be increased by my mother's presence as the "devil," so to speak.

When I returned to Austin and explained the arrangements, Mother was furious.

"You fool," she screamed at me. "I'm the one who will get the fifty-five percent, and it will be of the gross, not the net. I'm Madalyn Murray O'Hair, *the atheist.* I'll be the number one attraction people come to see. Why, I could do this with any preacher!"

Actually, I agreed with her but pointed out that I had Bob's commitment for one hundred percent of the financing. I assured her I could work the deal she wanted if we would offer to provide half the funds and share the risk. In the end Mother agreed to the forty-five/fifty-five split, with a $1,000 per night minimum for her.

The debates began the first week in August in Tennessee. From the beginning, each debate followed the same pattern. Advertisements, which announced a "Fight to the Finish" between the "demon-directed damsel" and "the chaplain of Bourbon Street," were run in local newspapers several days before each debate. Often Bob and Madalyn would arrive a day early to give interviews and appear on talk shows. The controversy and publicity produced a sizable crowd, the vast majority present being vehemently opposed to my mother. It was quite a show—more similar to a professional wrestling match than a debate.

A gospel band had been hired to stir the emotions of the crowd with familiar patriotic and religious tunes. When the spectators were warmed up and eager, an announcer would introduce Bob and my mother as though it were a prize fight—and they did make their entrance from opposite sides. Mother would speak first, inciting the audience with comments that derided God and the Bible. Predictably, she was booed and hooted. One night when the crowd was particularly nasty she said, "You're very rude, but that's to be expected from Christians." A man in the audience with a foghorn voice yelled back, "Praise the Lord!" The delighted crowd roared with laughter.

About the time Mother had said enough to prompt a crowd to consider lynching her, she would leave and Bob would take over. He, too, said little about his beliefs but spun off cute one-liners, such as "You people here who don't know God better get saved—look who you're going to hell with!" And, "Madalyn will be back out—she's just backstage getting her horns sharpened." The crowd loved this, and Bob ended his opening remarks by having the audience stand to recite the pledge of allegience. When the assembly reached the phrase "under God," on cue Mother dashed back on stage, and obviously enraged, tried to wrestle the microphone away from Bob. Supposedly she could not bear to hear those offensive words that violated her most hallowed principle: separation of church and state.

This usually drove the crowd berserk, and then Bob and Madalyn began the actual debate, which was more an extended exchange of insults. "You're all a bunch of fools," Madalyn would yell at the audience. Bob would chime in, "Well, if we are, we're fools for the Lord!" The crowd loved this and applauded and cheered until the walls shook. Sometimes the entire audience would chant, "We're fools for Christ, we're fools for Christ."

After an hour or more of this, Bob would mention that Madalyn, the "demon-directed damsel," was preparing the lawsuits to bar God from America's coins and the pledge. He planned to fight her at every point and that would take money. Envelopes were distributed and persons could "vote" for Bob ("God and country") or Madalyn ("No God and no country") by inserting coins, bills, or checks.

I attended the first few debates. I admired Bob for his

gold records and for his life story. Twenty years earlier he had been a top salesman, but his personal life had been plagued by problems, including one with drinking. Then Bob had become a Christian at a revival meeting in Alabama. Later he had become nationally known as a fiery foe of evil on New Orleans' infamous Bourbon Street.

My admiration for Bob was related to what I thought was his ability to stay off the bottle. I was relying heavily on alcohol to overcome (or escape) the confrontations with my mother, and I respected anyone who could stop drinking. Unfortunately, my regard for Bob disintegrated in Nashville when I went to his suite to help count the money. Bob opened a fresh bottle of Jack Daniel's and poured us each a drink.

The Nashville debate led to extensive bad publicity, especially for Bob. A local newspaper was suspicious of the whole spectacle and assigned a reporter to cover several of the later debates. His page 1 story three weeks later reported that the debates all had a similar pattern, including many of the same lines repeated exactly each time. Several more stories were written and finally the newspaper printed an editorial entitled "The Bob and Madalyn Show Is a Deplorable Thing." The editorial said in part, "Rehearsed like a soft-shoe routine, manipulated for money's sake, it is a debasing performance, a mocking of deeply held spiritual beliefs."

Other newspapers picked up this story, and thereafter the crowds declined. The show never again was quite as free wheeling and entertaining.

Bob rode the debate circuit in a large Double Eagle bus that was worth $150,000 and had been loaned to him by Larry Flynt, publisher of *Hustler* magazine. Coincidentally, Mother was involved in a lawsuit against Flynt at the time, and I think she was jealous of Bob's elegant rolling quarters. I was directed to purchase a thirty-foot Executive RV. This seemed a wise decision because the debates were making over $10,000 a week, but Mother had to pay her own travel and living expenses.

Indirectly, that RV contributed more to the final breakup

between Mother and me than any other factor. Mother had decided to send Robin to a private school in Arizona. I suspected that she did not want her associating with Val and me while she was touring with Harrington. I was thoroughly disillusioned and realized that when Robin left, I would have no reason to stay in Austin.

The week before Robin was to leave for Tucson, she, Valerie, and I drove Mother's new RV on a shakedown trip to Galveston. Mother and Garth planned to leave for another Harrington debate when we returned.

The three of us got back to Austin on a Friday night, and I stayed up late to wash the fitted sheets for the beds and to clean and refuel the rig. The next morning when I gave Mother the keys, she went in the RV, yanked all the sheets off the beds, and threw them in a heap on Valerie's desk. She attached a nasty note that stated in obscene terms that she would not sleep on sheets that might have been soiled by Val and me during sexual intercourse.

The note enraged me. I was completely fed up with Mother's ongoing attempts to demean my wife. I went to Mother's office red hot. "What the h__ is wrong with you?" I asked.

"I don't need your s___, Bill," she answered. "As far as I'm concerned you and that b__ of yours with that Rosemary's baby she is carrying can get out of here. *I'm* this organization," she said. "I'm Madalyn Murray O'Hair. I make $10,000 a week on the road with Harrington to run this place, and you don't do s___."

I turned and walked out of her office, stopping only long enough to kick my foot through a glass aquarium in her outer office. The water and fish poured out onto the carpet. I could hear her saying as I got Val and left the building, "My poor f___fish. That b__ is a nut. Someone call the cops."

It took two weeks for Mother to realize that I wasn't coming back. With no one to manage the office in her absence, problems cropped up and she started another controversy by firing the computer operator and then publicly announcing that the girl had stolen her mailing list. Interestingly, Mother then sent a newsletter, complete with computer labels, to her entire mailing list telling her supporters that the mailing list had been stolen.

In the midst of this commotion my daughter, Jade Amber Murray, was born. Somehow I had found the time to attend childbirth classes with Valerie, and we had chosen the Leboyer method. With this procedure the child is born naturally in normal room light rather than in the brilliance of a delivery room.

On Monday, October 10, Valerie began her labor. I drove her thirty miles north of Austin to the Georgetown hospital. At the time there were no hospitals in Austin that allowed a "natural" birth.

Valerie used no anesthesia, and early Tuesday morning Jade was born in a private room of the hospital. Less than ten minutes after her birth, the doctor handed her to me to bathe in warm water. Jade barely cried. I looked at her pretty little face and recalled the rotten thing her grandmother had said before her birth. Thinking of the way I had been treated and cursed for as long as I could remember, I could not stand the idea of her grandmother getting near her. I promised myself that the life of this sweet child would not be destroyed by Madalyn Murray O'Hair. I swore that Madalyn would never see, touch, or speak to Jade. There was no reason to allow her to destroy another human life.

I was not yet willing to believe, though, that all atheists were like Mother. Perhaps to prove this to myself, I decided to give the nonbelievers of the world one last chance. From personal correspondence I had the names and addresses of about 400 of my mother's 1,200 members. I wrote to them asking for support of positive rather than negative atheism. I suggested we use funds to establish atheist chairs at universities rather than to sue to have religious chairs removed. I recommended the construction of monuments and hospital wings.

A handful of people sent contributions out of habit. But the overwhelming majority of those who answered my letter pelted me with such abuse that I was stunned. Over and over I read that the principal goal of atheism was the destruction of religion and that this was no time to build.

During this same time my mother and brother were involved in defending themselves against lawsuits brought about by my mother's accusations against her employees just before I left Austin. Garth testified from the witness stand that he had seen me in a state of D.T.'s, even though he knew that was untrue. My mother wrote letters accusing me of being a heroin addict, and Garth said I was a homosexual. To stop me from having any contact with family members back north, my mother told them Valerie was black and that Jade was a "deformed idiot with one eye."

As I read about or heard of these things, I was infuriated but determined not to be drawn into an open battle with Mother.

It agitated me, though, that my brother and Mother seemed to have a favored legal position in the United States. They could libel or slander someone without appearing to have any fear. Mother's victims saw the courts favor her so often they did not even sue. It appeared to me that in this nation someone in her position could attack the government and its policies and avoid answering for behavior that otherwise would be questioned. For the authorities to prosecute such outspoken dissidents was to risk the charges of government "persecution" and "harassment."

Then (and now) my mother and brother lived in expensive homes owned by the alleged nonprofit Society of Separationists. They were paying no rent nor did they pay federal taxes for the value of the benefits they receive from the Society. Of course, both drove luxury cars owned by that same organization.

Radio, television, and newspapers continued to report both my mother's and brother's outrageous and obviously false accusations against me. Yet not one of these news orgainzations had the courage to report the truth about her activities.

But my rejection by the atheists was the final straw. I

could see no future in Austin. I placed our furniture in storage, and left town for Tucson. Valerie, Jade, and I arrived there about November 1. The first thing we did was visit Robin. For some reason I wanted to open a bookstore, which I did five miles from Robin's private school.

I did not realize how far I had slipped from reality in Austin. My ability to make business judgments had been severely damaged by my experiences with my mother. In addition I was now drinking nightly, oblivious to my self-destructive urges. The bookstore venture was doomed by simple customer traffic patterns, but I was too removed from reality to know it.

I named the new business the Jarob Bookstore (after Jade and Robin) and opened its door exactly thirty days before Christmas. I thought the Christmas rush would generate success. It did not. In fact the daily revenue never approached half of that needed for a break-even situation.

By mid-January I came face to face with failure. I told Valerie we would have to give up not only the store but our house as well. I would have to go back to Houston to find work with the aid of friends there. I used the last of my cash to send Jade and Valerie to Hawaii for a visit with her parents.

Perhaps what hurt the most was the fact that now I would be an embarrassment to Robin the way my Mother had been to me. I was going to have to bankrupt a business I had in part named after her.

A close friend of mine with Texas International Airlines promised me a position at the company's headquarters in Houston. I arrived in Houston with just a few hundred dollars and the knowledge that my new job would not start for six weeks. Just renting a small apartment on a month-to-month basis took most of my funds.

As I had two years before, I went to work selling cars to make ends meet until I could start the job with Texas International. In March Valerie and Jade joined me in Houston. No sooner had they arrived, than a call came from my friend. At Texas International they were playing management musical chairs, and he had been told to resign. Without his support, my chance for the $30,000 a year position was gone. I found a sales position with a word processing equipment manufacturer. The draw against my sales was only $1,000 a month. This just didn't cover the monthly obligations Valerie and I had. The rent and payments on the car and bank cards used up most of my take-home pay.

For the first time in my adult life I was nearly penniless. My printing equipment was gone and my furniture was sold. My frustration fed my hatred for my mother, her organization, and the people in it. I despised both my brother and mother. I concluded they no longer needed me now, after my business experience had built their little empire. It was easy to understand why Mother didn't want me around Austin. She had created the conflict over Valerie's then unborn child, intending to drive me out. I had been a threat to her throne. When I had been rebuilding her organization from a three-room, dirty office to a million dollar center she hadn't felt like queen of the mountain. Now with Bill Murray gone, she was once again the undisputed savior of the atheist world. I thought of her and Garth as two fat pigs waiting for the spike and wished them both the worst of everything.

Now when I drank late at night I poured shots of cheap bourbon, not Chivas Regal. I longed for revenge. I knew there had to be some retribution in the universe. Atheism, humanism, Marxism—each of these ideologies, I told myself, represented organized self-worship. In the midst of the "isms" was the great Madalyn Murray O'Hair, building her self-esteem.

In March I saw a note in the newspaper that told of Richard O'Hair's death. I did not even consider attending the funeral. I had no desire to witness again the same type of shenanigans that had surrounded Grandfather's death fifteen years ago. I remembered how Mother had voided the divorce with Richard, not for reasons of compassion or love but as a way of grabbing some government benefits. Yet it was this cold, selfish way of treating others that supposedly represented the beautiful, free atheistic life.

I still had some business sense, so I moved my family into an inexpensive four-room house that had only one window air conditioner.

Several months of struggle passed. I desperately wanted to return to the aviation industry that I had now been away from for three years. Finally, in August, the break came. I received word from a friend that a commuter airline, Universal Airways, was hiring at Hobby Airport.

I was hired by the Houston station manager, a lovable, overweight, retired Air Force master sergeant named Bill Simms. In less than sixty days I became Bill's superior when Tom Evans, the company's president, appointed me director of operations. When this happened, I thought that Bill, who had become my close friend, would be angry. But he only smiled and told me he had expected this from the day I was hired.

Before my promotion I had talked Tom into hiring Valerie as a reservationist. Now, once again, Valerie and I were working together.

Not until I moved into my office did I realize how deep a pit I had stepped into by accepting this position. Tom Evans ran Universal Airways the way my mother ran the Society of Separationists. Whatever doubts I may have had that there was distinct evil in the world were snuffed out by Tom Evans. I could not involve myself in many of the personal activities he dabbled in. Only his wealth, which I didn't share, kept him out of trouble.

I was not a model of virtue, of course, and now had a very serious problem with alcohol. I drank with Tom, and one night after he chug-a-lugged a pint of brandy, he tried to molest one of the girls who worked with Val. Because of the amount of money Tom paid me, I looked the other way. I hated him for what he did, and I hated myself for letting him get away with it. My anger from this incident caused me to stay off alcohol for weeks. But I couldn't stay away for good. I didn't have the strength.

One day while driving home from work the truth struck me. I thought, *There has to be a God because there certainly is a devil. I have met him, talked to him, and touched him. He is the personification of evil. He is Tom Evans, my mother, and others like them I have known.*

When I told Val of my thoughts a shocked look crossed her face. She told me she had hoped that one day I would believe and that she had never forsaken God, even during our experiences in Austin.

In January of 1979 I was told to open stations in New Orleans and Gulfport, Mississippi. This increased to six the cities Universal served in Texas, Louisiana, and now, Mississippi. I asked Bill Simms to take the position of regional manager over New Orleans and Gulfport.

To carry traffic on the new routes, Tom Evans leased a Queenair with executive configuration to make the six daily roundtrips between Gulfport and New Orleans. There was much excitement when the aircraft, a twin-engine craft with the identification 777 AE, was delivered to Houston. But when I climbed on board for the first time, a terrible chill spread over me. The thought pounded in my mind, *Beware of this ship, Bill; people will die aboard her.* From that moment I was afraid to fly in that plane.

The first week of February I flew to Gulfport to see Bill Simms and inspect the facilities he had set up. I was scheduled to return to New Orleans on the last flight of the day, but 777 AE's left engine would not start and the flight was cancelled.

Later that night Bill Simms and I went to the hanger to check on how the mechanic was doing with the repairs. My friend saw something and motioned to me impatiently.

"Bill, look at this. Look at this cargo door," he said.

The mechanic had left the door open while rotating the prop. There were large slice marks in the door where it had been hit.

"Bill," I said, "that could bring her down if it happened in the air. Make sure two men check that door before each departure to see that it's locked. I'll check on a modification when I get back to Houston."

I returned to Houston and consulted with our chief mechanic, who assured me it was impossible for the prop to rotate if the door was open. There was a safety switch activated by the door; when the door was open, no power could go to the starter. "Then how did the prop dents get in the door?" I asked. The mechanic shrugged his shoulders. He didn't know.

I checked the Aviation Directives from the FAA on Queenairs with the Excalibure modification to the engines. I discovered something. A plane owned by Ross Airlines in Arizona had gone down. The nose bin door had opened in flight, hitting a prop just after takeoff. The pilot had lost control and everyone on board had died. I directed my personnel to take all precautions, then asked Evans to ground the ship.

He laughed and said, "We're insured."

I was shocked. Then he said he was kidding and would order a modification. He laughed again and told me he was promoting me to assistant general manager. I was just one of his playthings, one of the devil's toys.

Evans did not make the additional modification I wanted made to the airplane, as he believed that the safety switch installed by Excalibure was adequate. I suggested that the cargo doors be welded shut, thus eliminating any possibility that they would open while the plane was airborne. Evans vetoed my idea, because the airline could haul revenue-producing freight in those compartments.

On February 28 Tom Evans and I became intoxicated at the same time. During an ensuing argument over 777 AE among other things, I told him I didn't want his job anymore. The next morning Bill Simms called me.

"Bill, you really didn't quit did you? he asked.

"Bill," I said, "that man is crazy. I'll starve before I'll work for him. I suppose you know some others quit this morning when they found out."

"I know, Bill," he said. "I'm headed back to Houston today. Evans thinks I'm coming back to take your job. Bill, I can't. I don't know what I'll do."

That afternoon all seven seats were full when 777 AE

lifted off the runway at Gulfport. Since the aircraft weighed less than 12,500 pounds, the FAA did not require a co-pilot. Because of that, Universal did not have any. Bill rode in the co-pilot's seat next to Universal's newest pilot, an ex-Navy fighter pilot. It was his first flight with passengers.

As the aircraft nose rotated up, the nose bin door popped open. The pilot cut the power on the left engine to idle and called the tower to say he was coming back. His landing gear still down, he turned into his good engine. Lift was lost, and the stall warning indicator sounded. The right wing pitched down. Struggling to gain control, the pilot drove his foot so hard onto the left peddle that he bent part of the mechanism. It was too late. With inadequate power to recover, the Queenair went into a full stall and plummeted to the ground with killing force. There was no fire. Only the passenger sitting in the last seat in the rear survived the crash, but he died forty-eight hours later from internal injuries. My friend Bill had taken his last flight.

I wanted to kill Tom Evans, because I blamed him almost totally for the crash. I also felt guilty myself. I could not shake the belief that not welding the nose bin door shut was the cause of the accident. But before I could take care of Evans, I had to help bury Bill. Both Tom and I had been asked to be pallbearers at Bill's funeral. Tom arrived late, having been delayed in traffic. As I helped carry Bill's coffin to the grave, I asked myself, *Why a good man? Why not Tom Evans? Why not my mother? Why not me? God, this is not right!*

I didn't have to kill Evans. In the fall of 1981 he was riding a sister ship of 777 AE on a flight from Houston to Dallas when a wing mysteriously fell off. Tom was thrown clear of the aircraft before it crashed and burned. There were no survivors.

The day after the crash that killed Bill Simms, I was hired as director of passenger services with Commutair, another commuter air carrier that operated out of Hobby Airport in Houston.

My emotions were still raw from the loss of my friend and the horrible tragedy. In the aftermath of the crash I was also extremely frightened, because I could not drag from my memory what action I had taken concerning the Aviation Directive on 777 AE. I blamed this memory block on the drinking episode that had ended in the early hours the day the aircraft went down. I was appalled that alcohol could affect my mind this way. Because of this I did not even look at a beer, much less drink one for three weeks.

During this period in March when I didn't drink, I realized how severe my dependence on alcohol had become. Each day I thirsted for a drink. I wanted to escape from the reality of who and what I was.

When I had quit at Universal, Valerie and two other reservationists had also left. I had become a close acquaintance of the Hughes Air West station manager at Hobby Airport, and as a favor, I asked him to interview the three girls. I did not tell him that one of the three was my wife, but he hired her.

Val left for California on April 1 to begin training for her new job. That evening, as I played with little Jade, I felt lonely and depressed. I could not rid myself of a foreboding that Val's new job would lead to the destruction of my family.

I thought getting drunk might help banish my fears, but that was impossible since I had to care for my two-year-old. Still I had to do something, so I went instead to one of the clubs for alcoholics in the Houston area. I thought I could learn there why I wanted to drink. I took Jade, who sat on my lap.

Before the meeting began I reflected that I must be an unusual candidate for Alcoholics Anonymous. I had not had a drink in almost thirty days and held a high level management position. My family lived in a nice townhouse near the airport. I had money in the bank and a wallet full of credit cards. My status did not match my image of an alcoholic.

As the discussion started, I noticed a small cross hanging on the wall and wondered what it had to do with conquering alcoholism. During the evening I learned that people drink for many reasons. A few of the "reasons" have some validity, but the others are just poor excuses. I learned, too, that only through reliance on God would I be able to conquer the drinking problem, even on a temporary basis. I pondered this idea for a while. I now found it relatively easy to accept the concept of a good God who could solve troubles and problems. There had to be good, because I had looked into the eyes of evil. There had to be a God, because I had held hands with the devil.

When the meeting ended, the group of about forty people all stood and recited the Lord's Prayer. Holding a sleepy Jade gently against my chest, I, too, repeated those words for the first time since I had been a schoolboy in Baltimore.

In the days that followed I heeded the instructions given at the meeting. To my surprise and joy I discovered that I could live without alcohol. I gave credit for this to God—who seemed to me to be a kind of "big buddy." I did not know His true nature or that He really existed and could be known intimately. I continued to attend the AA meetings, where I met men and women from all levels of society. I now knew that both the hard hat and the doctor shared this problem that cursed all levels of society.

As my head started to clear, I began to comprehend more

of what was happening around me. My productivity at work increased. In many ways I was a new man.

The past two or three years I had spent many (if not most) of my evenings drinking while watching television. Now the television shows bored me. One day while driving to work I was reflecting on how great I felt. The thought hit me: *How many of the sons and daughters of people like my mother had there been in history? How many were there now and how many would there be? How many people could I help out of lives of misery by sharing what had happened to me? Then, too, I thought, shouldn't America know the truth? How could I tell Americans that a huge portion of their history and heritage was lost because one woman could not admit to sin and failure and had decided to fight God?*

I had never intended to write a book on the subject, but suddenly I had plenty of spare time. So I started to write the truth—as I viewed it—about the previous fifteen years. Valerie had returned from her training and was now happily involved with her new job and new friends. Because we had only one car, I drove Val to work at 5:00 A.M., then dropped Jade at a daycare center at 6:30. I was in my office at 7:00 A.M., well ahead of anyone else. Before long Val began working double shifts almost daily. That meant I would pick up Jade at 5:00 P.M. and then go back for Valerie around 11:00 P.M. or midnight.

Valerie was at home so little that I don't think she realized I had not had a drink in nearly four months. This was my longest stretch without a drink since basic training in the army.

Because we were together so little, Val and I began to drift apart. The long days at work and caring for Jade drained us both, and incidents or disagreements that would have been minor irritations under normal conditions became sources of serious squabbling between us.

On a July evening in 1979, Val called me earlier than usual at about 8:00 P.M. and asked to be picked up. When we got home we argued for a few minutes, but she was so exhausted she threw up her hands and collapsed in bed.

I stayed up for a while and fumed. The more I thought about the state of my relationship with Val, the more angry I became. Finally, I found the checkbook, gathered up Jade, and stormed out of the house, intending to buy some snack food at a nearby grocery store. When I arrived at the store I was still raging mad. I noticed that next door to the grocery was a brightly lit liquor store. Without hesitating I entered the store and bought a fifth of scotch.

I drove home, put Jade in bed, then placed the bottle, a glass, and some ice on the kitchen table. I poured a double and took a long swallow. I had decided that Val must not like the sober, good-natured Bill Murray, so I would give her the other kind.

I stayed up most of the night drinking and nursing my frustration, anger, and bitterness with life. Filled with self-pity, I blamed Mother, Garth, Evans, Val, others—even God—for working overtime to make me miserable. I placed the manuscript I had been writing in front of me, and as the hours passed, I slowly shredded the 200 typed pages into tiny strips.

The next morning when Val got up, I was terribly drunk and in a very bad mood.

"What's wrong, Bill?" she asked.

"I'm having a few drinks."

"But why?"

"Because my mother is right. There is no God. It is all a bunch of s___. If there is a God, all He does is s___ on people anyway," I said.

"Does God make you drink like this? It seems to me you are pretty good at making your own problems." She turned and stomped from the room.

I followed her out, and we continued to argue viciously all morning. The fight ended at 11:00 when I physically threw Valerie out the front door. After not having a taste of alcohol in over four months, I had managed to drink an entire fifth in less than twelve hours.

I finally fell asleep in early afternoon but was awakened within an hour or so by the sound of metal clicking around the front door. My first thought was that Valerie had come back with a friend, maybe even a boyfriend, since I thought she might be cheating on me. In my drunken stupor I thought he might be armed. I took my Ruger automatic rifle from the shelf, slipped a shell in the chamber, and walked to the living room. I began to shake when I saw a man's hand just inside the door working to disconnect the chainlock.

I lifted the rifle and said, "Get out or I'll shoot." The hand remained, and I fired a warning shot through the top of the door.

Jade heard the noise and ran into the room crying.

"Come on, honey," I said. "You have to get dressed; we have to get out of here."

The phone rang. It was the police.

"How did you find out about this so fast?" I was stunned. I didn't know yet that the hand through my door belonged to a cop. Valerie had brought the police, not a friend.

"It was us you shot at. Come out with your hands up," the voice said sternly on the other end of the line.

I immediately called my attorney, Paul McGuffy, hoping he could negotiate the situation. The police were not interested. Finally, when Paul arrived, I surrendered and was taken to police headquarters.

When the police learned that I had a clean record, I was taken to a basement cell. One of the officers said, "The S.O.B. is clean. He'll get off without a day."

I knew I was about to pay for shooting at a cop. My arms were cuffed behind me at the wrists. One policeman gripped me by the neck. Another then beat me with a billy club in the stomach and the knees, and a third pounded his knee between my legs. They made me remove my shoes, then took turns stomping my bare feet.

The next day Ross Christian, the president of Commutair, and my attorney bailed me out. Ross was appalled by my condition. Paul, on the other hand, knew what went on at that time in the Houston Police Department. He was only surprised by the number of visible marks that showed on my body. "Normally they don't make it so obvious," he said. The two of them supported my arms so I could walk.

I asked Ross to drive me to the bank so I could reimburse him for the bail money. When I arrived, I was told my joint savings account was empty. Valerie had cleaned the money out after being advised to do so by one of the policemen who had come to the townhouse to get me. The cop had then asked her for a date.

The newspaper account didn't help my cause. The headline read, "Son of atheist tries to kill cop. Mother said he was always bad." No newspaper or TV station reported anything after that.

It turned out the prosecution had as many legal problems as I did. After all, a policeman minus a search warrant had tried to break into my home without identifying himself. In the process he had been shot at. These facts, combined with the injuries I had sustained, did not contribute to a strong case for the prosecution.

At my attorney's advice, during the next few weeks I tried to reconcile with Valerie. He told me we needed her testimony that the cop had tried to force open the door. Valerie was noncommittal. She wasn't sure she wanted to continue our relationship.

Finally, the district attorney offered to reduce the charge from attempted murder to simple assault if I would plead guilty to that charge. Paul explained to me that they would not let me off the hook completely because I would have grounds to sue the individuals involved as well as the city. I accepted the offer and eventually received a sentence of five years probation. Later the indictment and my guilty plea were both withdrawn. As far as the state was concerned, the incident had never happened.

I believed that my return to alcohol surely meant that God wanted nothing more to do with me, and in fact He had punished me with the incident involving Valerie and the police. As in the past I wanted to get "even" with the police and others. This lust for revenge overshadowed any inclination on my part to learn if God still wanted to help me. Once again I wanted to try to solve my problems by running away from them.

I began to look for employment outside Texas, confident

that with my aviation experience I could find something. I mailed 200 letters with resumes to department heads of commuter airlines and obtained interviews from airlines in Arizona, Alaska, and California.

Ultimately I was asked to become manager of the hub station for one of the largest commuter airlines in the country, Air Pacific. The job was in San Francisco, and I was eager to begin because Air Pacific had just obtained a new De Haviland Dash—7. The high wing, four-engine, fifty passenger aircraft intrigued me. Air Pacific was one of the first airlines to use the new plane.

Valerie decided to stay in Houston with Jade. Even though she had worked for Hughes Air West for less than six months, she did not want to lose the security of her union position. Our marriage was threatening to collapse.

After I arrived in San Francisco in August, I tried again to regain the euphoria and self-control I had experienced months before when I had first heard that God would give the power to lead a life free of compulsive behavior. I believed God—if he was really there—could do that, but I could not stop smoking several packs of cigarettes a day and constantly fought the desire to drink alcohol. My emotions climbed and dipped like a roller coaster. I wanted to please God with "good" behavior but seemed powerless to maintain any consistency.

I would not touch alcohol for weeks and would even attend church, trying to learn more about God. Then some crisis in my work or with Valerie would turn me off, and I would blame God and run away from Him. I would drink and smoke more than ever for a week or so, then burdened with guilt, wind up back in church. I didn't realize yet that God required more from me than just good intentions.

Once I attended a Unitarian Church. I talked to the minister about my dilemma and the problems I was having with my faith. He crisply told me I would have to find a solution within myself, because in all probability there was no God who answered prayer.

I tried earnestly to accept Christ intellectually. But even

attending three different Christian churches didn't work. There seemed to be some barrier I could not cross. Something was missing in my life.

Valerie and I still argued violently over the phone. I had placed the full blame on her for the incident with the police in Houston and had taken none myself.

In one fit of rage, brought on because no publisher would even look at a second manuscript I had written on the prayer case, I burned it. I wanted so much for the book to be of help to others, but faced with rejection, I destroyed the manuscript—making certain no one would benefit from it. I wasn't aware how selfish and self-defeating this was.

My anger with Mother would rekindle, too, when I heard or read of some of her activities. In September 1979 she and Garth filed a suit against, of all people, Pope John Paul II. Mother had sued Billy Graham some years before, accusing him of slandering her on a television show (the case was later dropped), but suing the Pope seemed to me to be even more ridiculous. Pope John was about to visit the United States, and Mother had become incensed because that "vicious and unprincipled man" was going to celebrate the "stupid, archaic" mass on public land. The Secretary of the Interior and the U.S. Parks Service were also named in the suit because a mass was to be held in a park between the Capitol and the Washington Monument in Washington, D.C.

I was not surprised that Mother was tangling with the Roman Catholic church and the Pope—she had for years despised them both because of her relationship with my father. But this issue seemed nonsensical. The courts apparently agreed, and the suit was dismissed. The Pope appeared to have an enjoyable visit, saying mass for thousands assembled in public places.

Just days before Christmas in 1979, I finally decided to read a book I had purchased some months before, *Dear and Glorious Physician*. I had read most of Taylor Caldwell's books, but not this one.

I was immediately intrigued with the book and read it rapidly. I identified strongly with its main character, Lucanas. He was not an atheist but had carried anger toward God since his childhood. His anger, though, was turned to love as he searched for and found God in Jesus Christ. By the time I finished the book, I would have willingly changed places in history with Lucanas, or as the Bible refers to him, Luke.

I was also affected by the fact that it was nearly Christmas, but being alone, I was not caught up in the holiday rush. I was free to observe the activities of the season and ponder their meaning. I noted that the cheerful shoppers were a far cry from the sick drunks puking in the gutters. I saw the beautiful, well-kept, clean churches I attended. In contrast was the filth in some of the bars.

Santa Claus stood outside the downtown Macy's collecting for the needy, while a few blocks away near the Hilton Hotel male and female hookers sold their services. Once again I could not ignore the existence of good and evil, of life and death, of God and Satan.

On Christmas Eve I boarded a flight to Houston where I planned to be with Valerie and Jade. In hand I had a copy of *Dear and Glorious Physician* for Valerie. The flight had a mechanical problem in Las Vegas, and while we were grounded for four hours, I got drunk and lost the book.

During the first week of January, two officers of Capitol Airways showed up in my office. After some opening pleasantries, they told me they were there to recruit me as station manager for their proposed operation at the San Francisco Airport. It was immensely satisfying to know that I had built a reputation that had led to an unsolicited job offer. Capitol was not a commuter but an international jet carrier. At once I knew I would accept the offer.

My career seemed to be on the upswing—perhaps I was a "comer." But I seemed to be a failure at doing the things I thought would make me a "good Christian." I attended church now and then, but I also got drunk now and then. I believed there was a God, and to a degree, I thought prayer worked. But many of the teachings of the Bible were not understandable to me, and I did not even own a Bible. I believed that Jesus had been a good man and great teacher who had decided to give his life so that others could have hope. I did not consider him to be God or the one who had conquered death by rising from the grave. My understanding of Christ was off base. Unknown to me there was still a great conflict raging within me, a war over my soul.

Then, on the night of January 24, 1980, an unusual event changed my life. I went to bed and, not long after falling asleep, experienced a consuming nightmare of unmentionable horror. Suddenly, the nightmare was sliced in half by a mighty, gleaming sword of gold and silver. The two halves of the nightmare peeled back as if a black and white photograph had been cut in half. A great winged angel stood with the sword in his hand. The blade of the sword pointed down, making it resemble a cross. On the sword's hilt were inscribed the words "IN HOC SIGNO VINCE." The tip of the sword's blade touched an open Bible.

Then I awoke, realizing that my quest for the truth would end within the pages of the Holy Bible, the very book my family had helped ban from devotional use in the public schools of America.

I knew that a psychiatrist might hear this dream related and say: "The subject was preoccupied with historically great figures and had a basic knowledge of Latin. The sword was tucked away in his mind along with his memories of the battle of Melvian Bridge. He has grandiose ideas and pictures himself as another Constantine. He had already made a decision to become a Christian, and this decision was only manifested in this dream."

Perhaps. Or had the hand and mind of God reached out and touched me?

Wide awake I climbed out of bed, dressed, and drove into San Francisco. Despite what any psychiatrist's interpretation might be, I believed this dream had told me two things. First, the answers to most if not all of my personal problems and dilemmas were in the book the sword had touched—the Bible. Second, only through the cross would I be able to conquer these problems ("IN HOC SIGNO VINCE" translates "By this symbol conquer.")

I drove to an all-night discount department store near

Fisherman's Wharf. There, under a stack of porno magazines in the "literature" section, I found a Bible.

I drove to my apartment and read the book of the Bible written by the great physician, Luke. There I found my answer—not the book itself, but Jesus Christ. I had heard many times in various churches that all one needed to do was to admit guilt and ask Jesus in. I had not made that one step, to ask Him into my heart. I knew I must take that step, and I did so that night. God was no longer a distant, impersonal "force." I now knew Him in a personal way.

Within days my life and attitudes began to change. I read in the Bible that anything asked in Jesus' name in prayer would be answered. On January 25, I asked God to remove from me the desire to drink alcohol. The desire left. Later I asked that the chains of my three-packs-a-day cigarette habit be broken. As if by a miracle, the desire for tobacco passed and along with it the bronchitis I had suffered with from my youth.

More importantly, though, my hatred began to vanish as the love of Christ took over my being. I no longer intensely hated my mother. Now I really *wanted* to be able to love her, whereas before I had only wanted revenge. I began to see my mother for what she truly was—a sinner, just like me. She blamed God and mankind for her personal sins and inadequacies rather than herself. She had demanded things of God, and when He had refused her demands, she had fought with Him openly.

Now I looked back at the devastation. My family, and particularly my mother and myself, had left a path of ruin behind us—ruined ideals, ruined lives. We had marched over both in quest of a victory that could not be won.

The only thing in my mind that was left undone was to apologize. I wanted to apologize to Susan and Robin, to Valerie and Jade. I wanted to apologize to my country for robbing a part of its heritage of righteousness by participating in the prayer and Bible reading case.

This desire consumed me until in March, at the age of thirty-three and almost twenty years exactly after the prayer case had begun, I did indeed apologize. I wrote two letters. One was to the newspaper in Austin, asking the people of that community to forgive me for helping to build the American Atheist Center in their city. The second letter was to the people of Baltimore and was printed in the Baltimore *Sun* on May 10, 1980. It read:

Editor:

This story began with a letter of defiance to the editor of this paper in the fall of 1960. It is my sincere hope that the story ends with this letter of both apology and forgiveness.

First, I would like to apologize to the people of the City of Baltimore for whatever part I played in the removal of Bible reading and praying from the public schools of that city. I now realize the value of this great tradition and the importance it has played in the past in keeping America a moral and lawful country. I can now see the damage this removal has caused to our nation in the form of loss of faith and moral decline.

Being raised as an atheist in the home of Madalyn O'Hair, I was not aware of faith or even the existence of God. As I now look back over 33 years of life wasted without faith in God, I pray only that I can, with His help, right some of the wrong and evil I have caused through my lack of faith.

Our nation, our people, now face a trying time in this world of chaos. It is only with a return to our traditional values and our faith in God that we will be able to survive as a people. If it were within my personal power to help to return this nation to its rightful place by placing God back in the classroom, I would do so.

I would also like to publicly forgive those who assaulted me and destroyed my property during those years that the case of Murray vs. Curlett moved through the courts. I do this even as I know that a loving God has already forgiven them.

William J. Murray

I mailed those letters with deep feelings of relief. My bonds of hate tying me to the past had been broken. Ahead lay the freedom and love found only through a new life with God.

y public apology offered through the letters to newspapers created a storm of publicity. The uproar in those first weeks brought back memories of similar events when the prayer story had been pushed by the media in 1960. Now, nearly twenty years later, my phone rang frequently as one news organization after another sought to learn what had happened. A number of pastors and religious broadcasters contacted me, too, many of them requesting that I come to speak or appear on their programs.

At first the attention was flattering, but before long I grew weary of it. I had to start saying no far more often than I could say yes. Ultimately, though, articles on my turn to God appeared in *Time* and *People* magazines, as well as in many newspapers and religious periodicals. I also was interviewed on a number of television and radio programs.

I'm certain that Madalyn and Jon Garth were shocked by the news, but publicly they said little to reporters about my conversion. A sarcastic statement by them was released to the press in which they accused me of having financial motives. Part of this press release read, "We are happy when any atheist gets some of that Christian scam money." I was angered by their untrue accusations but also had to laugh because I was nearly broke at the time.

One of the more memorable telephone calls came from Congressman Phil Crane's office in Washington, D.C. Congressman Crane was a sponsor of a bill that would remove jurisdiction over prayer in the public schools from the Supreme Court. A press conference concerning this legislation had been scheduled late in May, and Crane and others wanted me to come and make comments and answer questions. I prayed about this, and ultimately decided the trip would be worthwhile. At the press conference I met a number of congressmen and religious leaders.

Two months later, I returned to Washington and testified before a senate committee debating the Supreme Court Jurisdiction Act of 1979. In my testimony I argued that it was illogical to think there could be complete separation of church and state at all levels of government. Therefore, no segment of the government (such as the Supreme Court) should be allowed to dictate to all other segments at what point this separation (if any ever did exist) should occur. I noted that by precluding *all* religions advocating faith in God from public schools, the Federal Government was in fact establishing a materialist atheist religion by default.

After the initial flurry of publicity died down, I thought that at last I could pursue my career in aviation and live unbothered in the suburbs. I again had found employment in Houston and at last, I thought, was free of the atheism of Madalyn Murray O'Hair. Once more I was wrong.

Even before my testimony at the Congressional hearing, I had received many letters and other personal contacts supporting my statements that activities by anti-God atheists and humanists posed serious dangers to Americans.

I began to realize that because of my relationship to Madalyn Murray O'Hair and my past experiences, I had become something of a rallying symbol for many people who longed to do something about the moral chaos in our nation. In order to focus my own role in this, in July of 1980 I formed the William J. Murray Faith Ministries. The primary purpose of the ministry was to present the gospel to people who, like me, had been deceived by the lies of atheistic-humanistic philosophy.

I had always believed my experiences growing up in the

home of a famous dissident had been unique. But after the publicity of my conversion, I began to receive hundreds of letters from men and women who also had been raised in homes without God. Many had already found Him, while many others just wanted to know how I had found peace and had put the hatred for my mother behind me.

During the summer and fall of 1980 I thought it important to support political candidates whom I believed were sincerely advocating the need of our nation to repent and become obedient to God. This campaigning, as well as the television and personal appearances, soon demanded so much time that I had little left for my normal activities. I began to sense that I should work for God in ways I had not anticipated.

Since then, in an attempt to create public awareness of America's spiritual needs, I have traveled almost weekly to speak in churches and other forums throughout the country. Invariably when I reach a new city or town, I am contacted by newspaper and broadcast reporters. During these interviews I have the opportunity to tell both of my past and of my faith in Christ. Many persons still trapped in personal dilemmas have read or heard these interviews and have written to me seeking help.

Funds for this work are contributed by individuals who share a common concern for those influenced by atheistic and humanistic philosophies. Also, offerings are taken at most of the churches where I speak—these, too, are channeled into the ministry, which is a nonprofit institution.

Since the organization's birth in 1980, the Faith Ministries has sponsored prayer vigils in the same city—at the same time—as conventions of the American Atheists, and helped distribute over 250,000 folders bearing the Lord's Prayer and the Ten Commandments to public school children. We also have placed provocative advertising to capture the interest of atheists and explain the truth. On occasion the organization has stepped in to help in local communities where the activities of my mother or her organization (or some other group of atheists) have threatened to undermine positive activities, such as a recovery program for drug and alcohol abusers sponsored by Christians in public schools.

One of Faith Ministries' more exciting moments came in April 1982, when I and several others delivered to the White House petitions bearing the signatures of one million Americans who want religious freedom reestablished in our schools.

But undoubtedly the most satisfying aspect of my work is the counseling I do via mail, telephone, and in person with hundreds of people who face problems similar to those described in this book. Daily I receive word from former members of atheist and Communist organizations who now have found peace with God.

Developments in my own family have brought both joy and sadness. My uncle Irv, John Mays, has been led out of Austin and now lives comfortably in retirement in Houston. Unfortunately, Valerie filed for divorce, citing past "irreconcilable" differences. My daughter Jade, however, has been able to accompany me frequently on my speaking trips, and these times together have strengthened the faith of us both.

As for Mother, I have not spoken to her since that morning in 1977 when I parted from her. I have decided it is best for me to keep my distance. But each day I pray that she, too, will come to God.

WHAT I MUST DO. WHAT YOU CAN DO.

I had no intention of doing any work in ministry after I came to know Jesus Christ as my Lord and Savior. It was my belief I would become a Christian businessman and live quietly in the suburbs.

The Lord had other plans for me.

The various atheist groups in America tried to discredit my new way of life. Before I spoke even once publicly and while I was still employed by an airline, various atheist leaders accused me of everything from drug addiction to profiteering. The Lord said to me, "They do not attack you, they attack Me, for you are my servant now."

I knew then that I could not stand by and watch our nation and its Judeo-Christian foundation be destroyed. I knew with conviction that I would have to follow that which the Lord would have me do.

For this reason I founded the William J. Murray Faith Ministries. This ministry has as its major goal the revival of this land. Projects range from the very small to the very large. Television specials are produced to make America as a whole aware of many of the issues raised in this book. On the other hand, I do all I can to minister to individuals.

Newspaper ads telling what Christ has done for us have been run by me during conventions of the Freedom from Religion Foundation, the American Humanist Association and the American Atheists Association. Prayer vigils are conducted in cities where the various atheists conventions are held.

The Lord has placed me in His service. During revivals and

253

crusades conducted by Faith Ministries in 1982 and 1983, over twenty-five thousand men and women made first-time decisions for our Lord. Tens of thousands of others rededicated their lives to Christ.

Many former atheists have given up their misery for a life with Christ as a result of our tract and advertising programs. Some were even state directors of atheists groups before coming into a relationship with our Lord.

There are many ways in which you as a reader of this book can help in this cause for Christ. Knowing of my life and of my misery before I came to know Jesus, you can use my story as a witness for Him.

You can help directly as well. Workers are needed in various parts of the nation for this ministry. Perhaps you or your church can help in a crusade or other project. If so, I want to hear from you.

Maybe this book has in some way helped to lead you into a relationship with Christ. Now you want to know more about the Christian walk. I want to hear from you.

Please write directly to me. My address is:

WILLIAM J. MURRAY
P.O. BOX 28725
DALLAS, TEXAS 75228